Legal Usage in Drafting Corporate Agreements

KENNETH A. ADAMS

Q

QUORUM BOOKS
Westport, Connecticut • London

Library of Congress Cataloging-in-Publication Data

Adams, Kenneth A., 1961–
    Legal usage in drafting corporate agreements / Kenneth A. Adams.
        p. cm.
    Includes index.
    ISBN 1-56720-410-4 (alk. paper)
        1. Contracts—United States—Language. 2. Corporation law—United States—Language.
    3. Legal composition. I. Title.
    KF250 .A32 2001
    346.7302—dc21   00-051756

British Library Cataloguing in Publication Data is available.

Library of Congress Catalog Card Number: 00-051756
ISBN: 1-56720-410-4

First published in 2001

Quorum Books, 88 Post Road West, Westport, CT 06881
An imprint of Greenwood Publishing Group, Inc.
www.quorumbooks.com

Printed in the United States of America

∞™ The paper used in this book complies with the
Permanent Paper Standard issued by the National
Information Standards Organization (Z39.48-1984).

10 9 8 7 6 5 4 3 2 1

To Joanne

CONTENTS

SAMPLES AND TABLES

PREFACE

I imagine that usually one starts with some semblance of erudition, with the book following. In my case, the order was reversed.

In 1997 I was in Switzerland, winding up a stint at the Geneva office of an American law firm. I was soon to return to New York, where I had practiced for four years after graduating from law school in 1989. I got it into my head that I would write about contract drafting, and tentatively I started jotting down ideas.

Once back in New York and again subject to the rigors of practicing law there, I spent what time I could working on my fledgling manuscript. Over the course of three years I devoted holidays, weekends, and stolen hours to the task. With every part of this book the process was the same: I would start with some simplistic notions; my subsequent research and cogitation would show them to be largely or entirely inadequate; I would then grind out a new version that I would build on, in fits and starts, over the coming months and years. In effect, instead of simply being able to draw on a reservoir of drafting knowledge, as I had blithely assumed would be the case, I found that I had to teach myself the subject largely from scratch.

The principal contribution by others to this book was through the works I consulted on drafting and legal writing; as is manifest in my footnotes, I found particularly useful the various books written or edited by Bryan Garner. In addition, I am grateful to Carol Meltzer for her perceptive observations and encouragement, while Peter Sternberg's bare-knuckles comments prompted me to make many refinements. In terms of assistance from nonlawyers, Gerald Nelson, a grammarian, did his best to save me from blunders, and Jeremy Harmer's comments made for a tidier manuscript. The remaining shortcomings can be laid at my door.

I also owe thanks to Kramer Levin Naftalis & Frankel LLP for providing a civilized environment for my reintroduction to New York practice, and to the librarians at Kramer Levin for cheerfully and efficiently following up on my requests for research materials.

That this book is being published is due to the persistence of my agent, Theresa Stefanidis, and the enthusiasm of Eric Valentine of Greenwood Publishing Group. Robert Kowkabany of Doric Lay Publishers helped me fine-tune the manuscript and developed the design of the book.

On the home front, my wife Joanne and daughter Sydney tolerated with good humor and patience the time I spent away from them working on this book. Without Joanne's love and support I would never have been able to write it.

One of my hopes for this book is that it will encourage students of legal usage in drafting corporate agreements to come out of hiding. I welcome your comments or questions; you can send them to me at kadams@adamsdrafting.com.

INTRODUCTION

In this book I examine the conventions of language and structure used in drafting corporate agreements and suggest approaches to adopt and pitfalls to avoid.

My principal justification for this book is that little is available to the corporate lawyer looking for advice on basic principles of drafting corporate agreements. There are a number of worthwhile guides to legal writing in general,[1] but given their broad scope they are of little help to the contract drafter. Books on legislative drafting—a number of them published in British Commonwealth countries[2]—can provide guidance on a number of discrete issues that are potentially of interest to the contract drafter, but they cannot be used as guides to contract drafting. There are a few books dedicated to general principles of drafting—the majority intended for a British Commonwealth audience[3]—but none addresses questions of language and structure in the drafting of corporate agreements in sufficient detail to be of significant practical use to the corporate lawyer. Similarly, various works that focus on the drafting of contracts are, for one reason or another, of little help in this regard.[4] I have found the most useful volume to be *A Dictionary of Modern Legal Usage*,[5] but its breadth and dictionary format mean that it can offer only limited, and scattered, observations on contract drafting.

One might argue that if the legal profession does not have available to it a book that addresses in a comprehensive manner the issues of legal usage that arise in the drafting of corporate agreements, it could be that there is little need for such a book. The simplest retort would be that drafting contracts is, for corporate lawyers, so basic a task that such a book would have to come in handy. I will also offer a more pointed response: Lawyers have long been taken to task for how they write,[6] and in the considerable body of literature devoted to legal writing[7] it is for the most part taken as a given that "most lawyers write poorly."[8] Since drafting is simply a form of writing used in preparing legal instruments that seek to regulate conduct (principally statutes, regulations, wills, and contracts),[9] it should come as no surprise that many commentators think that most lawyers *draft* poorly.[10]

While I am wary of generalizations of this sort, I have come to the conclusion, based upon my experience as a corporate lawyer in private practice, that many contracts are in fact inexpertly drafted and that almost all show room for improvement. I do not mean by this that drafters demonstrate a less-than-perfect grasp of the law or of transaction mechanics, though that may or may not be the case. I mean instead that many contracts, to a greater or lesser extent, are structured in a way that makes them less accessible to the reader and use language that is less precise and efficient than it might be, in particular language that is unclear, wordy, archaic, pompous, or clumsy—in other words, "legalese." (Note that while the term "legalese" is not necessarily pejorative,[11] I, and others, use it as a convenient but entirely vague term for objectionable legal jargon.)[12]

You might ask whether it matters that many contracts are indifferently drafted. I suggest that it does, for three reasons. First, a party to a contract may discover, after signing, that due to a modest drafting flaw, such as a defined term that is ambiguous or an unthinking reliance on legalese, a given provision may not in fact mean what that party thought it meant. This could deprive that party of an anticipated benefit under the contract or result in a dispute leading to litigation; countless lawsuits have their origin in awkward drafting.[13]

Second, the more a contract is riddled with legalese and burdened with a clumsy structure, the more time-consuming and therefore expensive it will be to read, negotiate, and interpret.

Third, a poorly drafted contract serves to alienate the lay reader: as contract language strays from everyday English to legalese, the drafter becomes less the professional and more the occultist, muttering incantations over chicken entrails.[14] While the consequences of this are entirely intangible, when I hear a client making jibes about a particular bit of legalese I do not take it as a mark of respect for the legal profession.

I leave others to consider the root causes of the indifferent quality of much legal writing and, by extension, much drafting.[15] I will, however, suggest a factor that helps perpetuate indifferent drafting. The deleterious consequences of indifferent drafting are generally more subtle than mistaken interpretations of the law or problems relating to the structure of a transaction. As a result, many corporate lawyers are quick to dismiss questions of legal usage as going to form rather than substance[16] and are complacent about their own drafting abilities.[17] One consequence is that junior corporate lawyers often receive little training in the principles of drafting and rely on flawed form contracts, with the result that they unwittingly perpetuate poor drafting techniques.

The lack of a comprehensive guide to legal usage in the drafting of contracts is a symptom of the general indifference of the profession. It is also a factor contributing to that indifference: in the absence of critical evaluation of current drafting techniques, corporate lawyers have little in the way of standards against which to measure the effectiveness of their drafting. Due to a carrot-and-stick effect, such a book could have a significantly greater impact than that of any number of works on legal writing in general. The language and structure of contracts are inherently more limited and stylized than those of, say, an appellate brief, and so can be more readily mastered, given suitable reference tools. At the same time, the incentives to master drafting are greater than in the case of general legal writing: every provision of a contract carries weight and must stand or fall on its own, whereas in forms of legal writing other than drafting there is a much greater chance that a poorly crafted sentence will be borne along by the narrative.

This book represents my attempt to address this gap in the literature. It is organized as follows:

- Chapter 1 discusses that part of the contract that occurs before the body of the contract.
- Chapter 2 addresses the categories of language that occur in the body of the contract.
- Chapter 3 tackles the structure of the body of the contract.
- Chapter 4 concerns what follows the body of the contract.
- Chapter 5 examines usages relating to defined terms and definitions, numbers, references to time, and cross-references, and addresses issues of typography. It also examines an assortment of awkward usages and common drafting problems.
- Chapter 6 considers provisions specifying drafting conventions.
- Chapter 7 examines briefly some principles of effective general writing that apply to drafting.
- Chapter 8 discusses the process of drafting, focusing on use of form contracts and how to go about revising them.

- All notes are located in a separate section after the final chapter.

- To provide a better sense of the net effect of the approaches I advocate in this book, in the appendix are "before" and "after" versions of a simple contract.

Certain issues that I discuss, such as the form of the introductory clause,[18] are unique to corporate agreements. Issues that are also relevant to other forms of drafting, such as the use of defined terms,[19] I approach from the perspective of the corporate lawyer. I touch only briefly on those topics that are equally relevant to legal writing in general. While they are important—good writing skills provide a solid foundation for good drafting—they are addressed more comprehensively in any number of other works.

This book addresses the drafting of informal contracts, as opposed to formal contracts (such as negotiable instruments), which depend upon their form for their validity.[20] (Today, this distinction is of little significance.)[21] More specifically, this book is concerned with the drafting of long-form contracts and not letter agreements, and focuses on corporate agreements between ostensibly sophisticated parties represented by counsel. (By "corporate agreement," I mean nothing more specific than any agreement that you could comfortably ask the average corporate lawyer to draft.) Consequently, this book considers neither consumer contracts nor contracts involving other areas of law (real estate or trusts and estates, for example), although they would certainly benefit from application of the principles contained in this book.

While this book is written from the perspective of an American corporate lawyer, I hope it will prove of use to a broader constituency. For one thing, international transactions are often accomplished using contracts that are comparable to U.S.-style contracts. Also, any variations between American English usage and English usage elsewhere should be of limited significance for purposes of corporate agreements. That said, certain sections of this book—such as the discussion of the distinction between *representations* and *warranties*[22]—concern U.S. statutes and case law to a degree that may cause them to be of limited use for purposes of drafting agreements governed by the laws of other jurisdictions.

I explore in considerable detail some lesser issues, such as use of verbs in the introductory clause.[23] While this approach might seem excessive, it serves a purpose. When examining any issue of legal usage, you can use your intuition (what sounds right?) or you can lay out the underpinnings of that intuition. I could not expect readers to lend much credence to my views unless I were to follow the latter approach. (Similar reasoning explains my relatively copious use of notes.) I could, of course, ignore any issue if the space required to explore it seemed out of proportion to its significance, but drafting, like writing generally, benefits from mastery of both major principles and minor details.

It should already be apparent that this book is not a simple restatement of traditional principles of drafting. But like most corporate attorneys, I try to be pragmatic, and before recommending an unorthodox approach to any given issue I weigh the benefits of that approach against the resistance it is likely to encounter. In some contexts—for example, in connection with the many misuses of *shall*[24]—the accepted practice is sufficiently pernicious that I am willing to recommend wholesale change, no matter how firmly entrenched the accepted practice. Other flawed usages, such as using initial capitals in referring to agreements,[25] are sufficiently harmless and sufficiently widespread that for the time being I am willing to leave well enough alone.

Defenders of current standards of contract drafting could offer a number of arguments to rebut my assertion that many lawyers are indifferent drafters and that poor drafting can have damaging consequences. These counterarguments can be summarized as follows: that current standards of drafting are entirely adequate because legal documents reflecting those standards facilitate the countless transactions that are accomplished daily; that verbose and archaic contract language is the price that you pay for precision; that case law has settled the meaning of much legal vocabulary, leaving the drafter with little discretion; and that since the law is inherently complex, so too, inevitably, are contracts.[26]

I acknowledge that these arguments remain popular but I do not intend to rebut them. For one thing, others have done so and shown them to be myths or irrelevant.[27] More to the point, however, I find it unhelpful to deal in generalities. I prefer instead to assess the various ways of addressing any given drafting issue and then advocate the approach that seems the clearest or most efficient, my guiding principle being that unless there are cogent reasons to do otherwise, one should use standard English.

That said, I hesitate to call myself an advocate of "plain English" or "plain language." These terms refer to both an approach to legal writing and an associated "movement"[28] that has seen the enactment of statutes mandating clarity and simplicity in consumer contracts and insurance contracts, the establishment of bar committees to promote plain language, and the like.[29] Perhaps the most significant recent plain-English development is that the U.S. Securities and Exchange Commission has adopted regulations requiring that prospectuses be made more intelligible to the investing public.[30]

One reason for my ambivalence is that the term "plain English" can have different meanings. Some commentators have an expansive view of plain English that would encompass corporate agreements, and it would be hard to find fault with their recommendations.[31] Another view of plain English, however, is that it serves to "make complex legal documents intelligible to the average consumer while retaining the binding force of the original text."[32] Since corporate agreements are not intended for the average consumer, this definition would remove the principles of plain English from the scope of this book.

My principal reservation, however, is that while many of the issues I raise in this book would fall within the orbit of plain-English principles as broadly conceived (for example, my aversion to *witnesseth*),[33] many others, such as the ways to express conditions[34] and the subtleties involved in properly using defined terms,[35] do not. Consequently, it would not be accurate to say that this book is simply about drafting contracts in plain English.

Less well-known than plain English is the concept of "legal usage." It is commonplace to refer to "English usage" in connection with studies of different forms of speech.[36] This term has spawned the variant "legal usage," which applies to legal speech.[37] "Legal usage" describes better the scope of this book than does "plain English," and it also has the advantage of being not as loaded a term. That I take issue with many traditional usages does not render it any less applicable.

CHAPTER 1

Before the Body of the Contract

T HE BODY OF THE CONTRACT is preceded by the title, the introductory clause, and the recitals, as well as certain optional features.

THE TITLE

There is little mystery to the title of a contract. It appears at the top of every contract, usually in capital letters, and simply states without the benefit of a definite or indefinite article the kind of contract involved (distribution agreement, software license agreement, employment agreement, or other). (See sample 1.) The shorter, the better (*ASSET PURCHASE AGREEMENT* rather than *AGREEMENT FOR THE PUR-CHASE AND SALE OF ASSETS*, and *MERGER AGREEMENT* rather than *AGREEMENT AND PLAN OF MERGER*). That said, try to be more expansive than simple *AGREEMENT*.[38] Do not include in the title any additional information, such as party names.

Most corporate agreements use the word *agreement* in the title; one also sees *contract*, but much less frequently; I suspect that this is because *agreement* is free of the harsh consonants of *contract*, and so comes across as more genteel. The two words are not synonyms: while *contract* and *agreement* may both be used to mean a formal and legally enforceable arrangement, *agreement* may also refer to an informal arrangement not supported by consideration, such as an agreement between friends to play tennis on Saturday morning.[39] Since it is obvious that a corporate agreement does not represent an agreement in the broader informal sense, you may use either word in the title.[40] Likewise, in this book I use the two terms interchangeably.

The Introductory Clause

By convention, the title is followed by a paragraph containing a statement of the kind of agreement involved (this should be the same as the title), the date of the agreement, and a description of the parties to the agreement. Of the various alternatives, the term I prefer for this paragraph is "introductory clause."[41] (In a legal context, "clause" "generally refers vaguely to some unit of a legal instrument or statute,"[42] and that is the meaning "clause" conveys in "introductory clause." Occasionally in this book I use "clause" to convey its grammatical meaning—any group of words that contains a subject and a verb.)[43]

Of those contracts that have occasion to refer to the introductory clause, many refer to it as a "recital," however recitals are found after the introductory clause,[44] and others refer to it as the "preamble," a term best understood as the legislative equivalent of recitals.[45]

Sample 1 is an example of my preferred form of introductory clause. While the introductory clause is not a hotbed of drafting controversy, it raises a number of issues.

Reference to the Type of Agreement

In many contracts, the reference in the introductory clause to the type of agreement involved is often emphasized using all capitals (*This*

PREFERRED STOCK PURCHASE AGREEMENT

This Preferred Stock Purchase Agreement (this "Agreement") is dated December 14, 2000, and is between ACME PARENT, a Delaware corporation ("Parent"), ACME SUB, INC., a Delaware corporation ("Acme Sub"; together with Parent, each an "Acme Party"), and MIDAS INVESTMENT FUND, L.P., a New York limited partnership ("Midas").

SAMPLE 1   TITLE AND INTRODUCTORY CLAUSE

EMPLOYMENT AGREEMENT). Since the type of agreement is emphasized with all capitals in the title, which is immediately above the introductory clause, little is gained by so emphasizing it again. (See sample 1.)

Those contracts that do not use all capital letters to emphasize titles use initial capitals. In fact, drafters invariably use initial capitals throughout a contract when referring to an agreement. There is, however, no principled basis for this practice, which presumably derives from corporate lawyers seeking, consciously or otherwise, to ascribe particular significance to their stock-in-trade. If Acme and Excelsior sign a merger agreement, there is no reason for it to sprout initial capitals when referred to as being "between Acme and Excelsior."

This point is not as pedantic as it might seem: I have seen comment letters from the SEC requiring, as part of its enforcement of the plain-English rules,[46] that in a prospectus the registrant not use initial capitals when referring to any given agreement. While I now generally avoid using initial capitals when referring to agreements, as yet this approach has not been widely adopted for purposes of contract drafting; for all I know, I may be its only exponent. Unless you are filled with a pioneering spirit, you might want to be cautious about adopting it, since initial capitals cannot harm your clients' interests and fellow corporate lawyers might think you persnickety for doing away with them. That is why in sample 1 I refer to *This Preferred Stock Purchase Agreement*.

Verbs

Most drafters provide that an agreement is *made* or *entered into* on a given date. (Many drafters pointlessly use both verbs.) There are two problems with this formula: First, it is in the passive voice, and generally one should avoid using the passive voice.[47] Second, and more significantly, rephrasing this formula so that the parties *make* or *enter into* the agreement highlights that this formula makes inappropriate use of the simple present. Because *to make* and *to enter into* are dynamic verbs,[48] in this context *make* or *enter into* could represent only that form of the simple present tense known as the "instantaneous present," which occurs when the verb refers in the simple present to a single action begun and completed at approximately the moment of speech.[49] Use of these verbs in the introductory clause is not, however, consistent with the instantaneous present. Most pertinently, they are not performatives,[50] since there is no simultaneity of the event described and the speech event itself: a contract is not made by proclamation in the introductory clause, but upon signing, and the purpose of the introductory clause is the more mundane one of specifying the date of, and the signatories to, the contract.

A more intuitive way to explain the problem with stating that an agreement is *made* or *entered into* on a given date is to note that one would not normally say *This letter is sent by me today*, or even *I send this letter today*. Since one does say *I am sending this letter today*, one could conceivably use the present progressive in the introductory clause and provide that the parties *are making* the agreement on the date in question. The progressive serves, however, to convey that a happening has duration, and that the happening is not necessarily complete.[51] This is not helpful in the context of entering into a contract: one is either party to a contract, or one is not, and becoming a party to a contract should be thought of as occurring in an instant, rather than constituting a process.

By process of elimination, we are left with the approach exemplified by sample 1. This allows the introductory clause to serve its purpose, yet avoids disconcerting verb structures. And while *is dated December 14, 2000* is in the passive voice, it would be churlish to insist on *the parties date this Agreement December 14, 2000* or some such wording.

Many drafters use the following structure in the introductory clause: *Preferred Stock Purchase Agreement dated December 14, 2000, between* . . . . While this approach certainly avoids verb problems by omitting verbs entirely, it results in an introductory clause that is not a sentence, and it is preferable to draft in sentences.

Date

Many drafters use for the date in the introductory clause not the format *June 11, 2000*, but the format *this 11th day of June, 2000*. This usage is old-fashioned and long-winded. It is best to avoid using purely numerical dates: they are inappropriate in formal writing and are potentially confusing, given the different international conventions for expressing dates using numbers.[52] (For example, an American would assume that 5/7/01 means May 7, 2001, while to the English it means the fifth day of July.)

The date stated in the introductory clause is the date the contract becomes effective, unless the contract specifies otherwise. The introductory clause date may be the date the contract is actually signed by each party, but often the contract is signed before or after. This discrepancy is generally in the interests of convenience: when handling a transaction with many constituent components, it is often simplest to set a timetable for signing the different documents and to date all documents accordingly, even if logistics require that some or all of them be signed before or after the date they are given. Note, however, that in tax-sensitive transactions, the actual date the contract was signed can be important, and any attempt to suggest that it was signed, say, in a prior calendar year or before the effective date of a new tax law could result in civil or criminal penalties.

The conventional way of reflecting that one or more parties signed an agreement on a date other than the date specified in the introductory clause is to state that the agreement is dated *as of* the given date.[53] This allows lawyers to flag that the date of a given contract is a convenient legal fiction rather than the result of a mistake or sleight of hand. For a number of reasons, this is not a particularly significant usage.

First, while I can conceive of a party wishing to demonstrate to some third party, such as a governmental authority, that an agreement was in fact signed on the date stated in the introductory clause, it would seem less likely that a party would need to demonstrate that the date of execution was *not* in fact the date in the introductory clause. (Note that in the context of informal contracts, *to execute* simply means *to sign*, and *execution* is the act of signing.)[54]

Second, if the date an agreement was signed were somehow to become an issue, it is uncertain that an *as of* date would constitute persuasive proof that the agreement was not signed on that date, as contracts are very often dated *as of* a given date even if the contract was signed on that date, and conversely are often not dated *as of* when the date of signing is other than the date in the introductory clause. This confusion is compounded by the way concluding clauses generally refer to execution of the contract *as of* the date in the introductory clause, whether or not that date is an *as of* date.[55]

Third, it is likely that if required, more reliable evidence as to the actual date of signing would be available.

There would seem to be a paucity of litigation addressing this issue. For example, *Words and Phrases*[56] does not contain an entry for *dated as of*. This suggests that it matters little whether you give a contract an *as of* date. It also suggests, however, that using an *as of* date is essentially harmless. (Note that outside of the context of expressing the date of a given agreement, *as of* is often used when *on* would be the simpler and better choice:[57] "*As of* [read *on*] the date of this Agreement, there are outstanding 4,433,596 shares of Acme common stock.")

Another reason for a discrepancy between the date in the introductory clause and the date of signing is that the parties, for whatever reason, do not want the contract to be effective until some later time. If this is the case, it is clearer to put the date of signing in the introductory clause and provide in the body of the contract that it will not be effective until a specified later date.

In order to avoid conflicting dates for a contract, the only date stated should be that in the introductory clause. This means that you should generally avoid including a date in the concluding clause[58] or having signatories to a contract date their signatures. If, however, you anticipate that the signing of a contract will be spread over a week or more, you might want to omit any date from the introductory clause, have the signatories date their signatures, and provide that the contract only becomes effective once the last party signs.

Between *versus* Among

It is commonly held that while one speaks of an agreement *between* two parties, the correct preposition to use in the case of an agreement involving more than two parties is *among*.[59] *The Oxford English Dictionary* provides, however, that *between* can be "[u]sed in reference to any objective relation uniting two (or more) parties, and holding them in a certain connexion."[60] Furthermore, not only can you use *between* with more than two parties, it is in fact preferable that you use *between* instead of *among*:

> In all senses, *between* has been, from its earliest appearance, extended to more than two. . . . It is still the only word available to express the relation of a thing to many surrounding things severally and individually, *among* expressing them collectively and vaguely: we should not say . . . "a treaty among three powers" . . . .[61]

Among can be used when referring to relations within a group, as in "there were differences among Christians dating back to the Church Fathers,"[62] but there is no call for this usage in the introductory clause. Consequently, in the introductory clause I use only *between*, and never *among*.

That said, electing to use *between* rather than *among* in the introductory clause, or vice-versa, has no effect on meaning, as neither usage results in a party to an agreement somehow being any less of a party. I address this issue not so much to clear up confusion, but to eliminate a distraction: on those rare occasions when I hear corporate lawyers allude to an issue of legal usage, more often than not the topic is *between* versus *among*.

Finally, an agreement should not be *by and between* the parties; using *between* on its own is perfectly adequate.

Identifying the Parties

Each party should be identified in the introductory clause by the full name under which it is registered in the jurisdiction in which it was organized, rather than any alternative name under which it does business or by which it is commonly known. You can, if necessary, also refer to any such alternative name, as well as any name that a party was formerly known by. Include the designation of form of entity, whether it be *Inc.*, *LLC*, or something more exotic (*B.V.*, *S.A.*, *GIE*). Getting the name right would prevent disputes as to which of two or more similarly named affiliated entities is actually party to the contract.

To help them stand out, I state party names in all capitals.

Describing the Parties

As the jurisdiction of organization of a party to a contract is second only to its name as a means of identifying it, this information is generally included in the introductory clause. Many drafters refer to a party as, for instance, *a corporation organized under the laws of the State of Delaware*. Given that *a Delaware corporation* serves the purpose equally well, you do not need to use the longer formulation.[63] When dealing with non-U.S. entities, it is worth making the effort to refer to the correct legal form.

Some contracts squeeze additional information into the introductory clause, such as the address of each party; that Widgetco is represented by Jane Smith, its duly authorized representative; that Widgetco is duly organized and validly existing; that the agreement sets forth the binding agreement of the parties; or that the parties intend to be legally bound.[64] If such information is of use, it is much better placed in the body of the contract. This would leave the introductory clause uncluttered and would increase the likelihood of any such assertion being enforceable.

Defined Terms in the Introductory Clause

While I discuss defined terms in a later chapter,[65] their use in the introductory clause raises some discrete issues.

In the introductory clause, each party name is almost invariably given a defined term. The traditional way of giving Acme Corporation a defined term is to include after the full name of Acme Corporation something akin to the following: *(hereinafter referred to as "Acme")*. Unless the party names are confusingly similar, one could conceivably refer to a party by a shortened version of its name without explicitly defining that term.[66] I prefer, however, to warn the reader at the outset that references to *Acme* in fact mean Acme Corporation, even when there is no risk of confusion. The same applies to the names of individuals. Instead of not providing a defined term, pare down the parenthetical information to only the defined term, underlined (for emphasis) and in quotation marks: *("Acme")*.[67]

A surprisingly subtle question is where one should place the defined term when defining a party name. Take, for example, a reference to *Excelsior, a Delaware corporation*. As I suggest below, a term should generally be defined after the phrase representing its definition.[68] Since a party name constitutes a noun phrase unto itself and can therefore appropriately be regarded as the definition, the parenthetical *("Excelsior")* would normally be placed after *Excelsior Corporation*,[69] but there are factors favoring a different position.

One factor is that it does not seem particularly awkward to place a defined term after *a Delaware corporation*. The phrase *Excelsior Corporation, a Delaware corporation* is an example of what is known as apposition: *Excelsior Corporation* and *a Delaware corporation* are both noun phrases referring to the same thing.[70] This suggests why nine out of ten drafters would place the defined term for *Excelsior Corporation* after the second noun phrase. By contrast, if the reference were to *Excelsior Corporation, which is a Delaware corporation*, it would be difficult to justify placing the defined term after *corporation*.

A further factor to consider is that if, when creating a defined term, you also take the opportunity to create additional defined terms within the same parentheses,[71] placing the parentheses after the party name can make the jurisdiction reference seem like an awkward afterthought. (In sample 1, for example, imagine moving the parentheses defining "Acme Sub" and "Acme Party" to just after "ACME SUB, INC.") The upshot is that I define party names after the reference to jurisdiction, but do so as much out of expedience as out of principle.

In selecting defined terms for party names, there are two alternatives. You can select an abbreviated name based on the party name. In the case of individuals, this is generally the last name or, if the contract refers to two or more individuals with the same last name, the first name. As last names on their own can be rather stark, I generally add an appropriate honorific (*Mr.*, *Ms.*, *Dr.*). In the case of companies, you can select a word or two from the name (Alliance Metals Trading, Inc. could be referred to as *Alliance Metals* or simply *Alliance*). Alternatively, you can use an acronym or, as is more often the case, an initialism,[72] such as *AMT* in the case of Alliance Metals Trading, Inc. In the interest of readability, use whenever possible a defined term consisting of one or more words from an entity's name rather than an acronym or initialism.[73] Sometimes one has little choice but to use an acronym or initialism for a party name, such as when that party has similarly named affiliates or has a name based on an individual's name.

Often the defined term for a party is not based on its name but is instead a common noun that can be either blandly uninformative (*Company*) or indicative of the party's role in the transaction (*Seller*, *Employer*, *Lender*). It is preferable that the defined term for a party be based on the party's name, but common nouns are traditionally used for party names in certain kinds of contracts, such as credit agreements; are unobjectionable in an agreement that focuses on one entity, such as a limited liability company operating agreement; and are unavoidable when the identity of one or more of the signatories is unknown, as would be the case with an asset purchase agreement that is to be used in an auction context. Also, if a contract uses generic names it is easier to understand provisions taken out of context. To avoid unnecessarily confusing readers and to reduce the risk of your inadvertently using the wrong name, you should steer clear of paired defined terms that differ only in their final syllable (*Licensee–Licensor*; *Pledgee–Pledgor*; *Mortgagee–Mortgagor*).

If you elect to use a common noun as the defined term for a party name, you must decide whether to use a definite article. Once you have made your choice, be consistent; a surefire way to look like a sloppy drafter is to alternate randomly between, for example, *Purchaser* and *the Purchaser*. Doing without the definite article results in prose that is marginally more stilted than it would be with the definite article, but it also results in a marginally shorter document.[74] I generally prefer using the definite article.

Occasionally one finds party names defined in the following manner: *("Acme"* or the *"Company")* or *("Acme," sometimes referred to herein as the "Company").* This is a decidedly unhelpful practice because it places on the reader the burden of remembering that *Acme* and *the Company* are one and the same.

Drafters sometimes use all capitals for party names throughout a contract *(DOE hereby grants ROE).* All this does is render the contract harder to read, and it impairs, through overuse, the utility of emphasis.[75]

Often it is helpful to use a collective defined term such as *the Stockholders,* so as to be able to say *each Stockholder shall use its best efforts to do X,* rather than the more long-winded *each of Alpha, Beta, Charlie and Delta shall use its best efforts to do X.* Sample 1 contains the collective defined term *Acme Party.* I now avoid, however, using the defined term *Party.* It ostensibly spares one the effort of having to refer continually to *the parties to this Agreement,* but you should have no qualms about simply referring to *the parties,* because it would strain credulity to argue that you are thereby also referring to the parties to some other agreement.

After the introductory clause, most contracts refer to themselves as *this Agreement.* There is really no need to make *this Agreement* into a defined term: the *this* means that there could be no question as to which agreement is being referred to. Nevertheless, the vast majority of contracts do use *this Agreement* as a defined term, and generally it is defined in the introductory clause. I have in the past followed this practice because using this defined term can do no harm and dropping it could prompt fruitless discussion, and for those reasons I have included in sample 1 the defined term *this Agreement.* When I have free rein, however, I now forego using *this Agreement* as a defined term. (If you also forego using initial capitals when referring in the introductory clause to the type of agreement involved,[76] you should refer thereafter to *this agreement.)*

In sample 1, the definition of the defined term *this Agreement* is *This Preferred Stock Purchase Agreement.* Consequently, the position of the parenthetical *(this "Agreement")* complies with the precept that when defining a term, it should be placed at the end of the definition.[77] Placing the defined term for an agreement elsewhere in relation to its definition is warranted only if, as in contract references to other agreements, the date of the agreement and the party information constitute part of the definition. (See, for example, where the defined term *ABC Stock Purchase Agreement* is placed in the first recital in sample 2.)

In accordance with a Stock Purchase Agreement dated August 21, 2000, between ABC Holdings, Inc. ("ABC"), ABC Communications, Inc. (the "Seller"), Acme Sub, and ABC Acquisition Corporation ("ABC Sub"; that agreement, the "ABC Stock Purchase Agreement"), on September 18, 2000, ABC Sub acquired all the issued and outstanding stock of Acme Sub.

On November 27, 2000, ABC Sub merged into Parent, resulting in Acme Sub's becoming a direct wholly-owned subsidiary of Parent.

Parent wishes to sell to Midas, and Midas wishes to purchase from Parent, certain shares of capital stock of Parent.

Concurrently with execution of this Agreement, Parent, Midas, Dynamic Capital, Inc., and Octopus Holdings Limited are entering into a Stockholders Agreement in the form of Exhibit A (the "Stockholders Agreement") and Parent and Midas are entering into a Registration Rights Agreement in the form of Exhibit B (the "Registration Rights Agreement").

Parent, Acme Sub, and Midas therefore agree as follows:

SAMPLE 2 RECITALS

THE RECITALS

Most contracts of any length or complexity contain, following the title and before the body of the contract, a group of paragraphs known as the "recitals." The recitals in sample 2, which accompany the introductory clause in sample 1, reflect the form that I prefer.

Purpose

The recitals to an agreement essentially set the stage for that agreement.[78] One can identify different kinds of recitals providing different kinds of information. First come what I call "context recitals," which describe the circumstances leading up to the making of the agreement.[79] An asset purchase agreement providing for the sale of all the seller's assets might, for instance, contain context recitals stating that the seller is engaged in a given business and operates that business out of certain facilities. Context recitals can also provide basic details regarding previous transactions (see the first two recitals in sample 2).

Context recitals are generally followed by what I call the "purpose recital," which indicates very briefly and in broad terms what the parties wish to accomplish (see the third recital in sample 2).[80]

A set of recitals can also include a recital regarding transactions being entered into at the same time as the agreement containing the recitals (see the fourth recital in sample 2).

The last recital, known as the "lead-in,"[81] can be distinguished from the others in that it does not contain background information, but serves to introduce the body of the contract by indicating that the parties agree to what follows.

A complex agreement might have a dozen or more recitals. In a straightforward transaction, however, you can readily dispense with recitals. It is unnecessary to provide recitals that simply state, for instance, that Acme wants to sell the Shares to Investco, and that Investco wants to purchase the Shares from Acme, given that this information can readily be discerned from the contract title and the initial provisions of the body of the contract. You would still need a lead-in, though you would dispense with the *therefore*.

Do not address in any detail in the recitals the rights and obligations of the parties because courts regard recitals as subordinate to the body of the contract.[82] Bear in mind, however, that a court may use recitals to help determine the intent of the parties.[83]

Some lawyers recommend that no terms be defined in the recitals, since the recitals do not form part of the agreement proper. One authority, by contrast, advises that a principal function of recitals is to give the drafter the opportunity to define terms early on.[84] I do not favor either position: I often define some terms in the recitals, but I see no point in straining to do so and will sometimes avoid defining a given term in the recitals in order to keep them relatively succinct.

WITNESSETH, WHEREAS, *and* NOW, THEREFORE

More often than not, recitals are preceded by the centered heading *WITNESSETH*, with or without underlining, a space between each letter, and other embellishments. Such headings may be picturesque, but they are archaic and inane:

> [T]he modern use of *witnesseth* is premised on a mistake: that the word is a command in the imperative mood. Actually, it is the third-person singular verb—she sings = she *singeth*; he says = he *sayeth*; she witnesses = she *witnesseth*. The word at the outset of instruments is really just a remnant of a longer phrase, such as *This document witnesseth that . . . .* Hence to make WITNESSETH shout in all capitals from the top of a document makes no literal sense.[85]

In the majority of contracts, the recitals are independent clauses beginning with *WHEREAS* and linked by semicolons; recitals are, after all, commonly referred to as "whereas" clauses. This meaning of "whereas" is archaic,[86] and in drafting recitals you should dispense with *WHEREAS*, along with the accompanying semicolons.[87] You should also not be shy about using a conventional paragraph structure for your recitals rather than limiting each recital to a single sentence, as is traditional.

The lead-in indicates that what follows represents the agreement of the parties. Tradition requires that when the preceding recitals start with *WHEREAS*, the lead-in should begin *NOW, THEREFORE*. Once you rid yourself of *WHEREAS*, there is no reason to retain *NOW, THEREFORE*.

Heading

If you accept that the heading *WITNESSETH* is beyond the pale, *RECITALS* is a plausible alternative, *BACKGROUND* and *PRELIMINARY STATEMENTS* rather less so.[88] I do not use any heading. For one thing, any moderately sophisticated reader would be able to identify recitals based on their position, structure, and content and would not need them to be signposted. Also, the legal effect of recitals depends on their content rather than on how they are introduced. Furthermore, consistency would require that the heading *BODY OF THE CONTRACT*, or something similar, follow a heading for the recitals. (Occasionally recitals are followed by the heading *AGREEMENT*, which apart from anything else is a little misleading. "Agreement" is not a synonym for the body of the contract but applies to the contract as a whole.) And if one is going to indulge in a naming of the parts, why not give the introductory clause a heading? Ultimately, it is a matter of taste: if you do not share my preference for contracts stripped of bells and whistles, by all means give your recitals a heading.

Numbering or Lettering

Drafters who manage to wean themselves off recital archaisms often restore some clutter by using a number or letter to designate each recital. Numbering or lettering a paragraph serves a purpose only when you need to refer to that paragraph again, and it is unlikely that you should ever need to refer to an individual recital, as opposed to the recitals as a whole.

Consideration

Unlike the lead-in contained in the sample 2 recitals, most lead-ins refer to the consideration for the promises made by the parties to the contract. Such "recitals of consideration" can take many forms, but a relatively full-blown example is as follows: *NOW, THEREFORE, in consideration of the premises and the mutual covenants set forth herein and for other good and valuable consideration, the receipt and sufficiency of which are hereby acknowledged, the parties hereto covenant and agree as follows.* The wall-to-wall legalese is enough to suggest that such clauses are of dubious utility. This suspicion is well founded.

For one thing, *in consideration of the premises* is simply an archaic way of saying "therefore" and is superfluous given the preceding *THEREFORE*.[89] Also, it is sufficient that the parties *agree*; they do not need to *covenant* as well.[90]

The remainder of the lead-in, constituting the recital of consideration proper, is, however, of greater interest.

Recitals of consideration are included in contracts as a hedge against the possibility that the transaction might be found by a court to be unenforceable due to lack of consideration. Such clauses should, as a general rule, be redundant in a business context, because the likelihood of a contract lacking adequate consideration would seem remote. A more significant problem with such clauses, however, is that they are generally ineffective. A promise that is inherently unenforceable for lack of consideration, such as a gratuitous promise or a promise based on past consideration, does not become enforceable simply because a recital states that there was in fact consideration.[91] Also, a court that would refuse to enforce a promise on the grounds that the claimed consideration was a sham would not be dissuaded from doing so by a recital to the contrary.[92] Only in certain limited and, for our purposes, inapplicable circumstances will a recital of consideration be effective.[93]

Given that recitals of consideration are essentially ineffective, I recommend that you avoid them and use instead a lead-in of the sort contained in sample 2. If you find yourself in the exceptional situation of drafting a contract that a court might regard as lacking a bargained-for exchange, you should find ways of remedying that potential defect instead of relying on a recital of consideration.

The lead-in can raise other issues. It often contains additional extraneous matter such as a statement of the intent of the parties to be legally bound.[94] Additionally, the discussion below regarding the tense to use in "language of performance"[95] applies to the lead-in, since the lead-in itself constitutes language of performance.

COVER SHEET, TABLE OF CONTENTS, AND INDEX OF DEFINED TERMS

Once a contract is more than 20 or so pages long, I usually provide a table of contents that lists page numbers for articles and sections. Word-processing software makes it simple to create a table of contents and keep it up to date.

The table of contents is placed before the contract proper. Because no one wants the table of contents to be the face that a contract shows to the world, it is invariably preceded by a cover sheet on which is artfully spread what is basically a more concise version of the introductory clause.

If I use an index of defined terms,[96] I place it immediately after the table of contents.

CHAPTER 2

The Body of the Contract (Language)

B ETWEEN THE RECITALS AND THE CONCLUDING CLAUSE is the part of the contract that states the rights and obligations of the parties. The simplest term for this section is "the body of the contract."[97] While "the operative provisions," meaning those provisions having principal relevance,[98] is a possible alternative,[99] its is rather ponderous. I also avoid the term "substantive provisions": "substantive" is the counterpart of "procedural,"[100] and any given contract could contain both substantive *and* procedural provisions.

Since the body of the contract contains the bulk of the text and makes use of a broader variety of language than do the other sections, it is unsurprising that it is in the context of the body of the contract that most drafting issues arise. Many of these issues, including those discussed in chapter 5, can be addressed independently of one another. Other topics, such as the role of the word *shall* and which tense to use in any given context, are interrelated and are best addressed in the context of an analysis of the language of the body of the contract as a whole.

A clause or sentence in the body of the contract can serve one of a number of purposes. Each purpose requires its own category of language, and each category raises its own issues of usage. I discuss these categories below, as well as the question of how to express conditions by means of certain of those categories. This approach reflects my sense that understanding how contract language works requires that one break it down into its constituent components rather than tackle a series of discrete issues.

As part of this discussion, I provide tables containing examples of a particular category of language, with each example being followed by variations on that example. Each initial example is identified by two numbers within brackets and separated by a hyphen; the first number designates the number of the table, the second designates the number of the example within that table. (For example, [2-3] denotes the third example in table 2.) Each variation is given the same designation as the related initial example, with a lower-case letter added. (For example, [2-3b] denotes the second variation on [2-3].)

In addition, each example and each of its variations is annotated to indicate how acceptable I find it. I use the following symbols:

●● means that I recommend this usage

● means that this usage, while acceptable, can be improved upon; that it needs to be used with caution; or that how acceptable it is depends on the context in which it is used

○ means that I do not favor this usage, but acknowledge that many careful drafters do

○○ means that I recommend you avoid this usage

LANGUAGE OF PERFORMANCE

Contract language can serve to memorialize actions of the parties that are concurrent with the signing of the contract. I refer to this as "language of performance" (see table 1).

The simple present (Acme hereby *grants* the License to Smith) is without exception the tense used in language of performance, rather than the present progressive (Acme *is* hereby *granting* the License to Smith). The present progressive would convey, inappropriately, that a happening has duration and is not necessarily complete.[101]

Occasionally one finds *does* or *do* used as an auxiliary in language of performance, as in [1-1a]. This is an archaism.[102]

A further and more subtle issue relating to use of the simple present in language of performance is use of the compound adverb *hereby*.

TABLE 1		LANGUAGE OF PERFORMANCE
[1-1]	●●	Acme hereby grants the License to Smith.
[1-1a]	○○	Acme does hereby grant the License to Smith.
[1-1b]	●	Acme grants the License to Smith.
[1-1c]	○○	The License is hereby granted to Smith.
[1-1d]	○○	Acme shall grant the License to Smith as of the date of this Agreement.
[1-2]	●●	The Seller acknowledges that the Buyer would be irreparably harmed by any breach.
[1-2a]	●	The Seller hereby acknowledges that the Buyer would be irreparably harmed by any breach.
[1-2b]	○○	It is acknowledged by the Seller that the Buyer would be irreparably harmed by any breach.
[1-3]	●●	The Buyer does not hereby assume the Excluded Liabilities.
[1-3a]	○○	The Buyer hereby does not assume the Excluded Liabilities.

Like other *here-* and *there-* words,[103] *hereby* is often dismissed as an unhelpful archaism that one should avoid.[104] The role of *hereby* is, however, a little more complicated than it first appears.

First of all, there are two uses of *hereby*. In the phrase *Doe is authorized to consummate the transactions contemplated hereby*, the word *hereby* is located in the subordinate clause *contemplated hereby*. In this context, one can use the approved method of keeping to a minimum the number of *here-* and *there-* words and replace *hereby* with *by this Agreement*.[105] By contrast, in language of performance, *hereby* is located in the main clause. To understand the purpose that *hereby* serves in language of performance, one must be willing to delve rather deeply into aspects of the simple present.

There are various categories of the simple present, but the two that concern us here are the "habitual present" and the "instantaneous present." This is because the habitual present and the instantaneous present use dynamic verb meanings (She *makes* her own dresses) as opposed to stative verb meanings (Everest *is* the tallest mountain),[106] and language of performance requires dynamic verb meanings.

When they are used with the simple present, dynamic verb meanings most commonly refer, by means of the habitual present, to repeated events. (She always *eats* pasta for dinner. We *go* to London every year.)[107] By contrast, the instantaneous present occurs when the verb refers in the simple present to a single action begun and completed approximately at the moment of speech.[108] There are a number of forms of the instantaneous present, including "commentaries" (*Smith passes to Jackson. Jackson shoots!*),[109] but for our purposes the most significant is the "performative," which is characterized by simultaneity of the event described and the speech event itself.[110] There are two kinds of performatives, and each instance of language of performance falls into one or other category.

There are those performatives that use a verb of speaking (such as *apologize* or *request*) describing the speech act of which it is a part.[111] Every contract lead-in[112] is a performative, *agree* being a verb of speaking. If in a contract a party acknowledges a certain fact, that acknowledgment is a performative, *acknowledge* also being a verb of speaking.

The second kind of performative is that which describes ritual acts and is accepted as the outward sign that those acts are taking place.[113] This encompasses all other instances of language of performance, such as *Acme hereby grants Excelsior an exclusive license to the Patents.* I refer to these performatives as "ritual performatives."

It is in the context of ritual performatives that *hereby* has a role to play. Take the language of performance *Doe purchases the Shares.* While the context indicates that one is not dealing with a statement that Doe is in the habit of purchasing certain shares, or an observation that Doe is concurrently with, but independently of, the contract engaged in the act of purchasing those shares, in purely grammatical terms one cannot exclude those meanings. *Hereby* has come to act as a signal that the verb is being used as a performative verb,[114] and in the statement *Doe hereby purchases the Shares* it serves to indicate that one is not dealing with the habitual present or another form of the instantaneous present. Consequently, I find *hereby* reassuring, and to my ears a ritual performative lacking a *hereby* sounds odd. Others may disagree,[115] but they have perhaps not considered this aspect of *hereby*.

One commentator has argued that *hereby* serves no purpose in the phrase *I hereby resign the Office of the President of the United States.*[116] This view might be prompted by a simple aversion to *hereby*, whatever the context, but it might also be based upon the notion that one could not reasonably interpret this statement as meaning that I am in the habit of periodically resigning the office in question. Whatever the merits of this argument in other legal prose in the first person singular, I do not think it applies in the context of corporate agreements, where it would make little sense to treat *resign* differently from *purchase*. I would not hesitate to use in a contract *Smith hereby resigns*.

Notably absent from the above discussion of the utility of *hereby* is any reference to its use in performatives that use verbs of speaking. I agree with other commentators that one can do without *hereby* in, for example, the phrase *The parties declare*,[117] but my reasons are perhaps different. The likelihood of confusing ritual performatives with the habitual present or other forms of the instantaneous present is admittedly more theoretical than actual. In the context of performatives using verbs of speaking, confusion is even less likely, and it would strain credulity to suggest that *The parties declare* could possibly be construed as meaning that the parties habitually declare whatever it is that is being declared, or that their declaration is independent of the contract. Consequently, when a verb of speaking is involved you do not need to insert *hereby* to indicate that the verb is being used as a performative verb.[118] This is why I do not include *hereby* in my preferred form of lead-in,[119] an example of which is contained in sample 2. Note, however, that I base this distinction more on my own instinct than on clear-cut authority.

You might be tempted to use *by this Agreement* in language of performance instead of *hereby*. Resist the temptation: the better view is that the *here-* in *hereby* refers to the associated speech event, as opposed to the contract as a whole or any part of the contract.[120]

To summarize, if language of performance uses a performative verb that is a verb of speaking, as in [1-2], *hereby* would be redundant. If, however, the performative is other than a verb of speaking (in other words, if it is a ritual performative), use *hereby*, as in [1-1], to avoid any confusion, however theoretical, with the habitual present or other forms of the instantaneous present.

The modest implications of use or nonuse of *hereby* might not seem to merit the rather lengthy treatment I have afforded the topic. I am, however, less interested in changing how drafters use *hereby* than I am in cautioning against the sort of oversimplification that underlies sweeping assertions that *hereby* is redundant.

It is occasionally helpful to state that one or more parties are *not* taking a certain action. The only nuance is that it is preferable to negate the performative by placing *does not* before *hereby*, as in [1-3]. Placing it after *hereby*, as in [1-3a], would suggest, rather incongruously, that one could have a ritual action consisting of inaction.

Another issue that arises in the context of language of performance is what voice to use. It is best to avoid using the passive; this is standard advice in both general texts on English usage[121] and those concerned exclusively with legal writing.[122] One reason for this is that in the majority of passives (including [1-1c]), the passive agent is unexpressed.[123] This raises the possibility of confusion as to who is doing the performing. Even if it is clear from the context who is performing the action, or if the passive agent is explicit (as in [1-2b]), using the passive voice also results in a wordier sentence and disrupts the ordinary sequence of events in the reader's mind.[124]

Some drafters attempt to have language of obligation[125] (such as *Acme shall grant the License to Smith*) serve as language of performance by tacking on *as of the date of this Agreement.* (See [1-1d].) While doing so serves to require that Acme grant the license sometime on the day the agreement is entered into, that is a distant and potentially pernicious second-best to having the grant take place simultaneously with the signing of the agreement.

Finally, one might ask why the present tense is used in language of performance, rather than, say, the present perfect. (The vague adage that "[f]or the most part, the draftsman should stay in the present tense" does not apply in this context, but to "provisions of continuing effect," such as language of obligation and language of policy.)[126] Using the present tense is consistent with having a contract be the agreement of the parties; if you use the present perfect, you are treating the contract as a historical record of an agreement extrinsic to the contract. The former approach is the only one used, which is not surprising, because it is inherently simpler and more efficient.

LANGUAGE OF OBLIGATION

As the term implies, "language of obligation" serves to detail the obligations of one or more parties to a contract. As regards structure, language of obligation falls into two categories, depending upon whether the obligation is imposed on the subject of the sentence or on someone other than the subject.

Language of Obligation Imposed on the Subject of a Sentence

In the example in table 2, Widgetco is the subject of the sentence. The most widely accepted way of indicating that Widgetco has a duty to purchase the Shares from Jones is to use *shall*, as in [2-1]. Most commentators acknowledge this use of *shall*.[127]

TABLE 2		LANGUAGE OF OBLIGATION IMPOSED ON SUBJECT OF SENTENCE

[2-1]	●●	Widgetco shall purchase the Shares from Jones.
[2-1a]	○	Widgetco must purchase the Shares from Jones.
[2-1b]	○	Widgetco is obligated to purchase the Shares from Jones.
[2-1c]	○	Widgetco will purchase the Shares from Jones.
[2-1d]	○○	Widgetco agrees that it shall purchase the Shares from Jones.
[2-1e]	○○	Widgetco agrees to purchase the Shares from Jones.
[2-1f]	○○	Widgetco undertakes to purchase the Shares from Jones.
[2-1g]	○○	Widgetco covenants and agrees to purchase the Shares from Jones.
[2-1h]	○○	Widgetco shall be obligated to purchase the Shares from Jones.
[2-1i]	○○	Widgetco is responsible for purchasing the Shares from Jones.

It is worth considering how *shall* came to serve this function.[128] *Shall* is a modal auxiliary verb. The modal auxiliaries (*shall, will, must, can, may*) are so called because, unlike the other auxiliaries (*be, do, have*), they express modal meaning such as possibility, volition, and obligation. *Shall* originally meant obligation or compulsion and was a full verb (like *eat, walk,* and *play*), but now it is used only as an auxiliary, as is the modal *will*, which originally carried the sense of volition. Because obligations and intentions concern future conduct, and because English verbs lack a true future form, *shall* and *will* came to be used with future time, with the result that *shall* and *will* can now be used either to express modal meanings or to mark future time. There arose a set of exception-ridden rules to distinguish these two uses: one should use *shall* to express plain future in the first person, use *will* to express plain future in the second and third persons, and do the reverse to convey modal meanings.[129] These unmanageable rules have largely been abandoned; in common usage *shall* is rarely used to indicate plain future and barely survives in its modal form.[130] In the stylized context of legal drafting, which for the most part uses only the third person, *shall* continues to serve as a means of expressing obligations,[131] while *will* expresses simple futurity.

The complexity of the distinction between *shall* and *will* is doubtless the reason many drafters flit from one to the other and back again when imposing a duty on the subject of a sentence. I recall a moment in my second year of practice when it dawned on me that a contract I was drafting used *shall* and *will* at random, and that I had not the faintest idea how to distinguish between the two. I plowed on regardless, and had to wait several years to be enlightened.

The problem with the way drafters use *shall* is, however, not so much that they fail to use it when they should, but that they insist on using it inappropriately in other categories of contract language, as is discussed throughout this chapter. The result is that the way *shall* is used in most contracts violates the basic tenet of legal drafting that one should not use any given word or term in more than one sense.[132]

A small but influential group of American commentators advocate that one dispense with *shall* entirely.[133] They do so not because *shall* does not serve a purpose, but because "lawyers are not educable on the subject of *shall*, so the only solution is complete abstinence."[134] They recommended that instead of *shall*, one use *must*. This approach has been termed the "ABC rule" (in acknowledgment of the Australian, British, and Canadian drafters who were the first to champion this approach),[135] and contrasts with the "American rule," pursuant to which *shall* is used to mean *has a duty to*. A Dictionary of Modern Legal Usage says the following regarding the ABC rule:

> This view has much to be said for it. American lawyers and judges who try to restrict *shall* to the sense "has a duty to" find it difficult to apply the convention consistently. Indeed, few lawyers have the semantic acuity to identify correct and incorrect *shalls* even after a few hours of study. That being so, there can hardly be much hope of the profession's using *shall* consistently.[136]

What of the proposed alternative, *must*? In [2-1a], *must* means *is required to*.[137] (*Is required to* and *is obligated to* (see [2-1b]) are "*be*-verb circumlocutions" and inferior substitutes for *must*, one word being better than three.)[138] *Shall* and *must* are close in meaning,[139] but there remains a difference:

> [*Must*] does not directly create a duty; it merely asserts the existence of a duty, however it may have been created. Thus, anyone can say that all motorists *must* drive on the right, because the legislature has said they *shall*. But if the speaker has the power to command, then *must* has the force of a command, but only by inference. Hence, in directing commands to persons *shall* is better.[140]

Consequently, *shall* does have some value, and abandoning it would serve a purpose only if *must* presents distinct advantages.

The most significant benefit to using *must* is that it cannot be used to convey futurity and so would not be as prone to misuse as *shall*.[141] Using *must* to convey obligations would also be more in keeping with standard usage.

Must does, however, have its drawbacks. Using *must* to convey all obligations, whether imposed on the subject of the sentence or someone other than the subject of the sentence, rather than using *shall* for the former and *must* for the latter, "we do give up a potentially useful distinction."[142]

Also, the advantages of *must* would seem more apparent than real. While there is considerable case law concerning use of *shall*, the one commentator who has written in detail on the subject, Kimble, concludes that "lawyers' misuses, including the confusion of modal and future *shall*, are not the main problem."[143] Instead, the litigation concerns how strong *shall* is, namely whether it is mandatory, permissive (conveying the meaning of *may*) or "directory" (conveying the meaning of *should*, or a little stronger).[144] According to Kimble,

> We are still left without a word to express a mandatory, or absolute, duty, but I doubt that switching to *must* would do the job, because courts generally equate it with *shall* and seem equally willing to give it a soft interpretation. In a number of cases, *must* has been read as not being mandatory. Any number of other cases contain dicta that *must* is not always mandatory or can be read as *may* (and vice versa).[145]

A further drawback of *must* is a function of its tone. Use of *shall* to mark future time has softened the impact of *shall* as a means of conveying obligation. By contrast, *must* comes across as rather bossy,[146] and it is likely that most drafters would find it grating if used consistently instead of *shall*.

When considering the pros and cons of *must*, bear in mind that *shall* is firmly entrenched in corporate law circles. I cannot recall ever seeing *must* used in a corporate agreement to impose an obligation on the subject of a sentence, and while the ABC rule may, for purposes of the drafting of court rules, be "fast gaining ground in the U.S.,"[147] it is unlikely to gain acceptance in corporate law circles any time soon, particularly given its shortcomings. We are, after all, talking about a community that still uses *WITNESSETH*. (Note, however, that in one context, namely language of obligation used to express not duties but conditions, one can safely use *must*. This topic is discussed below.)[148]

Will has been proposed as a third way of imposing an obligation on the subject of a sentence, as in [2-1c]. Some commentators see it as a way of steering clear of *shall* while at the same time avoiding the stridency of *must*.[149] Other commentators are of the view that the agreement of the parties contained in the lead-in obviates the need for language of obligation, in the form of *shall*, and that the preferred alternative is *will*.[150]

Will would probably receive a more favorable response than *must* from the corporate law community, particularly because many drafters do not know the difference between *will* and *shall*. There are, however, two problems with this use of *will*.

First, according to customary usage, in the third person *will* does not convey obligation but simple futurity,[151] and agreement of the parties as to the terms of the body of the contract makes no difference in this regard. The view that the statement *X and Y agree* renders *shall* superfluous in what follows would seem to be based on the misapprehension that *X and Y agree* constitutes language of obligation,[152] whereas it is in fact language of performance.[153]

Second, using *will* to convey obligations of the subject of a sentence requires that one also use it to convey obligations of someone other than the subject of the sentence,[154] as well as to convey simple futurity. Using *will* in more than one sense would constitute just the sort of breach of the "Golden Rule" of drafting that jettisoning *shall* was ostensibly meant to cure.[155] Furthermore, the problem would be exacerbated if *will* were subject to the other misuses that afflict *shall*, which would doubtless be the case.

The upshot is that the cure, *will*, is more pernicious than the ailment, *shall*.

For purposes of my own drafting, I have mixed feelings about *shall*, because as long as it remains the principal means of indicating an obligation imposed on the subject of a sentence, legal prose will always be readily identifiable as such. I have not, however, elected to use *must* instead of *shall* to convey obligations of the subject of a sentence, largely because I like the additional level of precision that *shall* gives me, now that I finally know how to use it properly; because *shall* avoids the hectoring tone of *must*; and because it seems likely that switching to *must* would not resolve the issue underlying most litigation involving *shall*, namely whether it expresses that which is mandatory. The continued supremacy of *shall* in corporate law circles is also a factor.

Similarly, I have not elected to use *will* instead of *shall*, for doing so would require that I use *will* to convey both obligation and futurity.

Those who favor abandoning *shall* on the grounds that most drafters do not have the time, inclination, or acuity to figure out how to use it properly[156] may regard my approach as unsuited to general use because it is the product of close study of the subject. I am unwilling, however, to adopt or recommend to others, whatever the reason, a regime that I regard as less satisfactory. Furthermore, it is perhaps premature to give up on suggesting to the corporate legal community that it is best to use *shall* to mean only "has a duty to."

Because the parties state in the lead in that they agree to that which follows,[157] they do not need to state in the body of the contract that they agree to any given provision. Nevertheless, drafters tend to lard the body of the contract with such assertions, which can take various forms. (See, for example, [2-1d] through [2-1g].)

In this regard, I am particularly averse to the verb *to covenant*. It originally meant to enter into a covenant, namely a contract under seal.[158] In the context of corporate agreements, however, *covenant* is simply a synonym for agreement,[159] and *Acme covenants* is simply a fusty way of saying *Acme agrees*.[160] Many drafters remain attached to it, perhaps because of its Old Testament atmospherics, and they often make matters worse by having parties *covenant and agree* to a given provision, as in [2-1g].[161]

There are other less-than-perfect ways of expressing language of obligation imposed on the subject of a sentence. For example, *shall* is appropriate and *is obligated to* is adequate (barely), but joined, as in [2-1h], they mean, unhelpfully, "has a duty to be obligated." Also, *is responsible for* plus present participle, as in [2-1i], is long-winded and vague.

Language of Obligation Imposed on Someone Other Than the Subject of a Sentence

In a sentence expressing an obligation, the obligation is often placed on someone other than the subject of that sentence. There are five contexts in which this occurs.

First, it occurs when a sentence that would, in the active voice, have one or more parties to the contract as the subject is instead phrased in the passive voice, thereby causing the active object to become the pas-

TABLE 3		LANGUAGE OF OBLIGATION IMPOSED ON SOMEONE OTHER THAN SUBJECT OF SENTENCE
[3-1]	●	Notice of any claim must be given by the Indemnified Party to the Indemnifying Party.
[3-1a]	○○	Notice of any claim shall be given by the Indemnified Party to the Indemnifying Party.
[3-1b]	○	Notice of any claim will be given by the Indemnified Party to the Indemnifying Party.
[3-1c]	○	The Indemnifying Party is entitled to be notified by the Indemnified Party of any claim.
[3-1d]	○○	The Indemnifying Party shall be entitled to be notified by the Indemnified Party of any claim.
[3-1e]	●●	The Indemnified Party shall notify the Indemnifying Party of any claim.
[3-2]	○	The Consultant must be reimbursed for all authorized expenses.
[3-2a]	○○	The Consultant shall be reimbursed for all authorized expenses.
[3-2b]	○	The Consultant will be reimbursed for all authorized expenses.
[3-2c]	●	The Consultant must be reimbursed by the Company for all authorized expenses.
[3-2d]	○	The Consultant is entitled to be reimbursed for all authorized expenses.
[3-2e]	○	The Consultant shall be entitled to be reimbursed for all authorized expenses.
[3-2f]	●●	The Company shall reimburse the Consultant for all authorized expenses.
[3-3]	●	The Closing must take place at Acme's offices.
[3-3a]	○○	The Closing shall take place at Acme's offices.
[3-3b]	○	The Closing will take place at Acme's offices.
[3-3c]	●	The parties shall cause the Closing to take place at Acme's offices.
[3-3d]	●●	The parties shall hold the Closing at Acme's offices.
[3-4]	●	The auditors must examine the Financial Statements.
[3-4a]	○○	The auditors shall examine the Financial Statements.
[3-4b]	○	The auditors will examine the Financial Statements.
[3-4c]	●	The Financial Statements must be examined by the auditors.
[3-4d]	○○	The Financial Statements shall be examined by the auditors.
[3-4e]	○	The Financial Statements will be examined by the auditors.
[3-4f]	●	The Borrower shall cause the auditors to examine the Financial Statements.

continued

[3-5]	●	Jones must receive an annual salary in the amount of $100,000 a year.
[3-5a]	○○	Jones shall receive an annual salary in the amount of $100,000 a year.
[3-5b]	○○	Jones will receive an annual salary in the amount of $100,000 a year.
[3-5c]	○○	Jones is entitled to receive an annual salary in the amount of $100,000 a year.
[3-5d]	●●	Widgetco shall pay Jones an annual salary in the amount of $100,000 a year.
[3-6]	○	Doe is entitled to full credit for service performed on behalf of the Company.
[3-6a]	○○	Doe shall be entitled to full credit for service performed on behalf of the Company.
[3-6b]	●●	The Purchaser shall credit Doe fully for service performed on behalf of the Company.

sive subject and either turning the active subject into a *by*-agent, as in [3-1], or omitting it entirely, as in [3-2].

Second, it occurs when the subject of a sentence is an inanimate object, as in [3-3], and is therefore incapable of assuming a duty. (Such sentences are generally in the active voice.)

Third, it occurs in a sentence, whether in the active voice (see [3-4]) or passive voice (see [3-4c]), in which the active subject or *by*-agent (whether present or not) is a person or entity but is not a party, and so cannot be required to assume a duty.

Fourth, it occurs when, in a sentence in the active voice in which the subject is a party, the duty is in effect imposed on someone other than the subject, and the subject is passive, though in the literal rather than grammatical sense. The only instances of this I have encountered involve the verb *receive*, as in [3-5].

Fifth, it occurs when a main clause containing *is entitled to*, meaning "has a right to,"[162] is used with a thing, as in [3-6], or with a passive complement clause, as in [3-1c] and [3-2d]. In such constructions, it is implicit that another is required to provide what the subject is entitled to. (Note that *is entitled to* used with a complement clause in the active voice constitutes language of discretion.)[163]

The first four contexts above require a modal auxiliary. Which is preferable, *shall*, *must*, or *will*? The vast majority of corporate lawyers use *shall* in this context, just as they use it to convey an obligation imposed on the subject. This approach has been termed the "lax American rule."[164] This approach is also used in statutes, including those that corporate lawyers refer to constantly, such as the Delaware General Corporation Law[165] and the Securities Act of 1933.[166]

Dickerson has articulated arguments in favor of this usage:

> The command language of *shall* is not necessarily directed to the subject of the sentence. On the contrary, it is the very essence of the passive voice that a verb *not* be addressed to the natural subject of the sentence. It is enough if the target of the command is expressed or implied elsewhere in the sentence.[167]

From the analogous examples he provides, it is evident that Dickerson would favor [3-1a] and [3-2a] over the alternatives, on the grounds that it is express (in the former) and implied (in the latter) that the command is being directed elsewhere.[168]

Despite the near universal acceptance of this practice by the legal community, I am not in favor of having *shall* do double duty in this manner. Using *shall* to convey a duty imposed on the subject of a sentence is at least consistent with the historical role of *shall* in general English usage. By contrast, using *shall* in a sentence in the passive voice to indicate a duty imposed on a party represents an expansion that is limited to the legal community. It seems counterproductive to create new uses for a word that has largely been abandoned by most English speakers. Furthermore, while I agree that using *shall* in a passive sentence is not likely to result in confusion, having *shall* serve these two functions can only muddy its meaning.

The other examples in table 3 of the use of *shall* are even more questionable. I agree with Dickerson that the use of *shall* reflected in [3-5a] is "inept" because no duty is imposed on the active subject, *shall* and the active voice notwithstanding.[169] It is, however, unlikely that this sort of clumsiness could result in a misunderstanding. Potentially more confusing is the use of *shall* in [3-4a] and [3-4d]: the duty is imposed on neither the subject nor the object, but instead, one presumes, on the one or more entities whose finances are reflected in the Financial Statements. Nevertheless, most drafters would without hesitation use *shall* in this context.

Must, meaning *is required to*, is one alternative to *shall* for purposes of conveying an obligation imposed on someone other than the subject of a sentence. (Concision favors avoiding the synonyms *is required to* and *is obligated to*.)[170] Those who use *must* in this manner fall into two camps. First, there are those who do so while using *shall* to convey an obligation imposed on the subject of a sentence; by so doing, they are following what has been termed the "strict American rule."[171] Second, there are those who follow the ABC rule, which provides that one use *must* to convey not only duties imposed on the subject of the sentence,[172] but all duties, no matter whom they are imposed on.[173]

There are two advantages to using *must* in this context, and they are the mirror image of the disadvantages of using *shall*. First, doing so is more in keeping with general English usage. Second, it enhances clarity by allowing one to reserve *shall* for imposing a duty on the subject of a sentence. This is enough to cause me to favor using *must* for purposes of conveying an obligation imposed on someone other than the subject of a sentence. This, together with my championing of *shall* for purposes of conveying an obligation imposed on the subject of a sentence, makes me a follower of the strict American rule.

Followers of the ABC rule who elect to use *will* instead of *must*[174] would be required to use it for all duties regardless of whom they are imposed on.[175] In the context of duties imposed on someone other than the subject of a sentence, the weaknesses of *will* are the same as those apparent in the context of duties imposed on the subject of a sentence:[176] general usage has it that in the third person, *will* does not convey obligation but rather simple futurity, and using *will* to convey obligations as well as simple futurity would likely result in the sort of confusion that those who advocate abandoning *shall* are hoping to avoid.

While I favor the strict American rule, I recognize that following it rigorously requires application. But minding one's *shalls* and *musts* should really represent a minor part of the drafting process: you should have little need for *must*, because you would draft more clearly and concisely if you were to steer clear of imposing a duty on anyone other than the subject of the sentence. There are two ways to reduce to a bare minimum the need for *must*.

The principal way of doing so is to avoid using the passive voice. Eschewing the passive not only enhances clarity and concision,[177] it also, as an incidental benefit, significantly reduces the need for *must*. Consequently, of [3-1] and [3-2] and their variations, the preferred usage, by far, is that reflected in [3-1e] and [3-2f]. I recommend a similar fix for the effectively passive [3-5a]; see [3-5d].

A second way is to make explicit, in any sentence in which the active subject or *by*-agent is incapable of assuming a duty, such as [3-3], [3-4], and [3-4c], exactly who *does* owe the duty. One way to do this is by stating, as in [3-3c] and [3-4f], that the party owing the duty *shall cause* someone else to take a given action. The particular benefit of this usage is that it allows you to state explicitly who would be liable if the obligation is not met. It could, however, result in unacceptably leaden drafting. If, for example, [3-4f] were in a section containing numerous requirements regarding the auditors, resorting each time to *the Borrower shall cause* could be awkward. The same difficulty could arise in connection with provisions specifying how an arbitrator must act: it would not be feasible to state repeatedly that *the parties shall cause the arbitrator* to take a given action. In such situations, you can omit any reference to the party owing the duty and stick with either the active, as in [3-4], or the passive, as in [3-4c], using *must* in both cases. The passive would be acceptable if the thing done (examination of the Financial Statements) is more important than the doer (the auditors).[178] Note that by selecting your verbs judiciously, you can sometimes avoid altogether any need for *shall cause*; see [3-3d].

If you make the effort to ensure that whenever possible duties are imposed on the subject of a sentence, you will draft more clearly and will, in the process, limit your need to alternate between *shall* and *must*.

What of *is entitled to* used with a thing or a passive complement clause? Though it does not require a modal auxiliary, more often than not drafters incorrectly provide, as in [3-1d], [3-2e], and [3-6a], that a party *shall be entitled to* rather than *is entitled to*. This is an example of a phenomenon examined at greater length in the context of language of policy.[179]

What is more significant, however, is that provisions using *is entitled to* share the same defects as provisions that are in the passive voice.[180] The *by*-agent is often unexpressed, as is the case in [3-2d] and [3-6], and even when a provision using *is entitled to* makes it clear who bears the duty, as in [3-1c], it is at the cost of a certain wordiness. Furthermore, it seems counterintuitive to focus on the entitled party, and doing so could conceivably have unforeseen consequences: a statement that on a given date I am entitled to be paid an amount by Doe is not exactly equivalent to an obligation on the part of Doe to pay me, for one could argue that Doe is not required to pay me until I have indicated to Doe that I wish to be paid. Given these shortcomings, it is preferable to avoid using *is entitled to* in language of obligation and instead to focus on the party owing the duty, as in [3-1e], [3-2f], and [3-6b].

Language of obligation also serves, along with other categories of contract language, to convey contract conditions. I address this topic below.[181]

LANGUAGE OF DISCRETION

"Language of discretion" gives a party discretion to take or not to take a given action.

The principal vehicle for language of discretion is *may*. In this context, *may* expresses permission or sanction.[182] When used in an active construction, as in [4-1], *may* means "has discretion to, is permitted to"[183] or "is authorized to."[184] (Using any of these formulations as an alternative to *may*, as in [4-1a], would constitute circumlocution.)[185] *May* can also be used in a passive construction, in which case the one or more parties that have permission are present as a *by*-agent, as in [4-2], or are absent, as in [4-3]. For the reasons outlined above in the context of language of obligation,[186] you should avoid using the passive; [4-2a] represents an improvement over [4-2]. Often enough the likelihood of confusion is slim or nonexistent, as in the case of [4-3], but it is nevertheless better to use the active voice, as in [4-3a], if only to encourage good habits.

TABLE 4		LANGUAGE OF DISCRETION: *MAY*
[4-1]	●●	The indemnified party may at its expense retain separate co-counsel.
[4-1a]	○	The indemnified party is authorized to retain at its expense separate co-counsel.
[4-1b]	○	The indemnified party is entitled to retain at its expense separate co-counsel.
[4-1c]	○○	The indemnified party will have the option to retain at its expense separate co-counsel.
[4-1d]	○○	The indemnified party will be free to retain at its expense separate co-counsel.
[4-2]	●	The Option may be exercised by Smith any time prior to January 1, 2005.
[4-2a]	●●	Smith may exercise the Option any time prior to January 1, 2005.
[4-3]	●	This Agreement may be executed in any number of counterparts.
[4-3a]	●●	The parties may execute this Agreement in any number of counterparts.

One slight complication inherent in using *may* to connote permission is that it can also be read as indicating that something might come to pass.[187] Take the following provision: *During the term of this Agreement, the Investigator may provide the Sponsor with confidential information.* This could be read as meaning that the Investigator is authorized to provide the Sponsor with confidential information, but the intended meaning is that it is possible that the Investigator will do so. You can usually discern from the context which meaning is intended. Furthermore, the consequences of confusion are likely to be benign, because any action that the parties agree might occur would generally, at least implicitly, be permitted. You can reduce the frequency with which this ambiguity occurs by eliminating *may* when it is used superfluously to indicate what might come to pass, as in the following example: "Widgetco shall keep confidential any Evaluation Material that Target *may provide* [read *provides*] to Widgetco under this Agreement."

As with language of obligation, there are other, more long-winded alternatives to *may*. See, for example, [4–1c] and [4-1d].

A second vehicle of discretion is *is entitled to* used with a complement clause in the active voice. While more often than not this usage constitutes, as in [4-1b], a wordier and therefore inferior alternative to *may*, it can be distinguished from *may*.

As discussed above,[188] when *is entitled to* is used with a thing or a complement clause in the passive voice, it is implicit that another party is obligated to provide what the subject of the sentence is entitled to. Similarly, I suggest that *is entitled to* with an active complement clause is best used when it is in the power of another party to frustrate the party that is entitled to act. In [5-1], for example, Jones will be able to purchase the shares only if the party granting the option complies with

TABLE 5   LANGUAGE OF DISCRETION: *IS ENTITLED TO*

[5-1]	●●	If . . . occurs, then upon exercising the Option Jones will be entitled to purchase the number and kind of shares of capital stock . . . .
[5-1a]	○	If . . . occurs, then upon exercising the Option Jones may purchase the number and kind of shares of capital stock . . . .
[5-2]	●	Roe is entitled to serve on Acme's board of directors.
[5-2a]	○	Roe may serve on Acme's board of directors.
[5-2b]	●●	Acme shall at Roe's option appoint Roe a member of its board of directors.

any contract provisions regarding the closing of any sale. *Is entitled to* captures this nuance, *may* does not. (Note that [5-1] uses *will be entitled to* [and not *shall be entitled to*] rather than *is entitled to* because it follows a conditional clause.)[189]

A caveat: even if in a given context *is entitled to* conveys the meaning exemplified by [5-1], it would be best to use instead language of obligation if, as in [5-2], the entitlement consists of a party's ability to trigger an obligation of another party.

One can also convey a party's discretion by means of *is not required to* plus verb, which is the permissive analogue of the mandatory *shall* and *must*. (An alternative formulation is *In no event is Mr. Brown required to*.) One cannot simply dismiss *is not required to* as a *be*-verb circumlocution:[190] the only plausible alternative, *may not*, meaning in this context "is authorized to not," is too ambiguous for comfort.[191] *Is not required to* may be used in the active (see [6-1]) and the passive (see [6-2]). Again, the active (see [6-2a]) is preferable to the passive. Whatever your views on the use of *shall* in language of obligation, steer clear of the use of *shall* exemplified by [6-1a] and [6-2b], because *shall not be required to* represents an unlikely marriage of language of obligation and language of discretion. And it is better not to use *will not be required*, as in [6-1b]: even though the obligation will

TABLE 6		LANGUAGE OF DISCRETION: *IS NOT REQUIRED TO*
[6-1]	●●	Acme is not required to reimburse Consultant for annual expenses in excess of $10,000.
[6-1a]	○○	Acme shall not be required to reimburse Consultant for annual expenses in excess of $10,000.
[6-1b]	○○	Acme will not be required to reimburse Consultant for annual expenses in excess of $10,000.
[6-1c]	○○	Consultant's annual expenses must not exceed $10,000.
[6-1d]	○○	Reimbursement by Acme of Consultant's annual expenses is not required with respect to those expenses in excess of $10,000.
[6-2]	○	Amounts collected from Participants are not required to be held in a segregated account.
[6-2a]	●●	Widgetco is not required to hold in a segregated account any amounts collected from Participants.
[6-2b]	○○	Amounts collected from Participants shall not be required to be held in a segregated account.

continue into the future, it applies upon effectiveness of the agreement, and so the present tense is preferable.[192]

One does not often need *is not required to*, since contracts are more concerned with what the parties must do rather than what they do not have to do. It should, however, be used more often than it is. Drafters generally use language of obligation to require that a party remain within certain limits (see [6-1c]), whereas the aim should be not to restrict that party, but to free the other party from responsibility if that party does go beyond those limits (see [6-1]).

When drafters use *be*-verbs, they often end up "burying" other verbs by favoring nouns. I discuss this subject below,[193] but [6-1d] is an example of this phenomenon, with the noun *reimbursement* being used at the expense of the more succinct verb.

LANGUAGE OF PROHIBITION

One's need for language specifying what parties to a contract are prohibited from doing, or "language of prohibition," is generally met by *shall not*, meaning "has a duty not to,"[194] or *must not*, meaning "is required not to."[195] The question of when to use one or the other is deceptively simple: use *shall not* to convey prohibition where you would use *shall* to convey obligation, and do likewise with *must not* and *must* (or *will not* and *will* if, despite the problems,[196] you use *will* in language of obligation).

There are, inevitably, some nuances. First, *may not*, meaning "is not permitted to,"[197] achieves the same effect as *shall not* and *must not* because depriving a party of the authority to take a given action is essentially the same as requiring that party not to take that action.[198] Nevertheless, commentators favor *shall not* and *must not* over *may not*.[199] The reason for this would seem to be that the ambiguity that afflicts *may*[200] is aggravated in the case of *may not*, since *Acme may not transfer the Shares* can mean that Acme (1) may possibly not transfer the Shares, (2) is authorized not to transfer the Shares, or (3) is not authorized to transfer the Shares.[201] This is enough to make me favor *shall not* and *must not* over *may not*.

Second, a sentence may be given an exact opposite meaning by rendering negative either the subject or the verb.[202] Consequently, the opposite of *Stockholders may transfer their Shares* is not only *Stockholders may not transfer their Shares*, but also *No Stockholder may transfer its Shares*. (Rendering the subject negative is obviously only an option when it is a collective noun.) Many drafters similarly attempt to render negative the subject of a sentence containing *shall*, for instance by using *No Seller shall reveal any Confidential Information* rather than *The Sellers shall not reveal any Confidential Information* or the rarely used alternative, *A Seller shall not.*[203] Read literally, however, *No Seller shall* means "No Seller has a duty to" and is equivalent to "A Seller is not required to."[204] Since this is not at all what is intended, in this context it is preferable to use *No Seller may.*[205] This demonstrates that the relative merits of *shall* and *must*, on the one hand, and *may*, on the other, as a vehicle of prohibition depend on the context.

LANGUAGE OF POLICY

In addition to provisions stating what the parties are required to do, permitted to do, or prohibited from doing, a contract generally contains provisions that state additional rules that must be observed by the parties but that do not, at least expressly, require action or inaction on their part. One term for these rules is "policies."[206]

I can discern two categories of policy. First, there are those that state rules governing a given thing, event, or circumstance; see [7-1] and [7-7]. Second, there are those that address the scope, meaning, or duration of an agreement or part of an agreement; see [7-2], [7-3], [7-5], and [7-6]. One particularly prevalent form of the latter kind of policy is a sentence that contains the autonomous definition of a defined term;[207] see [7-4].

Regarding which tense to use in policies, it is best to use for those policies that apply upon effectiveness of the agreement (such as [7-2], [7-3], and [7-4]) the form of the simple present known as the "state present," even though the policy will continue to apply in the future.[208] The present tense is also appropriate for those policies (such as [7-5]) that state a time of effectiveness or lapsing of effectiveness, since one may use the simple present when a future event is set for a date certain.[209] If, however, the policy relates to future events that may or may not take place, as in [7-1] and [7-6], it is best to use *will.*

Some policies can be rephrased as language of obligation or language of discretion. In the case of such policies, "the difference between promise and policy is a matter of how a provision is phrased rather than the inherent nature of its substantive content."[210]

Policies of this sort I call "passive-type policies." They are often characterized by use of the suffix *-able* with transitive verbs to create

TABLE 7 LANGUAGE OF POLICY

[7-1]	○	Any attempted transfer of Shares in violation of this Agreement is void.
[7-1a]	●●	Any attempted transfer of Shares in violation of this Agreement will be void.
[7-1b]	○○	Any attempted transfer of Shares in violation of this Agreement shall be void.
[7-2]	●●	This Agreement is governed by New York law.
[7-2a]	○	This Agreement will be governed by New York law.
[7-2b]	○○	This Agreement shall be governed by New York law.
[7-3]	●●	This Agreement constitutes the entire agreement of the parties with respect to the subject matter hereof.
[7-3a]	○○	This Agreement shall constitute the entire agreement of the parties . . . .
[7-4]	●●	"Securities Act" means the Securities Act of 1933, as amended.
[7-4a]	○○	"Securities Act" shall mean the Securities Act of 1933, as amended.
[7-5]	●●	This Agreement terminates on December 31, 2002.
[7-5a]	○	This Agreement will terminate on December 31, 2002.
[7-5b]	○○	This Agreement shall terminate on December 31, 2002.
[7-6]	●●	This Agreement will terminate upon the closing of a Qualified IPO.
[7-6a]	○	This Agreement terminates upon the closing of a Qualified IPO.
[7-6b]	○○	This Agreement shall terminate upon the closing of a Qualified IPO.
[7-7]	●	Interest is payable at a rate of 8% per year.
[7-7a]	○○	Interest shall be payable at a rate of 8% per year.
[7-7b]	●●	The Borrower shall pay interest at a rate of 8% per year.

adjectives such as *exercisable* and *payable*. This usage is "fundamentally related to the passive," with *exercisable* being equivalent to *of the kind that can be exercised*.[211] As with passive verb phrases, the agent can be expressed by a *by*-phrase, but in contracts the agent is more often than not omitted (see [7-7]), leaving unstated the party responsible for performing the action. As with sentences in the passive voice, these policies are better rephrased as language of discretion, so that *the*

Option is exercisable becomes *Smith may exercise the Option*, or as language of obligation (see [7-7b]), depending on the adjective.

Passive-type policies come in other forms. Consider the policy *The First Installment is due on March 1, 2001*. It would be better expressed as language of obligation in the form *The Purchaser shall pay the First Installment on March 1, 2001*, on the grounds that the policy leaves unstated who is to pay the First Installment.

Some policies, such as [7-1], may resemble passive-type policies but cannot successfully be rephrased in the same manner. One could rephrase [7-1] as *No Stockholder may transfer any of its Shares in violation of this Agreement*. This conveys, however, a meaning different from that of [7-1], which does not address a prohibition imposed on Stockholders in connection with the transfer of Shares but instead addresses one consequence of Stockholder failure to comply with those obligations.

A large majority of drafters use *shall* when drafting policies, even though policies do not impose a duty. It has been suggested that lawyers make this mistake because they "wrongly tend to think that, because contracts and statutes apply into the future, they should be written in the future tense."[212] I have an additional explanation: because *shall* looms so large in contract drafting,[213] drafters have forgotten that it should be used only in language of obligation and have come to use it instead for all that is mandatory in a contract.[214]

EXPRESSING CONDITIONS

This section addresses not a category of contract language but a specialized use—expressing conditions—for certain categories of contract language.

Lawyers use the word "condition" to convey many different meanings.[215] The Restatement (Second) of Contracts provides that "[a] condition is an event, not certain to occur, which must occur, unless its non-occurrence is excused, before performance under a contract is due."[216] A condition has also been defined as "an operative fact, one on which the existence of some particular legal relation depends."[217] For my purposes the latter definition is the more helpful one, since it is more in keeping with general usage. Furthermore, unlike the Restatement definition, this definition does not suggest that conditions may be used only in the context of language of obligation, and so it is broad enough to encompass the three forms of usage described below.

Conditional Clauses

Conditional clauses do not fall within one of the categories of contract language discussed above, but serve to modify language of obligation, of discretion, of prohibition, and of policy. Conditional clauses raise issues of grammar that have not been adequately addressed in the literature on drafting.

A sentence containing a conditional clause consists of the conditional clause, including a subordinator, and the matrix clause. (In the sentence "*If Acme has not exercised the Option by December 31, 2000,* Smith may transfer the Shares to a Third Party," the italicized portion is the conditional clause, with *If* being the subordinator; the remainder of the sentence is the matrix clause.) The main function of conditional clauses (and the only function of concern here) is to express a direct condition: "[T]hey convey that the situation in the matrix clause is directly contingent on that of the conditional clause. Put another way, the truth of the proposition in the matrix clause is a consequence of the fulfillment of the condition in the conditional clause."[218] In general usage, the most common subordinator is *if*, and the negative subordinator *unless* is the next most common.[219] Other subordinators include *where, when, as long as, so long as,* and *on condition (that)*.[220]

Coode, the pioneering nineteenth-century English authority on statute drafting, distinguished between two kinds of conditional clauses (though he did not describe them as such), namely "cases" and "conditions."[221] According to Coode, a "case" is a statement of the circumstances in which a law operates and a "condition" is a statement of something that must be done before a law operates.[222] While some modern commentators based their discussion of conditional clauses on Coode's distinction,[223] I do not, because Coode's "cases" and "conditions" cannot be distinguished grammatically, and often cannot be distinguished at all.[224]

The problems of usage raised by conditional clauses involve verb use. First, there is the question of which verb to use in the conditional clause itself. *A Dictionary of Modern Legal Usage*, paraphrasing Coode,[225] states that one should "[u]se the *present tense* to express all facts and conditions required to be concurrent with the operation of the legal action," and should "[u]se the *present perfect tense* to express all facts and conditions required as precedents to the legal action."[226] While neither *A Dictionary of Modern Legal Usage* nor Coode states clearly the grammatical context, it is conditional clauses. *A Dictionary of Modern Legal Usage* offers, in slightly modified form, examples used by Coode. To illustrate appropriate use of the present tense, *A Diction-ary of Modern Legal Usage* gives "If by reason of the largeness of parish-es the inhabitants *cannot* reap the benefits of this Act, two or more overseers must be chosen," and as an example of appropriate use of the present perfect tense, gives "When the justices of the peace of any county assembled at quarter sessions *have agreed* that the ordinary peace officers are not sufficient to preserve the peace, the justices may appoint a chief constable."

The problem with this distinction is that on its own it is utterly cryptic, and neither Coode nor *A Dictionary of Modern Legal Usage* ex-plains, other than by limited examples, how to distinguish facts and conditions "required to be concurrent" from those that are "required as precedents." And this distinction bears an uncomfortably close re-semblance to Coode's problematic distinction between "cases" and "conditions."[227]

I will suggest what Coode might have had in mind. One could argue that certain conditional clauses are more conducive than others to use of the present perfect. Compare the following: "If the Company *termi-nates* [*has terminated*] Smith without cause, it shall pay Smith the Additional Compensation"; and "If Acme *has obtained* [*obtains*] all necessary consents, it may transfer the Shares." In the first conditional clause, the present tense is arguably more appropriate than the present perfect (in brackets); in the second, the present perfect is arguably more acceptable than the present (in brackets).

In the first example, payment of the Additional Compensation has no purpose other than to serve as a mechanism to compensate Smith for termination without cause, so it seems appropriate to give equal weight to both parts of the sentence. In the second, by contrast, transfer of the Shares is an end unto itself and an action that Acme might seek to ac-complish, rather than an automatic response to the obtaining of con-sents. As the present perfect conveys a sense of preliminary matters hav-ing been accomplished before the principal business at hand, it seems appropriate to use it in the conditional clause of the second example. This is also why the present perfect would seem better suited to [8-2a] than [8-1a]. This distinction only applies, however, to dynamic verbs. If a conditional clause contains a stative verb (for example, *If the Company is in good standing*, and [8-3]), you should use only the present tense.

There is a relatively straightforward way of expressing this distinc-tion: if a conditional clause using a dynamic verb precedes a matrix clause containing language of obligation or language of policy, use the

TABLE 8   CONDITIONAL CLAUSES

[8-1]	●●	If Acme receives a Violation Notice, it shall promptly notify Widgetco.
[8-1a]	○	If Acme has received a Violation Notice, ...
[8-1b]	○○	If Acme shall receive a Violation Notice, ...
[8-1c]	○○	If Acme shall have received a Violation Notice, ...
[8-1d]	○	If Acme should receive a Violation Notice, ...
[8-2]	●●	If Acme receives a Notice of Consent, it may transfer the Shares.
[8-2a]	●●	If Acme has received a Notice of Consent, ...
[8-2b]	○○	If Acme shall receive a Notice of Consent, ...
[8-2c]	○○	If Acme shall have received a Notice of Consent, ...
[8-3]	●	If Acme is in default, the Lender may accelerate the Loan.
[8-3a]	○○	If Acme shall be in default, ...
[8-3b]	●	If Acme is at any time in default, ...
[8-3c]	●●	If Acme defaults, ...

present tense in the conditional clause; if the conditional clause precedes a matrix clause containing language of discretion, use the present perfect tense. While this may not have been the distinction Coode had in mind, it is at least clear and grammar-based.

Having offered this distinction, I will now subvert it by suggesting that you can ignore it. While the present perfect might be slightly more effective than the present tense in some conditional clauses, the present is acceptable in all of them, including the examples cited by Coode and *A Dictionary of Modern Legal Usage* and those in table 8. That is why I have indicated that [8-2] and [8-2a] are equally acceptable.

The vast majority of drafters are oblivious of these nuances and instead use *shall* in either the modal auxiliary form (*shall* plus present participle; see [8-1b] and [8-2b]) or modal perfect form (*shall have* plus past participle; see [8-1c] and [8-2c]). Commentators disapprove of using *shall* in this manner.[228] This use of *shall* presumably has its origins in the fear that if a conditional clause in any given contract were in the present tense, then the matrix clause would operate only on conditions that are met at the moment the contract becomes effective.[229] When a conditional clause uses a dynamic verb meaning,[230]

TABLE 9 CONDITIONAL CLAUSES:
THE MATRIX CLAUSE

[9-1]	●●	If Jones ceases to be employed by the Company, the Parent will have an option to purchase the Shares from Jones.
[9-1a]	○○	If . . . , the Parent shall have an option . . . .
[9-1b]	○	If . . . , the Parent has an option . . . .
[9-2]	●●	If a Stockholder transfers all its Shares to a Person that is not a Stockholder, that transfer will be valid only if the Person acquiring those Shares agrees to be bound by the terms of this Agreement.
[9-2a]	○○	If . . . , that transfer shall be valid only . . . .
[9-2b]	○	If . . . , that transfer is valid only . . . .

this fear is unwarranted.[231] When a conditional clause uses a stative verb meaning,[232] as in [8-3], you can alleviate this fear by adding *at any time*, as in [8-3b]. Alternatively, you can often sidestep the issue by switching from a stative to dynamic verb meaning, as in [8-3c].

One occasionally sees *should* used in conditional clauses, as in [8-1d]. It adds nothing, other than unhelpful "overtones of tentativeness."[233] The present subjunctive also is apparently used in conditional clauses in legal contexts,[234] though I have yet to encounter it in a corporate agreement.

The second issue relating to verbs in conditional clauses is which verb to use in the matrix clause. If a verb in a matrix clause would, absent the conditional clause, be in the simple present, one should, as in [9-1] and [9-2], use *will* in its "habitual predictive" sense.[235] Almost invariably, drafters use *shall*, as in [9-1a] and [9-2a]. Others use the simple present, as in [9-1b] and [9-2b].[236] While this is an improvement on *shall*, it is not ideal. Note that the auxiliary verbs (*shall*, *may*, *must*) are unaffected by the presence of a conditional clause.

Conditional clauses have traditionally been placed at the beginning of a sentence,[237] but you should feel free to place them elsewhere if it would enhance readability to do so.[238] The longer the conditional clause, the more likely it is that the provision in question would be more readable with the matrix clause rather than the conditional clause at the front of the sentence.[239] If both the conditional clause and matrix clause contain more than one element, you would likely be better off expressing them as two sentences.[240]

Language of Policy Used to Express Conditions

When corporate lawyers refer to conditions, they have in mind not conditional clauses but closing conditions, namely a list of requirements introduced by a variation on the following: *The obligations of Acme under this Agreement are subject to satisfaction of the following conditions . . . .* Each condition is invariably a separate sentence using *shall* in either the modal auxiliary (*shall be*) or modal perfect (*shall have been*) form. These conditions constitute a specialized form of language of policy, but are worth considering apart, not only because lawyers consider them one of the principal building blocks of a contract, but also because of the particular drafting issues they raise.

There are some basic problems with this time-honored way of drafting conditions. First, when standard closing conditions are considered apart from the introductory language (the main clause), it is not evident that they constitute conditions. To express just one condition, rather than a list of them, the appropriate form of introduction would be *The obligations of Acme under this Agreement are subject to the condition that . . . .* In spite of this, standard closing conditions are never expressed as *that*-clauses, and as a result they can often be read as language of representation (see [10-1] and [10-2]), or even language of obligation (when used with *shall*). Expressing each closing condition as a tabulated enumerated[241] *that*-clause would make it clearer that one is dealing with conditions.

Second, the purpose of closing conditions is to provide that if certain circumstances do not apply at the time of closing, the closing will not take place. Consequently, it is inappropriate to use *shall*, as in [10-1a] and [10-2a], because one is not seeking to express an obligation. For the same reason, using *must* or *must have*,[242] as in [10-1b] and [10-2b], is no improvement. Using *will* or *will have*, as in [10-1c] and [10-2c], is also inappropriate: Determining whether the closing conditions have been satisfied requires that one inquire on the closing date into present, not future, circumstances. Just because the conditions are specified in advance of the closing date does not mean that they must be framed using future tenses.

If you accept that closing conditions should be expressed in the present, there remains a further question: should you use the indicative or subjunctive mood? The most common form of the subjunctive, the mandative subjunctive, is used in a *that*-clause following an expression of demand, recommendation, proposal, resolution, or inten-

TABLE 10   LANGUAGE OF POLICY USED TO
EXPRESS CONDITIONS

The Buyer's obligations under this Agreement are subject to satisfaction of the following conditions:

[10-1]	○○	Acme's representations are accurate at the Closing as though made at the Closing; . . . .
[10-1a]	○○	that Acme's representations shall be accurate . . . .
[10-1b]	○○	that Acme's representations must be accurate . . . .
[10-1c]	○○	that Acme's representations will be accurate . . . .
[10-1d]	○○	that Acme's representations be accurate . . . .
[10-1e]	●●	that Acme's representations are accurate . . . .
[10-2]	○○	the Buyer has received an opinion of Widget's counsel in the form of Exhibit A; . . . .
[10-2a]	○○	that the Buyer shall have received an opinion of Widget's counsel . . . .
[10-2b]	○○	that the Buyer must have received an opinion of Widget's counsel . . . .
[10-2c]	○○	that the Buyer will have received an opinion of Widget's counsel . . . .
[10-2d]	○○	that the Buyer have received an opinion of Widget's counsel . . . .
[10-2e]	●●	that the Buyer has received an opinion of Widget's counsel . . . .

---

tion.[243] While the mandative subjunctive might be an unfamiliar label, it is actually relatively prevalent in American English, as compared to British English.[244] Consequently, it would normally be appropriate, even desirable, to use the subjunctive in closing condition *that*-clauses, as in [10-1d] and [10-2d]. Placing closing-condition *that*-clauses at a remove from the related main clause as tabulated enumerated clauses has the effect, however, of preventing one from using the subjunctive, as does the structure of the main clause: readers tend to read the *that*-clause in isolation, and upon encountering the subjunctive assume that they have found a typographical error. I recommend that you use the indicative mood, as in [10-1e] and [10-2e].

Language of Obligation Used to Express Conditions

A third way of conveying a condition is to impose an obligation on the subject of a sentence, but by using *must* rather than *shall*.[245] While

TABLE 11		LANGUAGE OF OBLIGATION USED TO EXPRESS CONDITIONS
[11-1]	●●	To validly exercise the Option, Acme must submit the Option Notice to Widgetco no later than 30 days after the Option Date.
[11-1a]	○○	To validly exercise the Option, Acme shall submit the Option Notice to Widgetco no later than 30 days after the Option Date.
[11-1b]	○○	Acme must submit the Option Notice to Widgetco no later than 30 days after the Option Date.

in [11-1] Acme is required to submit the Option Notice to Widgetco in order to exercise the Option, Acme does not have a duty to do so, and Widgetco would not have a cause of action for Acme's failure to do so.

You should not, however, rely on *must*, as in [11-1b], to make it clear that you are expressing a condition. You should instead be explicit, whether by adding a *to-* infinitive clause, as in [11-1], or otherwise.[246]

LANGUAGE OF REPRESENTATION

A standard feature of corporate agreements is a section or article containing "representations and warranties," namely assertions by one or more parties as to past, present, or future circumstances. These assertions are traditionally preceded by a statement that the party or parties in question *represent and warrant as follows:* . . . .

The Distinction Between Representations and Warranties

I doubt many corporate lawyers have pondered the distinction between *representations* and *warranties*. I suspect that the following represents the conventional wisdom among those who have: "Representations . . . are limited to statements as to existing circumstances, whereas warranties may cover future circumstances. A party can, for instance, represent and warrant that as of a prior date his net worth was $75,000; he can also warrant that as of a future date his net worth will be that amount."[247] I do not think this is accurate, particularly as regards the meaning of *warranty*.

A representation has been defined as "[a] presentation of fact—either by words or by conduct—made to induce someone to act, [especially] to enter into a contract."[248] One of the requirements of an action for misrepresentation is that a party have made a false representation as to fact with regard to a past event or present circumstance, but not a future event,[249] because at the time a statement as to future circumstances is made there is no way of determining whether it is accurate or not. This suggests how some have come to view the term *representation* as applying only to statements of past or present facts and circumstances. It does not, however, necessarily follow that the meaning of *representation* must be linked to the elements of an action for misrepresentation, and indeed it is widely accepted that one can make a representation as to a future event.[250] Consequently, it would be unrealistic to insist that a statement as to future circumstances cannot be considered a representation.

Warranty is an altogether more problematic word. Like *condition*, it is a word with many meanings.[251] For purposes of contract law, a warranty has been generally defined as "[a]n express or implied promise that something in furtherance of the contract is guaranteed by one of the contracting parties; [especially], a seller's promise that the thing being sold is as represented or promised."[252] That a warranty can be a representation or a promise is reflected in Section 2-313(1)(a) of the Uniform Commercial Code, which provides that in the context of sale of goods, "[a]ny affirmation of fact or promise made by the seller to the buyer which relates to the goods and becomes part of the basis of the bargain creates an express warranty that the goods shall conform to the affirmation or promise."[253] *Affirmation* means effectively the same thing as *representation*.[254]

These definitions of *warranty* have the effect of making *warranty* very unhelpful as a label for distinguishing a particular category of contract language. On the basis of the U.C.C. definition, it simply cannot be used for this purpose, for "[t]he express warranty is merely a term of the contract having to do with the quality, description, or title of the goods, and it is not different in kind from other express terms such as price, delivery, or quantity."[255] Furthermore, outside the context of the sale of goods, one cannot state with any certainty just what warranty means. In particular, it is far from clear that a warranty simply constitutes a representation of past, present, or future facts or circumstances, as the conventional wisdom would have it.

Given that it is difficult to figure out exactly what *warranty* means for purposes of corporate agreements, and given that it is commonplace to use the term *representation* in connection with statements as to future circumstances, I have simply chosen to avoid using *warranty*, and I now refer only to the *representations* of a party and have that party *represent as follows*.

Traditionalists might wonder whether this usage could prejudice a party's interests. It is unlikely to, because any court should base its analysis of a contract provision not on how the contract labels that provision, but on the meaning the parties intended.[256]

That an action for misrepresentation requires a false representation as to a past event or present circumstances may not be enough to make me search for an alternative term to apply to representations as to future circumstances, but it does raise questions about the appropriateness of such representations.

There are two kinds of representations as to future circumstances: those relating to circumstances that are not under the control of the representing party, and those relating to circumstances that are.

Regarding the first category, there is something oddly oracular about having a party represent, for example, that the price of a given commodity will not fall below a stated value, that by some future date it will have received certain governmental approvals, or that an unrelated party will perform a certain act. Presumably the intention is to permit the nonrepresenting party to terminate the contract or to require that the terms be somehow adjusted in its favor; it is preferable to state as much directly rather than build on counterintuitive representations.

Some corporate lawyers would nevertheless insist that such representations are preferable to conditions, on the grounds that while a party has no cause of action if a condition is not satisfied, it can sue for damages if a representation is inaccurate. This argument relies on the questionable assumption that a court would respect the terminology used by the parties.[257] A court could instead hold that a representation as to future circumstances beyond the representing party's control constitutes neither a representation nor a condition but a prediction, and as such does not give rise to a cause of action for breach of contract.[258]

The second category of representations as to future circumstances is rather less disconcerting, since the representing party is in a position to determine, to a greater or lesser extent, whether or not the representation turns out to have been accurate. Nevertheless, such representations are flawed. Imagine that Acme represents that it will remain a corporation in good standing under Delaware law. This is best viewed not as a representation, but as an undertaking by Acme to pay its franchise taxes and do whatever else Delaware requires of a corporation for it to remain in good standing. Consequently, this representation, like all representations in this category, is better reworded and moved from Acme's representations and placed instead with Acme's obligations.

One Does Not Breach *a Representation*

It is standard practice to use the word *breach* for a party's failure to comply with a contractual obligation.[259] Many drafters also refer to a party's breach of its representations. This latter usage is less than ideal: A representation is a statement of fact and is either accurate or inaccurate when made, and nothing that the representing party does thereafter has any bearing on that. If I say that George did not chop down the cherry tree and it is later established that in fact he did chop it down, no one would say that I had breached my previous assertion. Instead, they would say that my previous assertion had been inaccurate. Likewise, it is preferable to refer to a representation as having been inaccurate rather than breached.

In the context of the Uniform Commercial Code, one usually refers to breach of a warranty.[260] Given the problems inherent in using *warranty* to describe a category of contract language,[261] this does not justify referring to breach of a representation.

Tenses Used in Representations

Representations (whether in the body of the contract or relegated to schedules) generally display the broadest range of tenses of any category of contract language: the simple present (*The Seller is in good standing*); the simple past (*The On-Site Contamination occurred in 1994*); the present perfect (*Acme has timely filed all tax returns*); and, as discussed above,[262] the simple future.

A FURTHER INSTANCE OF THE MISUSE OF "SHALL"

I discuss above the principal ways that drafters misuse *shall*. A further variety of misuse lurks in restrictive relative clauses. (In [12-1], the restrictive relative clause is *Acme specifies in writing*.) Most examples of this kind of misuse, including [12-1a], reflect the misguided fear, first encountered above,[263] that the present tense cannot be used to refer to events that will happen in the future. Sometimes, however, this use of *shall* would seem to represent an attempt to address a legitimate issue. Because [12-2] uses a stative rather than dynamic verb meaning,[264] it is not clear whether the transfer restrictions apply only to Shares owned on the date of the agreement or whether Shares acquired subsequently are also included. Referring to *Shares that it shall own* is not, however, the way to resolve this ambiguity; instead you should, as in [12-2b], make it explicit that after-acquired shares are included.

TABLE 12   MISUSE OF *SHALL* IN RESTRICTIVE RELATIVE CLAUSES

[12-1]	●●	Jones shall pay the Purchase Price by wire transfer to any account Acme specifies in writing.
[12-1a]	○○	. . . to any account Acme shall specify in writing.
[12-2]	●	No Stockholder may transfer any Shares that it owns except in accordance with the terms of this Agreement.
[12-2a]	○○	. . . any Shares that it shall own except . . . .
[12-2b]	●●	. . . any Shares that it currently owns, or any additional Shares that it acquires, except . . . .

CHAPTER 3

The Body of the Contract (Structure)

WHEN PREPARING THE BODY OF A CONTRACT, a drafter is faced with choices regarding the format to use and how the text should be arranged. While these decisions are nowhere near as subtle as those involving the language of the body of the contract and cannot alter a party's rights and obligations, they can have a dramatic effect on readability.

THE FORMAT OF THE BODY OF THE CONTRACT

The body of the contract could conceivably be presented as a solid block of text, with one provision running into another. Instead, drafters break it into sections, each of which may in turn consist of one or more subsections. Furthermore, one can subdivide the text of any section or subsection into what I call "enumerated clauses."[265] Subdividing contract text makes it much easier to read, permits cross-referencing, and allows readers to find their way around the document more efficiently.

Sections

Each section normally contains all provisions relating to a particular issue, although sometimes in the miscellaneous provisions at the end of a contract one finds lumped together in one section text relating to two or more unrelated topics.[266] Exactly what to put in any given section is a subjective decision, and no two drafters will necessarily adopt the same approach.

For ease of reference, each section is numbered (see sample 3). You

---

1.2   Sale of Shares. Axion hereby issues to Caspian, and Caspian hereby purchases from Axion, 1,400 shares of Axion Preferred Stock (the "Shares") for a purchase price (the "Purchase Price") consisting of the following:

(1) $5,000,000, $250,000 of which Caspian has already paid to Axion and the remaining $4,750,000 of which Caspian shall pay to Axion in immediately available funds in the amounts and on the dates stated in Schedule 1.2(a) (each installment of the remaining $4,750,000, a "Subsequent Payment");

(2)   200,000 shares of Caspian common stock (the "Purchase Price Shares"); and

(3)   a warrant for the purchase of a further 200,000 shares of Caspian common stock (the "Purchase Price Warrant").

1.3   Failure to Make Subsequent Payments. (a) If Caspian fails to timely make any Subsequent Payment, it may not make any further Subsequent Payments and it will be deemed to have surrendered to Axion a proportion of the Shares (with any fractional share rounded up) equal to the proportion of the dollar value of the Purchase Price that is represented by the missed Subsequent Payment and all other unpaid Subsequent Payments. This surrender will be Axion's sole remedy for the failure by Caspian to timely make any Subsequent Payment. For purposes of this Agreement, the dollar value of the Purchase Price is $6,795,000.

(b)   If Axion is dissolved and liquidated before Caspian has made each Subsequent Payment it is required to make under Section 1.2, the maximum Preferred Stock Liquidation Amount payable to Caspian will be calculated by multiplying the Preferred Stock Liquidation Amount that it would otherwise be entitled to by a fraction, the numerator of which is $1,795,000 plus $250,000 plus the amount of each Subsequent Payment made by Caspian, and the denominator of which is $6,795,000.

1.4   Dividend. Axion shall not distribute to its common stockholders as a dividend the Purchase Price Shares and the Purchase Price Warrant until such time as all holders of Axion common stock have made to Caspian customary investment representations in a form reasonably acceptable to Caspian.

SAMPLE 3   PREFERRED HYBRID FORMAT FOR
THE BODY OF THE CONTRACT

do not need to place "Section" in front of each section number. Drafters have the choice of simply numbering sections consecutively (1., 2., 3.) or grouping them into various articles and numbering the articles and sections using the multiple-numeration system (the sections of Article 1 being numbered 1.1, 1.2, 1.3, but *not* 1.01, 1.02, 1.03, with the unnecessary extra zero, or 1.1., 1.2., 1.3., with the superfluous extra period).[267] Which system you should choose for any given contract is a function of the length of the contract; there are no rules, but you might want to consider grouping sections into articles once you have more than 25 or so sections.

Some drafters also use the word "section" to describe each group of sections, but many—me included—prefer to distinguish between the components and the whole by using the word "article."[268] I use Arabic rather than Roman numerals for article numbers, and give each article a heading. (See sample 4.) Some drafters torture themselves and the reader and defeat the purpose of grouping sections into articles by attempting to reflect in article names all the sections contained in that article. You should give articles simple, all-encompassing headings: instead of *PURCHASE AND SALE, PURCHASE PRICE, ASSUMED LIABILITIES, RETAINED ASSETS, TRANSFER TAXES, ALLOCATION FOR TAX PURPOSES AND EXCLUSION FROM PURCHASED ASSETS*, use *PURCHASE OF ASSETS*.

You should use the automatic paragraph-numbering feature included in word-processing software. It allows you to delete or change the position of one or more articles or sections without having to spend an inordinate amount of time renumbering all the affected articles or sections, and you can also use it for subsections and enumerated clauses.

---

any untrue statement of a material fact or omit to state any material fact necessary in order to make the statements made therein, in light of the circumstances under which they were made, not misleading.

ARTICLE 5
CERTAIN OBLIGATIONS OF SSPI

5.1   Board Representation. From the Effective Time, SSPI shall use its best efforts to have two nominees of the Stockholders reasonably acceptable to SSPI appointed to SSPI's board of directors, either by appointing those nominees to any

---

SAMPLE 4   ARTICLE HEADING

For the layout of sections you can use either the "first-line-indent" or "hanging-indent" format. I prefer the former; based on the contracts I review, a majority of corporate lawyers share my preference. At the section level, hanging indents waste space without making text appreciably easier to read. In sample 3, Section 1.4 is in first-line-indent format, and both formats are shown side-by-side in sample 5.[269]

Each section is usually given a heading consisting of a word or short phrase in order to make it easier to find one's way around a document. Headings are invariably emphasized with underlining, boldface, italics, or any combination of the three; I prefer simple underlining.[270]

One's imagination is generally not taxed when formulating headings, since the same ones recur in contract after contract. Certain headings, such as *Arbitration* or *Confidentiality*, are a straightforward reflection of the contents of the section, while others, such as *Further Assurances*, represent a rather less-intuitive customary shorthand. If you need to create a heading, aim for brevity. Also, avoid using a heading that seems to promise more than the section actually delivers or is otherwise misleading, for courts have been known to refuse to enforce provisions with uninformative or misleading headings,[271] though this would seem to be an unlikely prospect when a contract is between ostensibly sophisticated parties represented by counsel. The miscellaneous provisions of longer agreements often include a provision stating that headings are for convenience only and are not intended to affect meaning;[272] you should not use the presence of such a provision as an excuse for being lax in formulating headings. If a section addresses two or more unrelated issues,[273] it is usual to give it a heading consisting of a word or short phrase for each issue, separate by a semicolon (such as *Amendment; Waiver*). Quite often one sees headings ending with *Etc.* (such as *Notices, Etc.*). Such headings smack of laziness, and the *Etc.* is always dispensable: if a section addresses more concepts than you can comfortably refer to in the heading, you should restructure the section as two or more separate sections.

As a rule, all text in the body of the contract should fall within a section, but there are exceptions. When Acme's representations constitute an article unto themselves, the introductory language—*Acme represents to Widgetco as follows*—is best placed after the article heading but before the sections proper. This allows the representations to be presented as sections, complete with headings, rather than subsections of a given section. The same principle applies when a party's conditions to closing constitute an entire article.

Subsections

Sections are frequently divided into two or more separate paragraphs known as subsections. A section is divided into subsections either because each subsection addresses different aspects of a single topic (such as conditions to closing) or because the section addresses a single topic that would be unwieldy unless broken down into digestible pieces (such as the steps required to effect a merger). Once you have waded through your first three-page, single-paragraph section, you tend to be in favor of drafters using subsections.

Subsections need to be numbered or lettered; I use the *(a)* hierarchy. If you run out of letters (which rarely happens), you can shift to the *(aa)* hierarchy.[274] Some drafters number subsections using the multiple-numeration system, with the subsections of Section 4.3 being numbered 4.3.1, 4.3.2, and so forth, but this system takes up more space than the *(a)* hierarchy and, if anything, makes it harder for the reader to distinguish between subsections.

I use the first-line-indent format for subsections, but place subsection designations one tab setting further in, to distinguish them from section numbers; see sample 3. The one exception I make is for the first subsection designation, which I place on the same line as the section heading; I see no point in wasting the better part of two lines of space by placing the *(a)* on a new line. Also, I am not fond of the way that starting the first subsection on a new line isolates the heading, while in my preferred scheme, headings in sections without subsections are followed immediately by text.

The preference for first-line-indent format over hanging-indent format that I express in the context of sections[275] is reinforced when an agreement contains subsections. The purpose of hanging indents is ostensibly to ensure that the reader quickly ascertains the hierarchy of paragraphs in any given section. Nothing is gained, however, by sharply distinguishing subsections from sections by using the staggered hanging-indent format shown in sample 5, with subsections indented one tab setting further in than sections. Subsections make up the entirety of the section to which they relate, rather than a subset, so there is no text further up the hierarchy with which subsection text might be confused. Furthermore, I find the staggered hanging-indent

1.2   Sale of Shares. Axion hereby issues to Caspian, and Caspian hereby purchases from Axion, 1,400 shares of Axion Preferred Stock (the "Shares") for a purchase price (the "Purchase Price") consisting of the following:

(1) $5,000,000, $250,000 of which Caspian has already paid to Axion and the remaining $4,750,000 of which Caspian shall pay to Axion in immediately available funds in the amounts and on the dates stated in Schedule 1.2(a) (each installment of the remaining $4,750,000, a "Subsequent Payment");

(2)   200,000 shares of Caspian common stock (the "Purchase Price Shares"); and

(3)   a warrant for the purchase of a further 200,000 shares of Caspian common stock (the "Purchase Price Warrant").

1.3   Failure to Make Subsequent Payments. (a) If Caspian fails to timely make any Subsequent Payment, it may not make any further Subsequent Payments and it will be deemed to have surrendered to Axion a proportion of the Shares (with any fractional share rounded up) equal to the proportion of the dollar value of the Purchase Price that is represented by the missed Subsequent Payment and all other unpaid Subsequent Payments. This surrender will be Axion's sole remedy for the failure by Caspian to timely make any Subsequent Payment. For purposes of this Agreement, the dollar value of the Purchase Price is $6,795,000.

(b)   If Axion is dissolved and liquidated before Caspian has made each Subsequent Payment it is required to make under Section 1.2, the maximum Preferred Stock Liquidation Amount payable to Caspian will be calculated by multiplying the Preferred Stock Liquidation Amount that it would otherwise be entitled to by a fraction, the numerator of which is $1,795,000 plus $250,000 plus the amount of each Subsequent Payment made by Caspian, and the denominator of which is $6,795,000.

1.4   Dividend. Axion shall not distribute to its common stockholders as a dividend the Purchase Price Shares and the Purchase Price Warrant until such time as all holders of Axion common stock have made to Caspian customary investment representations in a form reasonably acceptable to Caspian.

1.2   Sale of Shares. Axion hereby issues to Caspian, and Caspian hereby purchases from Axion, 1,400 shares of Axion Preferred Stock (the "Shares") for a purchase price (the "Purchase Price") consisting of the following:

(1) $5,000,000, $250,000 of which Caspian has already paid to Axion and the remaining $4,750,000 of which Caspian shall pay to Axion in immediately available funds in the amounts and on the dates stated in Schedule 1.2(a) (each installment of the remaining $4,750,000, a "Subsequent Payment");

(2)   200,000 shares of Caspian common stock (the "Purchase Price Shares"); and

(3)   a warrant for the purchase of a further 200,000 shares of Caspian common stock (the "Purchase Price Warrant").

1.3   Failure to Make Subsequent Payments.

(a)   If Caspian fails to timely make any Subsequent Payment, it may not make any further Subsequent Payments and it will be deemed to have surrendered to Axion a proportion of the Shares (with any fractional share rounded up) equal to the proportion of the dollar value of the Purchase Price that is represented by the missed Subsequent Payment and all other unpaid Subsequent Payments. This surrender will be Axion's sole remedy for the failure by Caspian to timely make any Subsequent Payment. For purposes of this Agreement, the dollar value of the Purchase Price is $6,795,000.

(b)   If Axion is dissolved and liquidated before Caspian has made each Subsequent Payment it is required to make under Section 1.2, the maximum Preferred Stock Liquidation Amount payable to Caspian will be calculated by multiplying the Preferred Stock Liquidation Amount that it would otherwise be entitled to by a fraction, the numerator of which is $1,795,000 plus $250,000 plus the amount of each Subsequent Payment made by Caspian, and the denominator of which is $6,795,000.

1.4   Dividend. Axion shall not distribute to its common stockholders as a dividend the Purchase Price Shares and the Purchase Price Warrant until such time as all holders of Axion common stock have made to Caspian customary investment representations in a form reasonably acceptable to Caspian.

SAMPLE 5   ALTERNATIVE FORMATS FOR THE BODY OF THE CONTRACT:
STAGGERED FIRST-LINE-INDENT FORMAT (TOP)
STAGGERED HANGING-INDENT FORMAT (BOTTOM)

format gives the left-hand edge of blocks of text a ragged look and disrupts the rhythm of the document.

Some drafters give headings to subsections. I do not, for the reason that whatever benefit a reader may derive from such headings is more than offset by the way they render section headings less effective.[276]

Enumerated Clauses

"Enumerated clause" is the term I use to describe the parts of a sentence in a section or subsection that are designated by a number or letter in parentheses, as in *The Purchaser shall make the Installment Payments on (1) February 1, 2002, (2) May 1, 2002, and (3) August 1, 2002.* Designating the parts of a sentence in this manner is entirely optional (the meaning of the immediately preceding example would not be impaired by deleting the enumerations), but it highlights and renders more readable the individual components of a list or series, and is recommended once a list or series is anything other than a short string of very simple items.

A drafter wishing to incorporate enumerated clauses in a sentence is faced with a number of choices. One of these is punctuation.

The first issue regarding punctuation is whether to use a colon to introduce the enumerated clauses. I use a colon when any set of enumerated clauses is more than about three lines long: the pause that it affords allows readers to catch their breath before tackling the enumerated clauses. The majority view, in which I concur, is that a colon should be used *only* to introduce a list if that which precedes the colon is a full independent clause. In other words, the colon should not, for example, be placed between a verb or preposition and its objects, for the effect is similar to hitting an unexpected pothole while cruising on the open road.[277] I consider that the following reflect inappropriate use of a colon: *Since March 30, 2001, the Company has not: (1) incurred any obligation . . . . ; and The Company shall deliver to each Purchaser: (1) unaudited financial statements . . . .* You can easily avoid using colons inappropriately, since any introductory statement that is not an independent clause can be reworked to make it one, often by adding *the following* or *as follows*. You can rephrase as follows the examples just cited: *Since March 30, 2000, the Company has not done any of the following: (1) incurred any obligation . . . . ; and The Company shall deliver the following to each Purchaser: (1) unaudited financial statements . . . .*

A drafter must next decide whether to use a comma or a semicolon to separate each enumerated clause from the next. The rule of thumb is that when items in a series are long and complex or involve internal punctuation, they should for the sake of clarity be separated by semi-colons;[278] otherwise, they should be separated by commas. Either way, the final enumerated clause should be preceded by *and* or *or*. Regarding how the use of semicolons or commas relates to the decision whether to precede enumerated clauses with a colon, my view is that if the enumerated clauses in any sentence are sufficiently complex or lengthy to warrant their being preceded by a colon, then they should also be separated by semicolons rather than commas. The corollary of this is that I do use commas, not semicolons, to separate enumerated clauses that are not preceded by a colon.

While a sentence containing enumerated clauses can constitute part of a paragraph, or a paragraph unto itself, you can make each enumerated clause stand alone. This is commonly referred to as "tabulation,"[279] although some call it "paragraphing."[280] I refer to each enumerated clause that is so treated as a "tabulated enumerated clause," as opposed to an "integrated enumerated clause"; Section 1.2 in sample 3 contains three tabulated enumerated clauses. The more enumerated clauses there are in a sentence, and the longer they are, the more likely it is that having them stand alone will make them easier to read. For purposes of comparison, sample 6 shows two versions of the same sample section, one with integrated enumerated clauses, the other with tabulated enumerated clauses.

Note, however, that I keep integrated those enumerated clauses that are not preceded by a colon and are separated by commas. I do this because, for one, I only forego colons and use commas as opposed to semicolons when the set of enumerated clauses in question is short and simple, and it would serve little purpose to tabulate such enumerated clauses. I would also find it mildly disconcerting to have the introductory statement end without punctuation and the tabulated enumerated clauses end with commas.

As well as having to determine what punctuation to use with enumerated clauses and whether they should be integrated or stand alone, a drafter must decide the enumeration hierarchy to use with enumerated clauses. The arrangement that I see more than any other is the *(a)* series followed by the *(i)* (generally referred to as "Romanette one" or—more of a mouthful—"little 'i' in the hole") series and then the *(A)* series, with the *(a)* series being dropped when the enumerated

Integrated Enumerated Clauses

1.2 <u>Sale of Shares</u>. Axion hereby issues to Caspian, and Caspian hereby purchases from Axion, 1,400 shares of Axion Preferred Stock (the "<u>Shares</u>") for a purchase price (the "<u>Purchase Price</u>") consisting of the following: (1) $5,000,000, $250,000 of which Caspian has already paid to Axion and the remaining $4,750,000 of which Caspian shall pay to Axion in immediately available funds in the amounts and on the dates stated in <u>Schedule 1.2(a)</u> (each installment of the remaining $4,750,000, a "<u>Subsequent Payment</u>"); (2) 200,000 shares of Caspian common stock (the "<u>Purchase Price Shares</u>"); and (3) a warrant for the purchase of a further 200,000 shares of Caspian common stock (the "<u>Purchase Price Warrant</u>").

Tabulated Enumerated Clauses

1.2 <u>Sale of Shares</u>. Axion hereby issues to Caspian, and Caspian hereby purchases from Axion, 1,400 shares of Axion Preferred Stock (the "<u>Shares</u>") for a purchase price (the "<u>Purchase Price</u>") consisting of the following:

(1) $5,000,000, $250,000 of which Caspian has already paid to Axion and the remaining $4,750,000 of which Caspian shall pay to Axion in immediately available funds in the amounts and on the dates stated in <u>Schedule 1.2(a)</u> (each installment of the remaining $4,750,000, a "<u>Subsequent Payment</u>");

(2) 200,000 shares of Caspian common stock (the "<u>Purchase Price Shares</u>"); and

(3) a warrant for the purchase of a further 200,000 shares of Caspian common stock (the "<u>Purchase Price Warrant</u>").

SAMPLE 6   INTEGRATED AND TABULATED ENUMERATED CLAUSES

clauses occur in a subsection. There are no clear favorites further down the hierarchy, largely because it is rare that a sentence needs to be divided into more than two levels of enumerated clauses.

I previously used this system but have recently adopted the hierarchy that some commentators recommend for legislative drafting:[281] the *(1)* series, followed by the *(A)* series, followed by the *(i)* series. I have done so for two reasons. First, I prefer reserving the *(a)* series for subsections, so as to enhance the distinction between subsections and enumerated clauses.[282] Second, I have, in the name of simplicity and modernity, promoted the *(1)* series at the expense of the *(i)* series. The SEC shares my aversion to Romanette: in enforcing the plain-English rules,[283] the SEC staff has taken to requiring that issuers purge registration statements of Romanette.

Do not use bullet points as an alternative to letters or numbers. While bullet points are useful in other documents, they are too informal for contracts and are not conducive to cross-referencing.

Tabulated enumerated clauses are best placed at the end of a sentence so as to avoid "dangling" text, which arises when the first part of a sentence consists of tabulated enumerated clauses and the remaining part starts flush left below the last enumerated clause.[284] (For an example of dangling text, see the text following the tabulated enumerated clauses in Section 5(a) of the "before" contract in the appendix.) By the same token, it is generally preferable to have a section or subsection end after a series of tabulated enumerated clauses.[285] It is also a good idea to avoid using more than one set of integrated enumerated clauses within any given section or subsection.

While I use the first-line-indent format for sections and subsections,[286] I use the hanging-indent format for tabulated enumerated clauses; see sample 3. (Because of this mixture, I refer to my preferred overall format as a "hybrid" format.) I do so for three reasons. First, while indenting the first line to different tab settings is sufficient to distinguish sections from subsections,[287] it is helpful to distinguish more explicitly tabulated clauses from subsections, as the former constitute subsets of the latter.

Second, indenting the first line is a way of denoting the beginning of a paragraph; a paragraph must contain one or more sentences; and a tabulated clause is not a sentence. Consequently, it is preferable not to use first-line indenting at the beginning of a tabulated clause.

Third, text starts to look a little odd if you indent the first line to the third or fourth tab setting and leave the rest flush left. Furthermore, if in a two-line first-line-indented tabulated clause the second line is only a word or two long, it is effectively marooned on the left margin, with blank space above, below, and to the right. For an example of this effect, see clause (ii) of Section 5(a) of the "before" contract in the appendix.

If a tabulated enumerated clause itself contains enumerated clauses and I choose to tabulate them, I again use the hanging-indent format but place each clause one tab setting further in from the left margin.

ARRANGING THE BODY OF THE CONTRACT

In addition to selecting the format for the text of a contract, you need to determine how you will arrange the text. Dickerson sees this as involving three separate issues:[288]

- *Division*, or the process of creating sections and, if applicable, articles.
- *Classification*, or the process of determining the section into which any given provision should be placed.
- *Sequence*, or the ordering of the sections and, if applicable, the articles.

Drafters rarely think in terms of division, classification, and sequence. For one thing, in drafting contracts one tends to address all three issues concurrently. More to the point, however, custom has already determined how the provisions of any commonly occurring kind of contract should be divided, classified, and ordered. In an acquisition agreement, for instance, the body of the contract is generally organized as follows: description of the transaction; representations; obligations; conditions to closing; termination; indemnification; and miscellaneous provisions.

Given that these customary arrangements are for the most part satisfactory, reinventing the wheel would serve little purpose. There is, however, room for improvement. With respect to division, one can often devise more rigorous alternatives to the traditional building blocks. For instance, using the article heading *COVENANTS OF THE SELLER* would seem unhelpful, given that *covenant* is simply an archaic word for *agreement*.[289] Where possible, I would use a more descriptive heading, such as *CONDUCT OF BUSINESS PRIOR TO CLOSING*. If the article is a mixed bag, I would use *CERTAIN OBLIGATIONS OF THE SELLER*. Note also my preference for placing the definition section at the end of a contract rather than at the beginning.[290]

In terms of classification, you should make a concerted effort to place each provision in its proper category. It is not unusual to find, for instance, language of obligation lurking in the representations; this sort of indiscipline can lead to confusion and could conceivably make it more difficult to enforce the provision in question.

Dickerson has also suggested some rules of thumb regarding sequence: (1) general provisions normally come before special provisions; (2) more important provisions normally come before less important provisions; (3) more frequently used provisions normally come before less frequently used provisions; (4) permanent provisions normally come before temporary provisions; and (5) "housekeeping" provisions normally come at the end.[291] Again, custom often determines the order of standard provisions. While following that order will not always result in provisions being ranked in the manner Dickerson suggests, I see little to be gained from tinkering with that order from transaction to transaction,[292] since I find it easier to come to grips with a draft agreement if the sections are ordered predictably.

CHAPTER 4

After the Body of the Contract

AFTER THE BODY OF THE CONTRACT come the concluding clause, the signature blocks, and any attachments.

THE CONCLUDING CLAUSE

Sample 7 provides an example of my preferred way of winding up a contract. The first element to consider is the preliminary sentence, which I refer to as the *concluding clause*. I have seen it referred to as the *closing*,[293] but I see no point in using a term that already has an established meaning in corporate transactions. *Conclusion*[294] also is unsatisfactory, in that the concluding clause does not offer any conclusions in the usual sense of the word, but is simply the final clause in the contract. Steer clear of *testimonium*, a hoary old term that only applies to sworn legal documents.[295]

For purposes of comparison with my preferred form, here is a slightly long-winded version of the traditional form of concluding clause: *IN WITNESS WHEREOF, the parties hereto, intending to be legally bound, have by their proper and duly authorized officers duly executed and delivered these presents as of the day and year first above written.*

To determine the appropriate form of concluding clause, it helps to consider what its function should *not* be. It should not contain agree-

Delta and Doe are executing this Agreement on the date stated in the introductory clause.

DELTA CORPORATION

By: _____
        Name:
        Title:

_____
JOHN DOE

SAMPLE 7   THE CONCLUDING CLAUSE AND
                 SIGNATURE BLOCKS

ments of or representations by the parties. To the extent that an assertion that the parties have caused the agreement to be executed by their proper and duly authorized officers serves any purpose (can an officer be duly authorized yet improper?), it would be better placed among the representations. Similarly, instead of a statement that the agreement has been duly executed and delivered, use standard representations as to corporate power and authorization.

While some elements of the traditional concluding clause should be placed elsewhere, others are best dispensed with. For example, the phrase *intending to be legally bound*[296] is ineffectual: it is not a condition to the enforceability of a contract that the parties have, or explicitly express, an intent to be legally bound.[297]

The traditional concluding clause also contains a number of archaisms: the musty *IN WITNESS WHEREOF* can, like *WITNESSETH*, be dispensed with, on the grounds that contracts rarely need to be witnessed;[298] *these presents*[299] is a ludicrous alternative to *this Agreement*; and the phrase *the day and year first above written* is long-winded and vague, while the usual alternative, *set forth above*, is also vague. Note also that most concluding clauses refer to execution of the contract *as of* the date in the introductory clause, whether or not that date is an *as of* date.[300] The two should be consistent.

I have wrestled with the question of which tense to use in the concluding clause. Drafters invariably use the present perfect (*have executed or have caused to be executed*), but using the present perfect is inconsistent with the requirements of narrative flow: it seems odd to have the parties assert in the concluding clause that they have signed the contract, given that the signature blocks do not precede that assertion, but follow it.

What are the alternatives? The simple present (*the parties hereby execute*) is inappropriate. For one thing, the concluding clause is not a performative,[301] for there is no simultaneity of the event described—the signing of the document—and the speech event itself. To execute a document, you cannot simply say you are doing so, you have to put pen to paper. The most plausible choice is the present progressive (*the parties are executing*). This is consistent with accepted usage: the concluding clause represents a statement in anticipation of a transitional event, with the result that one avoids the sense of duration normally associated with the progressive.[302]

Anyone who elects to join me in using the present progressive in the concluding clause should bear in mind that doing so could require conforming changes elsewhere in the contract. It is standard practice to include a representation that *This Agreement has been validly executed by Acme* (however, I would phrase it *Acme has validly executed this Agreement*). If you use the present progressive in the concluding clause, you should perhaps modify this representation to read *Acme is validly executing this Agreement*.

While most drafters refer in the concluding clause to the agreement having been executed *and* delivered, I prefer to omit any reference to delivery. Since the concluding clause serves to introduce the signatures, it seems gratuitous to introduce a further assertion regarding a post-execution act—delivery—particularly as an informal contract does not need to be delivered in order to be enforceable.[303]

If the parties to a contract are also parties to one or more other contracts, you can avoid confusion by referring in the concluding clause to the type of agreement involved instead of using "this Agreement." An alternative would be to state at the bottom of the signature page, in the following manner, the type of agreement involved: *[Signature page to Asset Purchase Agreement]*. To be certain of avoiding confusion you could add to any such statement the date of the agreement and party names.

Once you accept the above observations, you are left with my preferred form of concluding clause, at which point you would be entitled to ask whether you could dispense with it entirely, since all it does is say, in effect, "Here come the signatures!"[304] On balance, I prefer to retain the concluding clause. For one thing, it smooths what might otherwise be a slightly abrupt transition. Also, a concluding clause makes it clear that although other contracts may provide for each signature to be dated, this one does not. (Otherwise, little would be served by pointing out that the date of the contract is located elsewhere.)

THE SIGNATURE BLOCKS

As shown in sample 7, below the concluding clause is a signature block for each party. A signature block consists of a party's name accompanied by a signature line.

If the party is an entity, I place the entity's name in all capitals above the signature line. *By:* should be placed next to the signature line to emphasize that the signatory is not signing in his or her personal capacity, and the signatory's name and title should be noted under the signature. If you are certain of the name and title of the individual signing on behalf of an entity, having them input in the document under the appropriate signature line (instead of, rather than next to, *Name:* and *Title:*) would save the signatory (or, more likely, a junior lawyer or a paralegal) from having to write them in by hand.

If the party is an individual, I place his or her name under the signature line in all capital letters so as to distinguish it from the name of any individual signing on behalf of an entity, for which I use lowercase letters with initial capitals. If you are particularly eager to avoid confusion, you can add *in his* [or *her*] *own capacity* after the name of any individual signatory.

Signature blocks are usually aligned one above the other on the right-hand side of the page, as in sample 7. To save space, you can place them side by side.

Next to signature blocks one occasionally sees secondary signature lines marked *Attest*. The notation *Attest* would seem to represent a vestigial attestation clause and is intended to prompt signature by witnesses.[305] No corporate agreement, however, need be witnessed, except when required by statute. Similarly, in the absence of a statutory requirement, a signatory need not have his or her signature notarized and need not "acknowledge" a contract, in other words formally declare that signing the contract constitutes the signatory's free act and deed.[306] If a party insists that a signature be notarized, generally it is because it wants to eliminate the possibility of anyone questioning whether, or when, that person actually signed the contract.

The concluding clause and the signature blocks are often found on a page or pages by themselves. There are various possible reasons for this: (1) none of the signature blocks could fit on the page on which the body of the contract ends; (2) some of the signature blocks could not fit on that page, and it was sensibly thought best to avoid having the signature blocks spread over more pages than strictly necessary; or (3) one or more parties wanted to sign the agreement before it was finalized, and signing a signature page containing draft provisions leaves open the possibility that those provisions may thereafter be modified, or the location of the page break changed, which would render the signed pages unusable.

When the concluding clause and the signature blocks are on a page unto themselves, one sometimes sees, after the end of the body of the contract on the previous page, *[SIGNATURE PAGE FOLLOWS]* or the equivalent, or a typographic indication of finality such as a short row of asterisks. Such a device is generally used when there remains a significant amount of blank space on the page, and its function would seem to be to discourage anyone from surreptitiously tacking on further provisions after signing. This seems rather hopeful, as a party bent on forgery would have no great difficulty disposing of the final page of the body of the contract and inserting its own. The only effective way to protect yourself against forgery is to have a number of fully executed originals in different hands. (Having the parties sign or initial each page, as is done in British Commonwealth and civil-law countries, would add a further level of protection, but this practice has not been adopted in the United States.)

That said, using *[SIGNATURE PAGE FOLLOWS]* or the equivalent when the bulk of the last page of the body of the contract is blank does serve to counter the minor cognitive dissonance engendered in readers used to equating a partially blank page with finality. It also makes it clear that the blank space is not a mistake.

A further anti-forgery gimmick is to ensure that the signatures do not occupy a page by themselves, even if that requires truncating the previous page by carrying over to the signature page a couple of lines of text from the last provision of the body of the contract. While this would certainly prevent anyone from inserting anything in whatever blank space there may be between the main portion of that provision and the carryover lines, it is awkward and, furthermore, is unnecessary if there are multiple signed originals.

Attachments

Documents that are attached to the back of a contract are referred to generically as "attachments." There are two main kinds of attachment, "exhibits" and "schedules."

An exhibit is a stand-alone document.[307] It can be a document that is currently in effect, or one that the parties agree will be effective at some future date. In the former category are the organizational documents of Target Co. attached as exhibits to an acquisition agreement. Documents in the latter category are most often ancillary contracts that are to be entered into at the closing of the transaction provided for in the attaching contract. For example, the seller in a stock purchase agreement might require as a condition to the sale of his company that at closing he and the company enter into an employment agreement *in the form of Exhibit X* to the stock purchase agreement. (There is no need to say *in the form attached as Exhibit X*, for an exhibit is by definition attached. Similarly, I would avoid adding *hereto*.)[308]

Exhibits are generally numbered (*1, 2, 3*) or lettered (*A, B, C*). Number or letter exhibits consecutively in the order they are first encountered in the body of the contract, and attach the exhibits themselves to the contract in that order, with the exhibit designation marked in the top center or top right-hand corner of the first page of each exhibit. I find it helpful to make exhibit references in the contract stand out by underlining them.

Schedules, by contrast, consist of materials that are part of the contract proper but have been shunted to the back.[309] One kind of schedule is that containing factual information, such as details of ongoing litigation or lists of contracts. Each such schedule is often linked to the contract provision to which it relates (generally a representation) by means of a statement in that provision to the effect that *set forth on Schedule X are all instances of Y*, or that *other than as set forth on Schedule X, there are no instances of Y*. The latter formulation is generally used when Y is either undesirable or present in limited quantities. To avoid cluttering with exceptions a given set of representations, drafters often have the representing party state at the outset that the representations are subject to exceptions listed in an omnibus "disclosure schedule." Although it involves a little extra work, I generally prefer instead to flag for the reader any representation that is subject to one or more scheduled exceptions.

Drafters use such schedules for three reasons. First, the information included in schedules is often too voluminous to include in the body of the contract. Second, the process of collecting information regarding a company's operations involves an entirely different process, and usually different personnel, than the task of drafting and negotiating a contract, and so it simplifies matters to have that information presented in a separate set of documents. Third, if the information to be disclosed to the other side is sensitive, putting it in a set of schedules can help minimize the risk of wider disclosure: schedules are rarely attached to proxy statements or other similar disclosure documents and are often not filed with the SEC, even if the agreements are.[310]

Drafters also relegate to schedules entire contract sections, such as the definition section or the indemnification provisions. Doing so makes sense when you wish to incorporate into a negotiated contract with a minimum of effort standardized provisions that are not subject to negotiation. Also, if a contract is sufficiently long and complex, it might warrant a definition section that you can pull out and review side-by-side with the contract proper. Otherwise, I am not in favor of this practice, since it makes it less convenient to refer to the provisions in question. Some drafters are of the view that unpalatable provisions are more likely to escape scrutiny if they are stuck somewhere after the signature pages, a notion I find questionable and a little undignified. Some drafters also use schedules as a repository for contract sections that they regard as routine; such sections would be sufficiently out of the way if placed at the end of the body of the contract.

Schedules can be lettered or numbered consecutively, but once there are several of them, you are better off giving each schedule the number of the section to which it relates, with Schedule 6.22 containing the factual information or provisions referred to in Section 6.22. If a given section refers to information on a schedule, but in fact no such information exists, it is best to delete any reference to that schedule rather than force readers to flip to a schedule page that states *None or Not applicable*. Just as I underline contract references to exhibits, I also underline references to schedules.

If you need a way of referring generically to your attachments, I recommend "appendix," "annex," or "attachment." I see these most often when a contract has only one or two items attached.

CHAPTER 5

General Considerations

I N THIS CHAPTER I CONSIDER various features of legal usage that do not relate to any particular part of a contract. I also discuss a number of problematic usages.

NUMBERS

Most drafters still use both words and numerals to convey numbers: *forty (40) days*; *Ten Thousand Four Hundred and Twenty-Two Dollars and 46/100 ($10,422.46)*; *five percent (5%)*; and so forth. I suspect this practice arose because drafters valued the eye-catching quality of numerals yet recognized that they are more vulnerable to typographic errors than are words, and so decided that using both systems would afford the immediacy of numerals while providing insurance against a potentially drastic mistake. This insurance was rendered more effective by the now-standard canon of construction that the written-out number controls in the case of conflict.[311]

This belt-and-suspenders approach has few friends among commentators on legal writing.[312] Drafters rarely use it for every number,[313] which is just as well, because when it is observed scrupulously, the results can be faintly ludicrous. (I recall a credit agreement that required a party to make payments "not later than five (5) P.M. (New York time) on the date when due.") In most contexts, such as in a provision stating that a party is entitled to appoint "three (3) members of the board of directors," use of the words-and-numerals approach conveys that the drafter thought it necessary to insure against the possibility of profoundly slapdash work by the lawyers on the deal and their clients.

The words-and-numerals approach has doubtless saved the occasional contracting party (and its lawyer) from the adverse consequences of a misplaced decimal point or other error involving numerals, or would have done had it been used.[314] This benefit is, however, analogous to the protection afforded by wearing a crash helmet 24 hours a day: doing so might save your life in the off chance that you are struck by a falling brick, but it is very inconvenient and makes you look a little ridiculous.

All told, "[r]epetition is a poor substitute for proofreading."[315] It would be better to abandon the words-and-numerals approach, except perhaps in certain potentially sensitive contexts (such as a promissory note's statement of the principal amount of the indebtedness).[316] Instead, spell out whole numbers one through ten and use numerals for 11 onwards.[317] This approach applies to ordinal numbers (e.g., *fifth*, *18th*) as well as cardinal numbers. I use numerals for whole numbers below 11 in lists of numbers; when numbers occur frequently in the text; in percentages; and in statements of amounts of money or times of the day.[318] At the beginning of sentences I use words for numbers 11 and over.[319] Which system you adopt is, however, less important than ensuring that you do not distract the reader by being inconsistent.

DEFINED TERMS AND DEFINITIONS

As a rule, a corporate agreement will contain terms for which it provides definitions. Corporate lawyers invariably call these terms "defined terms," as do commentators.[320]

Purpose

The purpose of a defined term is to save wear-and-tear on the reader by allowing the drafter to use the shorter defined term instead of the longer definition. The corollary is that the purpose of definitions is "to explain the meaning that a term is intended to carry."[321]

Commentators have sought to identify two kinds of definition, namely "lexical" definitions and "stipulative" definitions.[322] Because I find their attempts to be as confusing as they are helpful, I offer some brief thoughts on the subject. Bear in mind, however, that this distinction is of no practical significance, as I indicate below.[323]

Dickerson explains the distinction as follows:

> [D]efinitions are called "lexical" insofar as they assert a meaning corresponding to actual usage in the given speech community. They are called "stipulative" insofar as they declare a meaning different from actual usage in that speech community. Lexical definitions attempt to record usage. Stipulative definitions attempt to create it.[324]

While others have followed this approach,[325] I find it not only more concise than I would like, but also potentially confusing. The references to "speech community" could be understood as meaning that a definition is lexical only if it corresponds to actual usage in one particular speech community. Such an approach would seem arbitrary. There are innumerable overlapping speech communities; why should you pick only one of them—presuming that it were feasible to do so—as the point of reference for determining what kind of definition you are dealing with? Distinguishing between lexical and stipulative definitions would in that case turn on whether a given definition was familiar to the speech community in question—presumably that of the drafter.

This reading of Dickerson's distinction might seem unlikely. That is, however, evidently how another commentator has interpreted it, since he suggests that because of its ostensible novelty, the aerodynamics term "wing-tip vortices" would, in legal drafting, require a stipulative definition,[326] never mind that the term would presumably have been standard in the aviation industry.

Given the limitations of Dickerson's distinction, it is not surprising that *A Dictionary of Modern Legal Usage* should attempt to put the distinction on a structural footing.[327] It succeeds, however, not in distinguishing lexical definitions from stipulative definitions, but "full" definitions from "enlarging" and "confining" definitions.[328]

If you must distinguish between lexical and stipulative definitions, you might find it more helpful to take a broader approach. Imagine that a drafter uses a particular term but is concerned that its meaning may not be clear to potential readers, or wishes to avoid any uncertainty or ambiguity, and so decides to provide a definition. The definition is secondary to the defined term, and reflects an accepted meaning of the defined term. I consider this definition a lexical definition. Corporate agreements make limited use of lexical definitions because drafters generally feel no need to define scientific, engineering, or other technical terms, such as "antisense" or "wind shear." Nevertheless, lexical definitions can be useful. For instance, an agreement that I drafted regarding the sale of collectibles included the following lexical definition: *"Collectible" means any tangible item that people accumulate as a hobby or for study and not for practical application or use, including without limitation stamps, coins, trading cards, posters, comic books, autographs, memorabilia, figurines, plates, and works of art.* Also, any noun phrase that is widely known by a defined term that is an acronym[329] (for example, *ERISA* or *GAAP*) or initialism[330] (such as *the SEC*) could be regarded as a lexical definition.

Imagine instead that the drafter needs to refer to a phrase several times in a contract and decides to make the contract more succinct by replacing that phrase with a word or a shorter phrase while keeping the original phrase as the definition of that word or shorter phrase, which thereby constitutes the defined term. The defined term is secondary to the definition. The definition does not reflect an accepted meaning of the defined term; this may be because the definition is broader or narrower than the accepted meaning of the defined term, or because the defined term is an acronym or initialism that is not widely known. I consider this definition a stipulative definition. In most agreements, stipulative definitions far outnumber lexical definitions.

The distinction between lexical and stipulative definitions might have modest value for drafters as a consciousness-raising exercise, but it has no practical significance since it does not reflect a meaningful structural difference. The clearest indication of this is that while in the sentence *"EPA" means the U.S. Environmental Protection Agency* the definition is best considered lexical,[331] it is stipulative if you change the defined term from *the EPA* to *the Agency*.[332] The shorthand *the EPA* would seem sufficiently widely recognized to make the definition lexical rather than stipulative, whereas a defined term such as *the Agency* could never have other than a stipulative definition. Drafters are unlikely to derive any practical drafting guidance from such an outcome.

The Form of Defined Terms

Defined terms are almost always nouns—common (*employee*) as well as proper (*Smith*)—and noun phrases (*material adverse change*), though occasionally I see a verb (*transfer*) or even a prepositional phrase (*to Acme's knowledge*). If the defined term is a common noun, it is generally preferable for purposes of defining it that it be singular.[333]

It is usually helpful in a contract to distinguish defined terms from words for which the contract does not provide a definition.[334] Doing so serves two purposes. First, readers would otherwise risk losing track of which are the defined terms and would need to refer more often to the definitions for guidance. Second, distinguishing defined terms allows a drafter to convey by means of the word or words of a defined term a meaning other than that reflected in the definition of the defined term.[335] The almost universal way of emphasizing defined terms is to use initial capitals.[336] An unsightly but rare alternative is boldface or italics.[337]

Unlike some drafters,[338] I generally use initial capitals for even routine defined terms, such as *subsidiary*. That said, when the one or more words of a defined term are not used to convey an alternative meaning elsewhere in a contract, I occasionally forego using initial capitals. For instance, often when drafting a stockholder agreement that uses the verb and noun *transfer* as a defined term I use a small "t" on the grounds that it would be unduly distracting to encounter it with a capital "T" at every turn.

Selecting Defined Terms

I suggest above, in the context of the introductory clause, considerations to bear in mind when selecting defined terms for party names.[339] I now provide some broader guidelines for selecting defined terms.

Commentators recommend avoiding definitions that give a word or term an extraordinary meaning, so that, for instance, "*Automobile*" *includes bicycles*.[340] The corollary is that you should avoid choosing for any given definition a defined term that is counterintuitive. In corporate agreements, this sort of awkwardness occurs infrequently and can generally be readily cured by changing the defined term: if you give a widely used defined term that has a generally accepted meaning (such as *EBIT*, meaning earnings before interest and taxes) a definition that is a little unorthodox, you might want to think of modifying the defined term appropriately (to *Adjusted EBIT*, for example).[341]

It has been suggested that you should not use in a definition the term being defined.[342] While this might be true in the case of lexical definitions (any dictionary definition of *dog* had best not include the word *dog*), repeating the defined term in the definition is standard practice in corporate agreements.[343] For example: "*Trademark*" *means a registered trademark or service mark or any trademark or service mark that is the subject of any application, registration, or renewal.*

Types of Definitions

Each defined term must somewhere in a contract be tethered to its definition. To do this, you can use either "autonomous" or "integrated" definitions. (The terminology is my own.)

Autonomous Definitions

An "autonomous" definition is linked to its defined term by a verb, which I refer to as the "definitional verb," with the definition, definitional verb, and defined term constituting a sentence or clause unto themselves. Drafters sometimes use the following kind of autonomous definition: *The time when the Merger becomes effective is referred to in this Agreement as the "Effective Time."* Far more common, however, is the kind of autonomous definition that begins with the defined term: for example, *"Preferred Stock" means the preferred stock, par value $.01 per share, of Acme Corporation.* It is this kind of autonomous definition that I consider in the following discussion. Either way, a defined term linked to an autonomous definition is invariably placed in quotation marks;[344] I also underline it so as to make it easier for readers to spot definitions.

As regards definitional verbs, there are a number of options. If the definition gives the entire meaning of the defined term (in other words, if the definition is "full" or "complete"),[345] you should use *means*.[346] In corporate agreements, the vast majority of autonomous definitions use *means*. Very occasionally one sees "enlarging" or "extending" definitions, in which only part of the intended meaning is expressed; these are introduced by *includes*.[347] I have yet to see in a corporate agreement a "confining" or "narrowing" definition, namely one that excludes something from the meaning of the defined term; these are introduced by *does not include*.[348] (Note that these various options bear no relation to the distinction between lexical and stipulative definitions[349] and could conceivably be used for either kind of definition.)

If the definitional verb is *means* or *includes*, the part of speech of the defined term should match that of the definition, whether verb, noun, or other.[350] Occasionally, that is not feasible; in that case, use *refers to*,[351] as in *"Continue," "Continuation," and "Continued" refer to the continuation of a Eurodollar Loan from one Interest Period to the next Interest Period.* A contract may contain a defined term that could be either a verb or a noun, and while the definition reflects only one part of speech, the contract uses the defined term sometimes as a noun, sometimes as a verb. A common example of this phenomenon is *transfer*, which is generally defined as a noun but is often used as a noun and as a verb. If you use a defined term as a noun and as a verb, that should be reflected in the definition. In the case of *transfer*, you could define it as a noun but start the definition as follows: *"Transfer," used as both a verb and a noun, refers to . . . .*

There is no point in replacing *means* with a dash, as in *"Code"—the Internal Revenue Code of 1986, as amended.* You sometimes see this usage in autonomous definitions placed in a definition section.[352]

Definitional sentences are examples of language of policy and as such should use the simple present tense.[353] Rather than *means*, many drafters use *shall mean* as the definitional verb in full definitions. *Shall mean* itself means "has a duty to mean" and as such makes no sense.[354]

One occasionally encounters *means and includes*. Do not use these definitional verbs together: "complete and incomplete meaning cannot be stipulated at one and the same time."[355] But it is permissible to tack on to a full definition, using *means*, a partial definition, using *includes* or *does not include*, so as to remove any doubt as to the meaning of the full definition.[356] The *includes* clause should not, however, "introduce matter beyond the reasonable scope of the 'means' clause or contradict the substance of the 'means' clause."[357]

Quite often autonomous definitions contain extraneous language, typically language of obligation. These definitions are described as "stuffed" or "loaded."[358] For example, rather than tacking on to the definition of *Acme Financial Statements* the nonrestrictive relative clause—with preceding comma—*which Acme shall deliver no later than three months after the end of each fiscal year of Acme*, state it separately as language of obligation.

The problem would be exacerbated if the extraneous language were phrased as the restrictive relative clause *that Acme delivers no later than three months after the end of each fiscal year of Acme.* Confusion could well result if in any year Acme delivers financial statements later than the specified date, since those financial statements would no longer satisfy the definition; it is unlikely that the parties would have intended such a result. Again, state as separate language of obligation any requirements regarding the timing of delivery.

One practice to avoid is that of including an integrated definition within an autonomous definition. For example: *"Environmental Report" means each of (1) . . . , (2) . . . , and (3) the Phase I report dated August 30, 1999, relating to the Smithtown Facility (the "Smithtown Report").* It is clearer to state the integrated definition separately as an autonomous definition.

Integrated Definitions

The alternative to autonomous definitions is "integrated" definitions. While an autonomous definition and the related defined term are set apart in a sentence unto themselves, an integrated definition is used once in the thick of the contract and the defined term is tucked at the end of the definition, in parentheses and quotation marks. An example: *At the Closing, the Buyer shall pay to the Seller $2,500,000 as the purchase price for the Acquired Assets (the "Purchase Price").* (I have seen integrated definitions referred to, perhaps rather archly, as "vest pocket definitions.")[359] While most commentators refer only to autonomous definitions,[360] integrated definitions are a routine feature of corporate agreements.

As with autonomous definitions, I underline the defined term and place it in quotation marks. Traditionally, the defined term has been introduced by a phrase such as *hereinafter referred to as*. Such language is unnecessary and nowadays is more often than not omitted.[361]

The principal source of confusion regarding integrated definitions is where to place the information in parentheses and what it should consist of. (In the examples below, I have stricken the inappropriate text and show my recommendations in italics.)

Drafters often incorrectly place the defined-term parentheses in the middle of the definition rather than at the end. In each of the following examples the defined term—a noun phrase—was placed in the middle of the noun phrase that constitutes the definition.

> The Company's board of directors has received a written opinion ~~(the "Fairness Opinion")~~ of the Financial Advisor stating that the proposed consideration to be received by the holders of Shares pursuant to the Offer and the Merger is fair from a financial point of view to the holders of Shares *(that opinion, the "Fairness Opinion)*.

> The registration statement on Form S-4 ~~(the "Registration Statement")~~ pursuant to which the shares of Parent Preferred Stock to be issued in connection with the Merger will be registered with the SEC *(that registration statement, the "Registration Statement")* will not, at the time the Registration Statement (including any amendments or supplements) is declared effective by the SEC, contain any untrue statement of a material fact . . . .

> Acme shall maintain confidential all information it obtains from Widgetco ~~(the "Confidential Information")~~ pursuant to this Agreement *(that information, the "Confidential Information")*.

Usually, all that results from mid-definition defined terms is awkwardness. Sometimes, however, they can change meaning. Take the following example:

> Schedule 4.11 contains an accurate list of all agreements, oral or written (~~"Contracts"~~), to which Widgetco is a party *(each such agreement, a "Contract")*.

As originally positioned, the defined term encompasses all agreements regardless of the identity of the parties. While this might be appropriate in another contract, in this case the drafter had intended to create a defined term to cover Widgetco's agreements.

The defined term is sometimes inappropriately placed beyond the definition. In the following examples, the defined term is separated by a verb phrase from the noun phrase constituting the definition:

> The lease for Blackacre *(the "Lease")* must be substantially in the form of Exhibit B ~~(the "Blackacre Lease")~~.

> The purchase price for the Acme Shares *(the "Purchase Price")* is $2,500,000 ~~(the "Purchase Price")~~.

Garner recommends that one avoid integrated definitions because "the end-of-the-phrase parenthetical . . . does not clearly say how far back the definition goes."[362] Any uncertainty as to the scope of the definition can, however, generally be avoided by referring, in the defined-term parentheses just before the defined term, to the pertinent noun in the definition: *(that litigation, the "Acme Litigation"); (those employees, the "Continuing Employees"); (any such Lien, a "Permitted Lien")*. This technique is used in most of the above examples.

If you comply rigorously with the precept that in integrated definitions the defined terms should come at the end, you will occasionally need to define more than one term within a given set of parentheses: *With respect to any further monitoring and possible cleanup of PCE contamination at the facility located at 277 Acacia Drive, Smithville, New York (the "Smithville Facility"; that contamination, the "Smithville Contamination"), ...* Occasionally, this can get out of hand: *Jones desires to sell to Smith 20,000 shares of common stock, par value $1.00 per share, of Widget Corporation ("Widget"; that common stock, the "Common Stock"; those shares, the "Shares").* In such cases it should be easy enough to define one or more terms elsewhere.

In the same vein, with integrated definitions you can define a term and then define a second term that is somehow linked to the first: *Schedule 3.11 lists all real property and interests in real property leased by Widgetco (collectively, the "Leased Real Property"; the Owned Real Property together with the Leased Real Property, the "Real Property").*

As is the case with autonomous definitions, in integrated definitions the part of speech of the defined term should match that of the definition. Mismatch occurs more with integrated definitions; this is presumably due to drafters shoehorning defined-term parentheses into existing text. An example of such a mismatch: *At the Effective Time, Merger Sub will merge into Acme (the "Merger").* Adding transition language before the defined term can generally cure this; one could supplement the defined-term parentheses in the previous example to read as follows: *(the merger thus effected, the "Merger").* In any given instance, however, it might be simpler to restructure the definition or define the term elsewhere.

Which Type of Definition to Use

How to present any given definition is partly a function of its length. If a definition is relatively succinct, it is probably more efficient to present it as an integrated definition than as an autonomous definition. The longer the definition, the more likely it is that it would be best as an autonomous definition. Also a factor in determining which type of definition to use is whether the definition would best be placed in a definition section, an issue discussed immediately below.

The Definition Section

A drafter can use a definition "on site," in other words place it, in the form of an integrated or autonomous definition, close to a provision that uses the related defined term. (An on-site autonomous definition can simply constitute another sentence in the section or subsection, or can be placed in a separate subsection.) Alternatively, that definition can be placed in a definition section, which lists autonomous definitions in alphabetical order by defined term. In longer documents, the definition section can constitute an article unto itself, and in particularly lengthy contracts it can be thirty or more pages long.

Drafters have traditionally tended to favor placing definitions in definition sections. This has the signal disadvantage of requiring that a reader who encounters an unfamiliar defined term flip to the definition section to read the definition of that term; from there, the reader may be required to consult the definition of one or more other defined terms referred to in that definition before being able to return to the starting point. The longer the document, the greater the number of defined terms, and the greater the complexity of the definitions, the more wearing this process becomes.[363]

Definition sections do, however, serve a purpose. While it is best to have unfamiliar terms defined on site, since it is distracting to continually refer to the definition section, it is also distracting to continually encounter definitions of familiar terms. Consequently, to determine which terms can be relegated to a definition section, you should assess the degree to which they can be understood independently of their definition.

Some terms, such as *GAAP* or *ERISA*, have a universally accepted meaning. Somewhat less inherently comprehensible is a defined term such as *Lien, Governmental Authority, Intellectual Property*, and *Subsidiary*; to know its exact meaning you need to read the definition, but the defined term on its own gives a good general sense of its meaning. Your understanding of the provisions in which such a defined term occurs should in general not be unduly compromised if you have not read the definition. At the other end of the spectrum are those defined terms, such as *Equity Infusion* or *Excess Insurance Proceeds*, that are entirely a creature of the transaction and cannot be understood without reference to the definition. I suggest that terms in the first and second category are best placed in the definition section, so that they do not unnecessarily clutter up the text. Any term in the third category is best defined on site.

Definition sections have traditionally been used to provide, in addition to definitions, references to the sections where other terms are defined. Definition sections are not, however, suited to this task, since the cross-references are rather cumbersome (the typical format is *"Stipulated Value" has the meaning given that term in Section 3.6*), are interspersed with actual definitions, and are generally spread out over several pages. A much more efficient vehicle for helping readers quickly find their way around the definitions is an index of the defined terms. An index of defined terms lists the defined terms in alphabetical order and indicates the page where the definition of each term is located; it is best placed after the table of contents. (A page number is more useful than a section number. First, one can find a page number more quickly than a section number. Second, sections are routinely spread over more than one page.) Despite their efficiency, indexes of defined terms are still something of a rarity.

The definition section has traditionally been placed at the beginning of the body of the contract, presumably with the thought that comprehension would be enhanced if readers could familiarize themselves with the defined terms at the outset. While this view still has its adherents,[364] it is problematic. For one thing, it does not take into account that "most readers don't begin by plowing through definitions," but instead turn first to the main provisions.[365] Furthermore, those readers who do tackle the definitions head-on are not well served: "Defined terms are difficult to understand if they are not immediately used, yet the reader [of a definition section] must usually wait many pages before seeing how the defined term fits into the text."[366]

If you pare the definition section down to those terms that are inherently familiar, as I suggest, there remains no possible justification for keeping it at the beginning of the body of the contract, since readers would only need to refer to it to fine-tune their understanding. In fact, keeping it at the beginning would delay the reader from coming to grips with the contract. The definition section should be moved to the back of the contract, where, in its slimmer form, it may be slight enough to constitute a single section rather than an entire article.

For reasons outlined above,[367] one solution I am not fond of is placing the definition section in an attachment.[368]

Finally, do not give each definition a subsection designation (or section designation, if the definition section does constitute an article). Alphabetical order provides all the order one needs.

Cross-Referencing Definitions

While I discuss below cross-referencing generally,[369] it is an issue that also arises in the context of definitions.

When the definition section is located someplace other than at the beginning of the body of a contract, one often sees as the first section a statement to the effect that all or some defined terms are defined in section such-and-such, namely the definition section. I am not fond of such provisions, in that they run counter to the notion that the more important provisions should come first.[370] Furthermore, when the definition section contains only some of the definitions, as is generally the case, this sort of provision is not particularly helpful. I prefer instead to rely, in longer contracts, on readers using an index of defined terms to find their way around.

For defined terms that are not defined in a definition section, it is traditional to place the definition where the defined term is first used so that the reader does not have to flip through the following pages looking for the definition. Sometimes the context does not permit this; it also happens that revisions to a contract result in a defined term being inserted upstream of its definition, and it is not thought worthwhile to move the definition. In these situations it is traditional to place in parentheses, after the first use of the defined term, the unhelpfully vague *as defined below*, the more precise *as defined in Section X*, or some variation. In shorter contracts I have no objection to complying with this convention. In longer contracts I try to avoid it. For one thing, these references were devised for the minority of readers who start at the top of the contract and work their way methodically through to the end. (These are presumably the same stalwarts who read the definition section straight through.) I suggest that most readers, either during their first reading or when they subsequently refer to the contract, skim through the text and refer to whichever provisions happen to be of interest; for them, it would be a matter of luck whether or not any such cross-references happen to be of use. Also, it is a tedious business to check each of your drafts to ensure that every defined term that precedes its definition is given a cross-reference the first time it is used. The simplest way to avoid these annoyances is to drop such cross-references in favor of an index of defined terms.

Using Defined Terms Sparingly

You should not create a defined term if you do not use it after having defined it. You should also not create a defined term if you use it only once or twice after defining it, unless the definition is so awkward that expressing it more than once is unbearable.[371] When you use defined terms you pay a price in terms of readability, and you need to use any given defined term a certain number of times in order to get your money's worth.

That said, it is sometimes expedient to create a defined term that you use less than you ought to. I have over time developed a core set of representations and a definition section that lists the defined terms contained in those representations, and I use them repeatedly in my drafting. In longer contracts I end up using those defined terms several times; in shorter contracts I may use any given term only a couple of times, but generally do not feel it worthwhile to go back and eliminate that defined term on grounds of insufficient use.

REFERENCES TO TIME

A contract may refer to future time for purposes of indicating what the term of the contract is, or when a party may or must take or not take a particular action. Contracts also divide future time into units for purposes of setting a limit, per unit of time, to any given obligation or right of a party. The discussion that follows represents my attempt to make sense of this topic.

For Specifying the Term of a Contract or Stating When a Party May or Must Take a Particular Action

For purposes of specifying in a contract what the contract term is or when a party may or must take a particular action, drafters refer to time in two ways. First, as a point in time (as in *This Agreement terminates on September 22, 2003*). Often points in time are paired to reflect the beginning and end of a period of time (as in *Smith may exercise the Option any time after March 31, 2001, and before June 1, 2001*). Second, as a period of time of a stated length. Such periods of time begin or end at a stated point in time (as in *Acme shall employ Smith for the two years from the date of this Agreement*).

The distinction between periods of time and points in time is largely one of phrasing; paired points in time can generally be restated, with varying degrees of awkwardness, as a point in time beginning or ending a period of time, and vice-versa. (You can, for example, restate the above examples as *Smith may exercise the Option any time during the 30 days after March 31, 2001*, and *Acme shall employ Smith from the date of this Agreement until the second anniversary of the date of this Agreement.*)

Points in Time

Drafters generally fix a point in time by reference to a given day. This day may be either a date certain (such as *November 22, 2004* or *the date of this Agreement*) or the date of a contingent future event. Either way, caution is required when specifying a point in time by reference to only its date, since most prepositions are not up to the task of indicating with certainty on exactly which day falls any given point in time.

The most common preposition for purposes of denoting a beginning point in time is *from*. If I say that I will be on holiday *from April 1, 2000*, it is not entirely clear whether my holiday starts on April 1 or April 2, as in general usage "[t]he date *from* which one reckons may be either inclusive or exclusive."[372] If the *from* is inclusive, my holiday will start one day earlier than it would if the *from* were exclusive. Case law, however, indicates that courts now regard *from* as exclusive unless there is something in the context or circumstances to indicate a different intention, in which case courts are willing to include the day from which a period of time is to be reckoned.[373]

Some commentators have greater confidence that *after April 1* is unambiguously exclusive,[374] but case law indicates that *after* has also been considered both exclusive and inclusive.[375] By contrast, *starting April 1* is unlikely to be construed as anything other than inclusive.[376] Similarly, in the phrase *The Option Period will commence on April 1, 2001*, the *on* would likely be considered inclusive.[377]

Ambiguity also infects certain prepositions used to denote an ending point in time, namely *to* and *until*,[378] as well as *by*.[379] Similarly, in the phrase *The Option Period will end on October 3, 2001*, it is uncertain whether the option may be exercised on October 3 itself, and if a period is described as *ending on October 3*, it is not clear if October 3 is included in that period. By contrast, it appears that there is little dispute that *before October 3* is exclusive,[380] and you could reasonably expect that any court would hold that *through October 3* includes October 3.[381]

Between serves to link beginning and ending points in time. While the majority of courts have treated *between* as exclusive,[382] there nevertheless exists the possibility of confusion.[383] Pairing *from* and *to*, as in *from June 18, 2000 to August 13, 2000*, can serve the same purpose, but not without the ambiguity inherent in *from* and *to*. The same applies to *after June 18, 2000, and before August 13, 2000*.

Specifying a point in time is obviously fraught with uncertainty. You can, however, avoid ambiguity by making explicit whether the date for a given point in time is inclusive or exclusive. You could, for example, provide that *Acme may exercise the Option any time from April 13, 1998, exclusive, to April 25, 2001, inclusive*. The added precision more than compensates for the inelegance. You could also avoid ambiguity when referring to a point in time by specifying a time of day, which is generally what I do; I discuss this below.[384] (Refer also to my form of provision specifying drafting conventions governing references to time, but bear in mind it was prepared as a discussion piece rather than for use in a contract.)[385]

Even if it is certain on which day any stated point in time is to occur, there remains the question of when on the day in question it is to occur. It is accepted that in this context *day* means a calendar day of

24 hours from one midnight to the next.[386] Consequently, unless otherwise specified, a beginning point in time occurs at midnight at the beginning of the day in question (if it is inclusive) or at the end of the day in question (if it is exclusive), while an ending point in time occurs at midnight at the beginning of the day in question (if it is exclusive) or at the end of the day in question (if it is inclusive).

Periods of Time

A period of time can run either forward or backward from a point in time. A forward-running period of time is usually indicated by *from, following,* or *after* (as in *Smith may exercise the Option any time during the 10 days from his receipt of* [or *following his receipt of* or *after he receives*] *the Option Notice*). For purposes of determining the ending date of a forward-running period of time, the general rule is that you leave out the day from which you are counting and include the last day of the specified period, unless it is clear that the period must consist of a certain number of entire days, in which case both the first and last days are excluded.[387] Applying this rule to the preceding example, if Smith receives the Option Notice on January 1, the first day of the 10-day period is January 2 and Smith must exercise the Option before midnight at the end of January 11.

This rule does not apply if the parties intend that the first day be included.[388] For example, if a consulting agreement is signed on October 1 and specifies that it has a term of 30 days from the date of the agreement, it is likely that the parties intend October 1 to be the first day of the term. If that is the case, the agreement will terminate on midnight at the end of October 30.[389] If you were to apply instead the first-day-excluded, last-day-included rule, the term would expire on midnight at the end of October 31.

A backward-running period of time is usually indicated by *before* and *prior to* (as in *If Acme wishes to extend the Exclusivity Period, it must at least 10 days prior to expiration of the Exclusivity Period* [or *10 days before the Exclusivity Period expires*] *submit to Widgetco a request for an extension*). To determine the beginning date of a backward-running period of time, the general rule is that you count one of the days at both ends of the period, and do not count the other.[390] Using the preceding example, if the Exclusivity Period expires December 31, the tenth day before expiration is December 21, and a request given on that day satisfies the requirement.

Note, however, that case law is not entirely consistent, since some courts have held that you do not count either of the days at both ends of the period.[391] Applied to the example in the previous paragraph, this would mean that Acme submitted a request only nine days prior to expiration of the Exclusivity Period and therefore failed to satisfy the requirement for extension.

Like the rule with respect to forward-running periods, the rule with respect to backward-running periods contains an exception for periods that must consist of a certain number of entire days.[392] This exception arises principally in connection with provisions requiring advance notice. Take the provision *Smith shall provide Jones with at least 30 days' prior notice of any Proposed Transfer*. It requires that Jones must for at least 30 full days have been aware of the Proposed Transfer. Consequently, instead of not counting just one of the terminal dates, you exclude both the date of the Proposed Transfer and the date that Jones was notified of the Proposed Transfer. To satisfy the provision, Jones must be notified, at the latest, on the 31st day before the Proposed Transfer; if the date of the proposed transfer is December 31, Smith must give Jones notice on November 30 or earlier. Note that if instead the requirement is that *Smith shall give Jones notice of any Proposed Transfer at least 30 days before the date of that Proposed Transfer*, Smith would be able to give Jones notice one day later, on December 1.

There is some disagreement as to when this exception applies. Take, for instance, a contract that requires that an act take place *at least* a certain number of days before a known future date. While some courts have held that it is implicit that those days must be clear days and the first and last terminal days are excluded,[393] most courts have only excluded both days if it was clearly the intent of the parties that the period consist of a certain number of clear days.[394]

When drafting a provision referring to a period of time, you need to determine not only when the period begins or ends and how long it lasts, but also what unit of time it is stated in.

The smallest unit is the day, consisting of the 24 hours from one midnight to the next.[395] When denoting periods of time in days, I generally use *business days* rather than simply *days*. A business day is generally defined in contracts to mean any day other than a weekend or a public holiday in a given jurisdiction, or any day that banks generally are, or a named bank is, open for business. Using business days would ensure that the last day of a notice period is a business day. This would spare any party the awkwardness of learning, for example, that according to the notice provisions of its contract, the fax it sent on Sunday, the last day of the notice period, must be considered to have been received on Monday, too late to constitute the valid notification. Note that this latter issue could be addressed in a provision specifying drafting conventions.

You do not have to count periods of time in days. For example, drafters occasionally use periods of time calibrated in weeks. In this context, *week* is generally defined as a span of any seven consecutive days, irrespective of the time from which it is reckoned, rather than seven successive days beginning with the day traditionally fixed as the first day of the week, namely Sunday.[396]

You can also state periods of time in months. A period of a month counting forward from any given date ends at midnight at the end of the corresponding day of the following month, the day from which one is counting having been excluded.[397] If there is no corresponding day of the next month, the period ends on the last day of that month. In other words, a period of a month counting from March 31 ends on April 30. Since one can quickly determine without referring to a calendar the end date of a period denoted in months, I generally prefer to use months to provide for periods of time of 30 days or more.

A period of time can also last one or more years, in which case it runs through the day before the appropriate anniversary of the first day included.[398]

Some drafters are reluctant to express periods of time in months or years for fear that a court will construe *month* to mean one of the 12 months of the year, starting on the first day of that month, or *year* to mean a period of 12 consecutive months starting January 1.[399] But avoiding this slight risk comes at a cost, in that it forces the drafter to figure out that the 18 months from January 12, 2001, is 546 days, or that five years from November 12, 2000, is 1,826 days (including one day to reflect that 2004 is a leap year); more importantly, it forces the reader to figure out the reverse.

Due to the ambiguity inherent in *month* and *year*, some drafters avoid expressing periods of time in years and instead use months. The rationale is apparently that if, despite the prevailing usage, a court interpreting a given provision construes *month* to mean one of the 12 months of the year, the impact would likely be less than if the period of time were denoted in years and the court were to construe *year* to mean a period of 12 consecutive months starting January 1. Expressing periods of time in months rather than years is less awkward than expressing periods of time in days rather than months or years, but I do not find particularly compelling the risk avoidance that it offers.

Finally, I indicate above that a period of time must be anchored to a stated beginning or ending point in time, but when a certain act or event must take place *on* a certain date, the period of time is the 24 hours of the day in question. Consequently, no beginning or ending point in time need be explicitly stated; they are midnight at the beginning and end of that day, respectively.

The Time of Day

The main reason for including in a contract references to the time of day is to supplement references to points in time. You can, in other words, say *from 9:00 A.M. on September 25, 2000* instead of *from September 25, 2000*. You can also refer to the time of day indirectly, as in *at the close of business on April 20, 2001*, it being implicit that the exact time is to be determined by reference to the practice of the business in question. Adding the time of day to points in time would allow you to avoid the ambiguity that often results from identifying points in time solely by reference to their dates.[400] In the preceding examples, for instance, including the time of day would allow you to sidestep the question of whether the *from* and *on* are inclusive or exclusive.

Including the time of day is how I prefer to avoid the ambiguity that afflicts many references to points in time, but generally the time of day I specify is midnight. This is because I prefer to deal in entire days. Besides being simpler, it minimizes the chances of any dispute as to, for example, the time at which any notice or payment was received. That said, you should bear in mind the following points when referring to midnight of any given day.

First, you should not refer to midnight, or noon for that matter, as *12:00 A.M.* or *12:00 P.M.*[401] Just as noon is not part of either the set of 12 *ante meridiem* (before noon) hours or the set of 12 *post meridiem* (after noon) hours, but represents the boundary between the two, midnight is the boundary between any set of *post meridiem* hours and the following set of *ante meridiem* hours.

Second, while simply referring to noon of a given day avoids any confusion as to which day is intended, since each day only has one noon, referring to midnight of a given day begs the question whether you are referring to the midnight that precedes that day or the midnight that follows it.[402] There is a convention that *midnight of August 15* refers to the midnight that follows August 15,[403] but I am not convinced that this convention is universally accepted or that the parties to any given contract will be aware of it. You should address this ambiguity when stating explicitly that a period of time begins or ends at midnight. A 24-hour notation would work (for the midnight at the end of August 15, either *2400 August 15* or *0000 August 16*),[404] but in the United States drafters use the 12-hour system. A second alternative would be to indicate both the preceding and following day (for the midnight at the end of August 15, *midnight August 15–16*).[405] A third alternative would be to move any midnight beginning point in time forward by one minute to 12:01 A.M., and any midnight ending point in time back by one minute to 11:59 P.M.,[406] but this has the effect of creating awkward leftover minutes. A clever—perhaps too clever—variant is to provide that a midnight beginning point in time occurs at one minute prior to 12:01 A.M. and a midnight ending point in time occurs at one minute after 11:59 P.M. A fourth alternative would be to refer to *midnight at the beginning [or end] of August 15*. This is what I do.

If you need to refer to a time of day in a contract providing for transactions that cross time zones, you should specify which time zone is to be used for determining when that time of day has come. I do so by stating that the time of an appropriate location applies (as in *The Purchase Price must be credited to the Seller's account by 5:00 P.M. New York time on the Closing Date*). I recommend that you avoid using a time-zone designation when specifying a time of day for an unknown date in the future: you may not be in a position to anticipate whether (in the case of New York time) Eastern Standard Time or Eastern Daylight Saving Time will apply, even if you happen to remember exactly when the clocks move forward and back.

For Limiting, Per Unit of Time, an Obligation or Right

In drafting contracts you will periodically need to refer to units of time not for purposes of specifying what the contract term is or when a party may or must take or not take a particular action, but to set a limit, per unit of time, to any given obligation or right of a party. An example of a provision that serves this function: *Acme may not exercise the Option more than twice a year*. Another example: *Widget is not required to reimburse Smith for expenses in excess of $2,000 a month*.

In such provisions the word *year* can be ambiguous. On July 1, 2000, Acme and Jones sign an employment agreement that simply states that *Jones is entitled to four weeks of vacation a year.* Jones takes one week of vacation between July 1, 2000, and the end of the year, and a further three weeks of vacation in the first half of 2001. He then asks to take a further three weeks of vacation in the second half of 2001. Is he entitled to those additional three weeks of vacation? The case law suggests that most courts would hold that he is entitled to only one further week of vacation, on the grounds that in this context *year* means the 12-month period from January 1 rather than 365 days starting July 1.[407]

Given this case law, it is likely that courts would hold that in such provisions *month* means one of the twelve months of the year, starting on the first day of that month, rather than the period from any given date to midnight at the end of the corresponding day of the next month.

You can avoid this kind of ambiguity by stating what *year* or *month* mean for purposes of the provision in question. Also, instead of using *year* in any given provision, you can use *period of 12 consecutive months beginning January 1.* Furthermore, it can be helpful to state how a short period between the signing date and the beginning of the next month or year should be treated. To return to the preceding example, Jones's employment agreement could have specified that Jones could be entitled to two weeks of vacation during the balance of 2000. If the issue is a party's share of an annual amount that is only determined after the end of each year, you could provide that for the short first year of the contract the amount in question will be prorated.

Using the term *calendar year* would also seem a plausible way of avoiding this kind of ambiguity. *Calendar year* has indeed been construed in several cases to indicate the period from January 1 through December 31, but there are cases that hold otherwise.[408] Given that *year* poses only a limited risk of ambiguity, and given that you can clearly and simply eliminate even that limited risk, you should not need to use the term *calendar year.*

Be careful about using *calendar month* to avoid ambiguity in this kind of provision. While there is some authority suggesting that it means one of the twelve months of the year,[409] most courts that have considered the question have held that it means the period from any given date through the corresponding day of the next month.[410] I have seen both meanings used in contracts. You could avoid this ambiguity by defining the term *calendar month*, but I prefer not to use it.

CROSS-REFERENCES

Another feature of contract topography is the cross-reference, namely a reference in a contract to a provision of that contract (in which case the reference is known as an internal cross-reference) or another contract. Here are some suggestions for streamlining internal cross-references and making them more effective.

In order to make it clear that a reference to *Section X* is an internal cross-reference rather than a reference to a section of some other contract, drafters generally tack a *hereof* on to the internal cross-reference. It can get a little tiresome to encounter *hereof* at every turn, so I have dispensed with it. If you are uncertain about the consequences of following suit, you can address the issue in a section on drafting conventions.[411]

It is often the case that internal cross-references are correct in the first draft of a contract but are rendered incorrect when the contract is subsequently modified and are only fixed shortly before signing. That is not ideal; cross-references, like the table of contents, are most useful during the drafting process, as opposed to after the contract is signed. Using your word-processing software's automatic cross-referencing function is a simple way of ensuring that your cross-references remain up to date.

Drafters sometimes underline internal cross-references. This would come in handy if you do not use automatic cross-referencing and need to check internal cross-references manually, since underlining would help ensure that you do not miss any. Otherwise, underlining internal cross-references serves no purpose.

When referring to an enumerated clause that does not constitute a grammatical sentence, I generally prefer to use the format *clause (2) of Section 4(b)* rather than referring to *Section 4(b)(2)*, in order to make it clear that I am referring to a fragment of a larger provision.

TYPOGRAPHY

Word-processing software has given drafters all manner of options for making a contract more readable or, conversely, impenetrable. Here are a few points to consider.

Line Spacing

I prefer lines of text to be single-spaced; double spacing results in thicker contracts and is, to my mind, more difficult to read. Double

Single Spacing

If Axion is dissolved and liquidated before Caspian has made each Subsequent Payment it is required to make under Section 1.2, the maximum Preferred Stock Liquidation Amount payable to Caspian will be calculated by multiplying the Preferred Stock Liquidation Amount that it would otherwise be entitled to by a fraction, the numerator of which is $1,795,000 plus $250,000 plus the amount of each Subsequent Payment made by Caspian, and the denominator of which is $6,795,000.

Line-and-a-Half Spacing

If Axion is dissolved and liquidated before Caspian has made each Subsequent Payment it is required to make under Section 1.2, the maximum Preferred Stock Liquidation Amount payable to Caspian will be calculated by multiplying the Preferred Stock Liquidation Amount that it would otherwise be entitled to by a fraction, the numerator of which is $1,795,000 plus $250,000 plus the amount of each Subsequent Payment made by Caspian, and the denominator of which is $6,795,000.

Double Spacing

If Axion is dissolved and liquidated before Caspian has made each Subsequent Payment it is required to make under Section 1.2, the maximum Preferred Stock Liquidation Amount payable to Caspian will be calculated by multiplying the Preferred Stock Liquidation Amount that it would otherwise be entitled to by a fraction, the numerator of which is $1,795,000 plus $250,000 plus the amount of each Subsequent Payment made by Caspian, and the denominator of which is $6,795,000.

SAMPLE 8   LINE SPACING

spacing does allow more room for handwritten comments, but you can achieve the same effect with a single-spaced document by marking your comments on a slightly reduced photocopy on standard-size paper. Of course, word-processing software would allow you to change the space between lines, or "leading," in much smaller increments,[412] including line-and-a-half, but I have not as yet been tempted to do so. (See sample 8.)

Left Justification

If Axion is dissolved and liquidated before Caspian has made each Subsequent Payment it is required to make under Section 1.2, the maximum Preferred Stock Liquidation Amount payable to Caspian will be calculated by multiplying the Preferred Stock Liquidation Amount that it would otherwise be entitled to by a fraction, the numerator of which is $1,795,000 plus $250,000 plus the amount of each Subsequent Payment made by Caspian, and the denominator of which is $6,795,000.

Full Justification

If Axion is dissolved and liquidated before Caspian has made each Subsequent Payment it is required to make under Section 1.2, the maximum Preferred Stock Liquidation Amount payable to Caspian will be calculated by multiplying the Preferred Stock Liquidation Amount that it would otherwise be entitled to by a fraction, the numerator of which is $1,795,000 plus $250,000 plus the amount of each Subsequent Payment made by Caspian, and the denominator of which is $6,795,000.

SAMPLE 9   JUSTIFICATION

Justification

In formatting text you can use either full justification, with text aligned at both left and right margins, or left justification, which leaves the right margin ragged. (See sample 9.) Based on a highly unscientific survey, I estimate that the world of corporate lawyers is evenly split between those who favor full justification and those who prefer left justification. Those drafters who use full justification should consider switching to left justification: while they might feel that full justification gives contracts a more professional look, it also makes them harder to read.[413]

Typeface

Word-processing software has made a wide range of typefaces available to the drafter. One typeface I would avoid is Courier, the standard typewriter typeface. (Sample 10 includes a Courier variant.) Courier characters have the uniform width and fine line required by typewriters, but these attributes lost their utility with the advent of the laser printer, and Courier otherwise has little to recommend itself.[414]

Selecting which of the many alternative typefaces to use requires that one decide whether to use a *serif* or *sans serif* typeface.[415] I prefer *serif* typefaces, such as Times New Roman, as opposed to a *sans serif*

Times New Roman 9pt

If Axion is dissolved and liquidated before Caspian has made each Subsequent Payment it is required to make under Section 1.2, the maximum Preferred Stock Liquidation Amount payable to Caspian will be calculated by multiplying the Preferred Stock Liquidation Amount that it would otherwise be entitled to by a fraction, the numerator of which is $1,795,000 plus $250,000 plus the amount of each Subsequent Payment made by Caspian, and the denominator of which is $6,795,000.

Helvetica 9pt

If Axion is dissolved and liquidated before Caspian has made each Subsequent Payment it is required to make under Section 1.2, the maximum Preferred Stock Liquidation Amount payable to Caspian will be calculated by multiplying the Preferred Stock Liquidation Amount that it would otherwise be entitled to by a fraction, the numerator of which is $1,795,000 plus $250,000 plus the amount of each Subsequent Payment made by Caspian, and the denominator of which is $6,795,000.

Courier New 9pt

```
If Axion is dissolved and liquidated before Caspian has
made each Subsequent Payment it is required to make under
Section 1.2, the maximum Preferred Stock Liquidation
Amount payable to Caspian will be calculated by multiply-
ing the Preferred Stock Liquidation Amount that it would
otherwise be entitled to by a fraction, the numerator of
which is $1,795,000 plus $250,000 plus the amount of each
Subsequent Payment made by Caspian, and the denominator
of which is $6,795,000.
```

SAMPLE 10   TYPEFACE

typeface such as Helvetica. (See sample 10.) I find *serif* typefaces easier to read, perhaps because they are invariably used in legal publications.[416] Others share this preference.[417]

Emphasis

You can choose to make certain words, phrases, or paragraphs of a contract particularly conspicuous. You would need to decide, however, which text warrants being emphasized, and whether it should be emphasized by using italics, boldface, capital letters, underlining, or a combination of any two or more of them. Sample 11 demonstrates the effect of the more sober possibilities.

For my part, I emphasize the title, as one generally does any sort of

No Emphasis

If Axion is dissolved and liquidated before Caspian has made each Subsequent Payment it is required to make under Section 1.2, the maximum Preferred Stock Liquidation Amount payable to Caspian will be calculated by multiplying the Preferred Stock Liquidation Amount that it would otherwise be entitled to by a fraction, the numerator of which is $1,795,000 plus $250,000 plus the amount of each Subsequent Payment made by Caspian, and the denominator of which is $6,795,000.

All Capitals

IF AXION IS DISSOLVED AND LIQUIDATED BEFORE CASPIAN HAS MADE EACH SUBSEQUENT PAYMENT IT IS REQUIRED TO MAKE UNDER SECTION 1.2, THE MAXIMUM PREFERRED STOCK LIQUIDATION AMOUNT PAYABLE TO CASPIAN WILL BE CALCULATED BY MULTIPLYING THE PREFERRED STOCK LIQUIDATION AMOUNT THAT IT WOULD OTHERWISE BE ENTITLED TO BY A FRACTION, THE NUMERATOR OF WHICH IS $1,795,000 PLUS $250,000 PLUS THE AMOUNT OF EACH SUBSEQUENT PAYMENT MADE BY CASPIAN, AND THE DENOMINATOR OF WHICH IS $6,795,000.

Underlining

<u>If Axion is dissolved and liquidated before Caspian has made each Subsequent Payment it is required to make under Section 1.2, the maximum Preferred Stock Liquidation Amount payable to Caspian will be calculated by multiplying the Preferred Stock Liquidation Amount that it would otherwise be entitled to by a fraction, the numerator of which is $1,795,000 plus $250,000 plus the amount of each Subsequent Payment made by Caspian, and the denominator of which is $6,795,000.</u>

Italics

If Axion is dissolved and liquidated before Caspian has made each Subsequent Payment it is required to make under Section 1.2, the maximum Preferred Stock Liquidation Amount payable to Caspian will be calculated by multiplying the Preferred Stock Liquidation Amount that it would otherwise be entitled to by a fraction, the numerator of which is $1,795,000 plus $250,000 plus the amount of each Subsequent Payment made by Caspian, and the denominator of which is $6,795,000.

Bold

If Axion is dissolved and liquidated before Caspian has made each Subsequent Payment it is required to make under Section 1.2, the maximum Preferred Stock Liquidation Amount payable to Caspian will be calculated by multiplying the Preferred Stock Liquidation Amount that it would otherwise be entitled to by a fraction, the numerator of which is $1,795,000 plus $250,000 plus the amount of each Subsequent Payment made by Caspian, and the denominator of which is $6,795,000.

Bold and Italics

If Axion is dissolved and liquidated before Caspian has made each Subsequent Payment it is required to make under Section 1.2, the maximum Preferred Stock Liquidation Amount payable to Caspian will be calculated by multiplying the Preferred Stock Liquidation Amount that it would otherwise be entitled to by a fraction, the numerator of which is $1,795,000 plus $250,000 plus the amount of each Subsequent Payment made by Caspian, and the denominator of which is $6,795,000.

1.   <u>Defined Terms</u>. Defined terms used but not defined in this Amendment are defined in the Development Agreement.

2.   <u>Amendments to Section 1</u>. Section 1 of the Development Agreement is hereby amended as follows:

(1)   by adding at the end of Section 1.5 the words *"not specially sized for use with the Occuspan Unit"*;

(2)   by deleting Section 1.6 in its entirety, and substituting in lieu thereof the following:

> *1.6   "<u>Occuspan Consumable</u>" means any single-use disposable or reusable component used in the operation of the Occuspan Unit, which components include, based upon the Occuspan Unit as currently configured, (1) the Occuspan Handpiece, (2) the pump cartridge, (3) the pump collection bag, (4) the irrigation and aspiration tube set, (5) the Occuspan Handpiece tube set, (6) the incision sizing probe, (7) the entry probe, (8) the Occuspan irrigation needle, (9) the bottle or pouch of sterile balanced salt solution, and (10) any surgical knife specially sized for use with the Occuspan Unit.*

> *1.7   "<u>Occuspan Handpiece</u>" means a single-use disposable tissue removal device incorporating a high-speed rotary cutter using integrated irrigation aspiration, the current configuration of which device is represented by Visex part number 59572 Revision A.*

(3)   by renumbering Sections 1.7 through 1.10 as Sections 1.8 through 1.11.

SAMPLE 12   USE OF ITALICS IN AMENDMENTS

---

title. In the introduction I emphasize the names of the parties. I also emphasize article headings. In the signature blocks I emphasize again the names of the parties, partly as a nod to convention but also to help distinguish the name of a party from the name of an individual or entity signing on behalf of a party. In each of these cases I achieve emphasis by using all capital letters. Capitalized text impairs readability because the eye cannot easily differentiate characters that are all of a uniform size,[418] so capitalization is best avoided, but in any contract I use it sufficiently sparingly that its effect on readability is negligible.

I emphasize all section headings by underlining them. I also underline each defined term when I define it, as well as references to exhibits or schedules. Underlining creates its own readability problems,[419] but I do not use it enough for that to become an issue.

I do not emphasize any part of the provisions proper; I think it would be unnecessary and distracting to lead the reader by the nose in that manner.[420] Sometimes, however, statutes require that entire provisions be emphasized. A prime example is a disclaimer of the implied warranty of merchantability, which the Uniform Commercial Code states must be "conspicuous."[421]

Additionally, in response to case law many drafters emphasize waivers of jury trial. The case law addressing whether waivers of jury trial need to be conspicuous is, however, inconsistent. In New York, for instance, a waiver of jury trial may be printed in the same size type as the rest of the contract,[422] while courts in some other jurisdictions, in holding a waiver of jury trial to be enforceable, have noted that the waiver of jury trial was in boldfaced type or in uppercase letters.[423] Unless you are able to do the necessary research, the cautious approach would be to make all waivers of jury trial conspicuous regardless of the law governing the contract.

Drafters sometimes emphasize sections in all capitals in an attempt to draw the attention of the parties to a particularly significant provision, the aim being to prevent any party from thereafter claiming that it had been unaware of that provision. This is presumably what lies behind the emphasized governing-law provisions and consent-to-jurisdiction provisions that one occasionally sees, despite the lack of any statute or case law requiring that such provisions be particularly conspicuous. I would not add such emphasis unless there is a substantial disparity of bargaining power and sophistication between the parties.

While it is occasionally appropriate to emphasize an entire provision, the paradox is that drafters invariably emphasize such provisions by using all capitals, which is guaranteed to make them nearly impenetrable. Wherever possible, I prefer to use instead both italics and boldface. Note, however, that depending on the applicable state case law, italics and boldface may not be sufficiently conspicuous for an implied warranty of merchantability.[424]

When an agreement specifies the legend that is to appear on stock certificates, the legend is almost always in all capitals and is an ordeal to read. I prefer to use italics instead, both in the agreement and on the stock certificates. Also, I use italics in amendments, to distinguish from the language around it the new language that is to be added to the original agreement. (See sample 12.)

You will have gathered from the above account that not only am I relatively austere in my use of emphasis, but I also make scant use of the font-appearance features of word-processing software, in that I do

Times New Roman 10pt

If Axion is dissolved and liquidated before Caspian has made each Subsequent Payment it is required to make under Section 1.2, the maximum Preferred Stock Liquidation Amount payable to Caspian will be calculated by multiplying the Preferred Stock Liquidation Amount that it would otherwise be entitled to by a fraction, the numerator of which is $1,795,000 plus $250,000 plus the amount of each Subsequent Payment made by Caspian, and the denominator of which is $6,795,000.

Times New Roman 12pt

If Axion is dissolved and liquidated before Caspian has made each Subsequent Payment it is required to make under Section 1.2, the maximum Preferred Stock Liquidation Amount payable to Caspian will be calculated by multiplying the Preferred Stock Liquidation Amount that it would otherwise be entitled to by a fraction, the numerator of which is $1,795,000 plus $250,000 plus the amount of each Subsequent Payment made by Caspian, and the denominator of which is $6,795,000.

Times New Roman 14pt

If Axion is dissolved and liquidated before Caspian has made each Subsequent Payment it is required to make under Section 1.2, the maximum Preferred Stock Liquidation Amount payable to Caspian will be calculated by multiplying the Preferred Stock Liquidation Amount that it would otherwise be entitled to by a fraction, the numerator of which is $1,795,000 plus $250,000 plus the amount of each Subsequent Payment made by Caspian, and the denominator of which is $6,795,000.

SAMPLE 13   FONT SIZE

not use boldface and italics (except for purposes of emphasizing entire sections, when I use both, and emphasizing stock certificate legends and amendments, when I use italics). I find that boldface is too emphatic: when used sparingly it makes words leap off the page; when it is used in excess it turns reading into a bumpy ride. As for text in italics, I find that it is too subtle.

Font Size

I have yet to tinker with font size. Every word-processing system I have used offered a 12-point font as the default option, and judging from the contracts I review the vast majority of drafters are, like me, satisfied with using a 12-point font size.[425] I have occasionally been presented with contracts in 14-point text and have found the larger font size more distracting than helpful. (See sample 13.)

Characters Per Line

For optimum readability, the number of characters per line should not exceed 70.[426] A line of 12-point Times New Roman on letter-size paper with one-inch margins contains approximately 80 characters. While this is not ideal, I have not felt the need to compensate by increasing the font size or margins, changing to a hanging-indent format, or using columns, each of which has drawbacks. In particular, I think that corporate agreements, with their tabulated and hierarchized text, are ill-suited to a column format.

MISCELLANEOUS OTHER ISSUES

Redundant Synonyms

For centuries, lawyers have strung together synonyms.[427] Corporate lawyers have inherited this tradition, and rare is the contract that does not include redundant synonyms or near-synonyms. Many of the synonym doublet and triplets one finds in contracts, such as *successors and assigns*, are traditional.[428] I truncate most of them. For instance, generally I no longer refer to a party's *right, title, and interest* in any particular property, but simply to its *interest*,[429] and I now prefer to have a party represent that it has the *power* to do something, rather than the *power and authority*.[430]

But many synonym strings appear to be improvisations. This suggests that many lawyers still assume that the liberal use of synonyms is an integral part of drafting. That this practice spares drafters the often-awkward task of selecting the best word for a given provision may help explain why it lives on.

Here is an example of this phenomenon: *Smith shall purchase from Jones, and Jones shall sell, convey, assign, transfer and deliver to Smith, the Shares on the Closing Date.* Just as *purchase* is adequate to reflect the transaction from the perspective of Smith, Jones can simply *sell* the Shares. *Convey, assign,* and *transfer* reflect concepts that are implicit in a sale, while any concerns Jones might have regarding delivery would be best addressed by listing in a separate section what needs to be delivered at closing. Furthermore, Jones would presumably be representing that as of the closing date he will have good and marketable title to the Shares free of any liens, and that title will pass to Smith free of any liens. This would take care of any of Smith's concerns far more effectively than searching out different ways to characterize the transaction.

Governing-law provisions are another fruitful source of such redundancy. Take the following example: *This Agreement shall in all respects be interpreted, construed and governed by and in accordance with the laws of the State of New York.* It is entirely adequate to state that the agreement *is governed by* the stated laws, and *in all respects* adds nothing, since the provision is sufficiently comprehensive without it. (Not much would be gained by eschewing the passive voice in favor of *The laws of the State of New York govern this Agreement.*)

Here is a final example of redundancy: An agreement states, as many do, that it is a condition to closing that a party's representations be *true, correct, and complete.* One or other of *true* and *correct* can be dispensed with, since a representation cannot be true but incorrect, or untrue but correct. *Complete* presumably represents an attempt to ensure that no information is missing from the contract proper or the schedules; again, if such information is correct or true it will also be complete, meaning that you can do without *complete.* I would, in fact, get rid of all three adjectives and use *accurate* instead.

Some might argue that unnecessary synonyms are essentially harmless and could be left well enough alone, but the air of pomposity they lend to drafting by itself warrants purging contracts of unnecessary synonyms. Furthermore, "the canon of construing legal documents that states that every word is to be given meaning and nothing is to be read as mere surplusage" can result in synonyms being "given unforeseen meanings by clever interpreters,"[431] particularly if a contract attempts to use a changing cast of synonyms to convey a consistent meaning.

So before turning your contract into a legal thesaurus by using a multiplicity of overlapping terms, ask yourself whether any given term conveys a meaning that is both sufficiently apt and sufficiently distinct from any accompanying terms that it warrants your retaining it.

Provisos

A common feature of contract topography is the "proviso."[432] In contracts and legislation, the traditional proviso is a clause introduced by *provided that* and set off from the preceding clause by a colon or semicolon. As often as not, corporate lawyers throw in *however* and underlining to introduce provisos by means of a semicolon and *provided, however, that*, with any immediately following proviso being introduced by a semicolon and *provided further, however, that* or some variation.

In this context, *provided that* is a truncation of the "term of enactment" (and language of performance)[433] *it is provided that*, which was used into the nineteenth century to introduce statutory provisions.[434] As such, *provided that* is analogous to a contract lead-in,[435] and strictly speaking using *provided that* in this manner in the body of a contract is as redundant as using *the parties agree* outside of the lead-in.[436] (Do not confuse this use of *provided* with its use as a conjunction meaning *if*, as in "I will join you for dinner, provided I get home on time" and "Acme may thereafter transfer the Shares to any Person, provided Acme gives the other Stockholders at least 30 days' prior written notice.")[437]

Given its derivation, it is not surprising that *provided that* is not an effective way of conveying the relationship between two adjoined contract provisions. The problem is that "the phrase means too many different things: *provided that* may create an exception, a limitation, a condition, or a mere addition."[438] There are many clearer alternatives to *provided that*:

> For all [situations using *provided that*] a perfectly good conjunction
> is available. In some cases a semicolon, colon or period would be
> much better than a conjunction. And in many instances, instead of
> adding a clause, it would be better to insert a phrase or other
> modifier somewhere in the body of the main sentence.[439]

In this spirit, below are some provisos, one for each of the categories of meaning drafters seek to convey by means of provisos; in each, the clearer alternative to the italicized text incorporating *provided that* is noted in italics in the brackets that immediately follow.

- *Exception:* No party may assign any of its rights and obligations under this Agreement without the prior written consent of the other *parties; provided, however, that* [read *parties, except that*] Buyer may assign any of its rights and obligations under this Agreement to any Affiliate.

- *Limitation:* The Closing must take place at the offices of the Purchaser's counsel as soon as possible after the date of this *Agreement; provided, however, that the Closing must occur* [read *Agreement, and in any event*] no later than December 1, 2000, at 5:00 P.M. New York time, unless the parties agree to another date.

- *Condition:* Acme may assign to any Person its rights and obligations under this *Agreement; provided, however, that* [read *Agreement, on condition that*] prior to any such assignment Acme must obtain the prior written consent of each of the other parties.

- *Addition:* The Company or the Purchaser shall promptly notify the Seller after any set-off and *application; provided, however, that failure* [read *application. Failure*] to so notify the Seller will not affect the validity of any such set-off and application.

If the syntactical limitations of provisos were not enough, I would also avoid them on stylistic grounds, in that *provided, however, that* interrupts, with a grinding of gears, the flow of a sentence. I also find grating the idiosyncratic punctuation and underlining.

All told, it is not surprising that commentators exhibit a marked distaste for provisos.[440] One should, however, be careful not to overstate the problem. While *provided that* may fail to convey clearly the relationship between adjoined clauses, that relationship can generally be deduced from the clauses themselves. That explains how *provided that* has managed to survive.

Such *Used as a Pointing Word*

When in corporate agreements drafters use *such* in conjunction with a noun phrase echoing an antecedent noun phrase, it is sometimes used appropriately to mean "of this kind,"[441] particularly when prefaced by *any* or *no*, as in "The Escrow Agent shall give written notice of any *such* deposit to the Purchaser and the Sellers" and "No *such* default or breach now exists."

Much more often, however, drafters use *such* instead of the demonstrative determiners, or "pointing words," *this, that, these,* and *those.*[442] This is one of the hallmarks of legalese.[443]

An example selected at random: "'<u>Affiliate</u>' means, with respect to any Person, any other Person controlling, controlled by, or under common control with *such* Person." I would use *that* instead of *such*.

A further example: "Widgetco shall complete its review within 10 days. If Widgetco has not within *such* 10-day period notified the Licensee, in writing, of its disapproval and the reasons for *such* disapproval, the Licensee may, in its sole discretion, publish the Licensee Work." I would replace the first *such* with *that*, and would use *its* instead of the second *such*.

Inappropriate use of *such* also arises in the context of modification of a plural noun. Take the following example: "Acme has purchased all shares of Common Stock held by the Widgetco stockholders listed on <u>Exhibit A</u>, and has received from each of *such* stockholders a certificate representing its shares of Common Stock." I would use *those* instead of *such*.

A further problem that arises with *such* is that often there is no antecedent noun phrase to which *such* could relate, as in the following example from a set of recitals: "The Sellers are, however, willing to sell to the Purchaser all the outstanding shares of Common Stock held by them, and the Purchaser has agreed to *such* purchase." Replacing *such* with *that* would not be a suitable remedy; say instead, "the Purchaser has agreed to purchase those [*and not* such] shares."

Sometimes a pointing-word *that* is preceded by the *that* of a *that*-clause: "The Manager will not be liable to the Company or to any Member for any loss or damage sustained by the Company or any Member except to the extent *that that* loss or damage is the result of the Manager's gross negligence, willful misconduct, or breach of this Agreement." While *that that* is awkward, I regard it as a lesser evil than *that such*. Often, however, there is a quick fix: replace the pointing-word *that* with *the*, as there would still be no doubt what loss or damage—in the case of the preceding example—is being referred to.

Notwithstanding *and* Subject To

Notwithstanding is a regular fixture in corporate agreements; it occurs in sentences such as "Notwithstanding any provision of Section 3.2, Acme may own 1% or less of a publicly traded company." In this sentence, *notwithstanding* means "in spite of" or "despite"[444] and serves to indicate that while the subject matter of Section 3.2 overlaps with that of the quoted sentence, the quoted sentence should be read and interpreted as if Section 3.2 did not exist.

Similarly, you can subordinate an entire agreement to a given provision by placing before that provision the old chestnut *notwithstanding anything herein to the contrary*, while *notwithstanding the foregoing* allows you to subordinate the preceding text.

For a number of reasons, I recommend you avoid *notwithstanding*. For one thing, the one or more provisions that it subverts could be at a remove from it. A reader could blithely accept at face value a given contract provision, unaware that it is undercut by a *notwithstanding* several pages later.

Furthermore, while a *notwithstanding* clause that refers to a particular section at least warns the careful reader what is being undercut, one that encompasses the entire agreement leaves to the reader the often awkward task of determining which provisions are affected. Often enough, the answer is none: lazy or harried drafters tend to throw in *notwithstanding anything herein to the contrary* to inoculate particularly significant provisions against conflicting provisions, whether or not there in fact are any.

Finally, while *notwithstanding the foregoing* might seem relatively benign, in that the provision that is undercut is specified and is close at hand, I am uncomfortable with *the foregoing*, since it could conceivably refer to the previous sentence, to the entirety of the preceding part of the body of the contract, or to something in between.

All told, I concur that "*notwithstanding* is a dangerous word even for lawyers. The writing lawyer is too apt to throw it in without considering all of its side effects; the careful, reading lawyer is compelled to examine its possibilities. Readers at large must inevitably regard *notwithstanding* as a warning of legal trickery."[445]

There is an alternative to *notwithstanding*. A contract provision, call it Section 4, requires that Acme pay the Purchase Price to Jones, and another, Section 5, requires that Acme pay $10,000 of the Purchase Price to Smith if the Closing occurs after a given date. Instead of prefacing the latter provision with *Notwithstanding Section 4*, qualify the former provision with *Subject to Section 5*.[446] Using *subject to* allows you to signal the reader, in the context of any given provision, that the provision is undercut by another provision; you do not have to hope that the reader spots a *notwithstanding* elsewhere in the contract.

Note, however, that when you are proposing a change to the other side's draft that would undercut one or more other provisions, using *notwithstanding* rather than *subject to* would allow that change to be self-contained and, in all likelihood, more discreet. Consequently, even drafters who normally use *subject to* sometimes have use for *notwithstanding*.

Key language of performance (*Acme hereby grants Pharmaco a license . . .*) and key language of obligation (*the parties shall cause Cyberco to merge into Digitalco . . .*) is often preceded by *Subject to the terms of this Agreement*. This phrase is the obverse of *notwithstanding anything herein to the contrary* and often is equally superfluous, as the rights and obligations of the parties to a contract are determined by considering the contract as a whole rather than each provision in isolation. If, for example, a party grants an option in one section and states in one or more other sections the exercise price and the exercise period, it does not follow that the grant should be made "subject to the terms" of that contract, since it would be inconceivable for the party that is granted the option to claim that there is no exercise price or that the option is exercisable indefinitely. *Subject to* is best used when a provision is undercut, rather than supplemented, by another provision, in which case the provision doing the undercutting should generally be specified. That said, when a given key obligation—for example, the obligation to cause Cyberco to merge into Digitalco—is subject to the satisfaction of certain conditions and the right of one or more parties to terminate the agreement in certain circumstances, it is generally simpler to state at the outset that the obligation is *Subject to the terms of this Agreement* rather than specify at greater length the sections containing those conditions and termination rights.

Deem

In contracts, as in statutes, *deem* means "to treat [a thing] as being something that it is not, or as possessing certain qualities that it does not possess."[447] In other words, it is used to create a legal fiction.

In contracts, *deem* is always used in the passive and almost always with *shall*, as in *The failure to receive any such consent shall be deemed a breach of this Section 4*. Because no duty is being imposed, it is inappropriate to use *shall* with *deem*. Instead, *deem* is a sign that one is dealing with language of policy. As in all language of policy, you should use either the simple present or the simple future tense.[448] Use the simple present when the policy applies upon effectiveness of the agreement: *This Agreement may be executed in counterparts, each of which is an original and all of which together are deemed one and the same instrument.*

Use the simple future when the policy relates to future events: *Failure to obtain any such consent will be deemed a breach of this Section 4.*

There is something to be said for using *deem* in the active rather than passive voice: it is only the parties to a contract who are doing the deeming, rather than, say, any judge who may preside over any future dispute. One could also argue that because the parties are in fact doing all their deeming at the time the agreement becomes effective, it would always be preferable to use *deem* in the present tense. Applying these approaches to the immediately preceding example would yield the following: *The parties deem that failure to obtain any such consent will be a breach of this Section 4.* But it would be unduly formalistic to insist that drafters adopt these approaches.

Deem is overused. Consider how it is used in the following provision: *Any violation of the restrictions set forth in this Section 4.2 by any officer or director of Acme or any investment banker, attorney, or other advisor or representative of Acme will be deemed to be a breach by Acme of this Section 4.2.* It would be a stretch to call this provision a legal fiction; use *will constitute* rather than *will be deemed to be*.

Here- and There- Words

Corporate lawyers are fond of *here-* words (such as *hereby, herein,* and *hereof*) and their *there-* counterparts.[449] Except in the case of *hereby* used in language of performance,[450] I recommend that you avoid these words and use them "only as a last resort to avoid awkward phrasing."[451] (An example of the legitimate use of a *here-* word: "all contracts to which Acme is party that are listed on Schedule 3.6, including any amendments *thereto*.") My objection is not so much that it may be uncertain what the *here-* refers to in a phrase such as *the transactions contemplated hereby*,[452] for in my experience corporate lawyers invariably use *here-* to refer to an entire agreement rather than a section or other component of an agreement. Instead, I dislike the "musty legal smell" they give off[453] and also find it tiresome to encounter endless references to *Section, Article,* or *Schedule X hereof*.

There are two fixes. First, instead of the *here-* in *hereby* and *herein*, use the defined term for the agreement in question, as in *the transactions contemplated by this Agreement.* The effect is sufficiently salutary to warrant the additional few words. Second, you can for the most part dispense with *hereof* entirely because it would be obtuse to argue that unless one tacks on a *hereof*, a contract reference to, say, Schedule 3.12 could refer to a schedule of either that contract or of some entirely different contract. To avoid any uncertainty, you could address this issue in a section specifying global drafting conventions.[454]

Syntactical Ambiguity

A contract provision is ambiguous if it is capable of being given more than one meaning. While there are various kinds of ambiguity,[455] certain of which I refer to elsewhere in this book,[456] the most obvious ambiguities that I encounter in reviewing contracts are syntactical ambiguities, which arise from a less-than-ideal arrangement of words and phrases.

One example: *The Company shall credit the Shares to the DTC account designated by the Purchaser upon receipt by the Escrow Agent of payment for the Draw Down.* While this sentence suggests that the Purchaser designates the DTC account after the Escrow Agent receives payment, what the drafter intended to express is that the Shares will be credited after receipt of payment. To avoid this ambiguity, the sentence could be rephrased as follows: *Upon receipt by the Escrow Agent of payment for the Draw Down, the Company shall credit the Shares to the DTC account designated by the Purchaser.*

A second example: *"NDA" means a new drug application, product license application, or its equivalent filed with any Governmental Authority seeking approval to make and sell a Licensed Product in the Territory.* Since no Governmental Authority is seeking approval, this sentence would be better rephrased as follows: *"NDA" means a new drug application, product license application or its equivalent that is filed with any Governmental Authority and seeks approval to make and sell a Licensed Product in the Territory.*

The ambiguity in each of these examples is "patent," in that there is little or no danger of the meaning being unclear. Ambiguity can also be "latent" and give rise to real uncertainty as to meaning. Take the following example: *If Acme stockholders do not approve issuance of the Second Installment Shares on or before March 31, 2002 . . . .* While this clause apparently refers to the timing of issuance, the drafter had in fact intended to address the timing of stockholder approval, and so should have provided as follows: *If prior to April 1, 2002, Acme stockholders do not approve issuance of the Second Installment Shares . . . .* While latent ambiguity is more pernicious than patent ambiguity, both kinds of ambiguity detract from the provision involved.[457]

A type of syntactical ambiguity that occurs frequently in contracts involves the use of modifiers[458] in a series. This kind of ambiguity comes in two related forms.[459] The first involves an adjective or other modifier used before two or more nouns. *Jones is selling his company to Widgetco and undertakes not to engage in the sale of collectibles, except that his sale of sports memorabilia and trading cards will not fall within the scope of that restriction.* It is not, however, clear whether Jones could sell non-sports trading cards. If it is intended that he be able to do so, the provision should refer to *sports memorabilia and sports trading cards.* If the intention is to prevent him from selling any trading cards, it would be better to reverse the order of the two nouns so as to have the exception cover *trading cards and sports memorabilia.*

The second form of this type of syntactical ambiguity arises when a qualifying phrase *follows* two or more nouns. A contract provides that *Acme may not incur any debt or make any capital expenditure in excess of $500,000.* In interpreting this prohibition, a court could well apply what is commonly referred to as "the Rule of the Last Antecedent," which provides that a qualifying phrase relates to the word or phrase immediately preceding it and is not to be construed as extending to others more remote.[460] This would likely lead a court to conclude that Acme may not incur any debt, no matter what the amount. To ensure that the threshold amount applies also to Acme's incurring debt, the provision would need to be rephrased to provide that *Acme may not incur any debt in excess of $500,000 or make any capital expenditure in excess of $500,000.*

The Ambiguous Or *and* And

The word *or* has two senses, in that it can be "inclusive" (A or B, or both) or "exclusive" (A or B, but not both).[461] While in some contexts (for example, *He will arrive on Sunday or Monday*) it could have only the exclusive sense, in others (for example, *You may give your tickets to Paul or Ellen*) it is not always clear which sense is intended. According to Dickerson, in legal usage *or* is mostly used in the inclusive sense.[462] In general usage, however, the converse is true.[463] Given this uncertainty, it is often a good idea for drafters to be explicit as to which sense they mean to convey.

A device many drafters rely on to this end is *and/or*, which they use when they want to convey the sense of the inclusive *or*.[464] While more general authorities suggest that *and/or* has its uses,[465] commentators on legal writing tend to wax indignant.[466] For my part, I regard it as one of the more benign drafting evils. It does, after all, have a specific meaning (*X and/or Y* means *X or Y or both*)[467] and is succinct. Furthermore, the difficulties associated with *and/or* are more apparent than real. For example, while commentators have expressed concern that the phrase *Acme shall purchase A and/or B and/or C* in a contract would give rise to seven possible combinations of A, B, and C,[468] this could well be exactly what the parties intend.

There are, however, two drawbacks to *and/or*. First, when used thoughtlessly it results in "a joining of impossibles,"[469] as in *Any sublicensee must be a corporation and/or a limited liability company*. Second, I find *and/or* too clunky to use in my general writing,[470] and in this case see no reason to hold my drafting to a different standard. Given these shortcomings, I try to avoid using *and/or* in my drafting and use instead *X or Y or both*, or, when more than three items are involved, *one or more of A, B, and C*.

Using *either . . . or* can sometimes help convey the exclusive sense of *or*.[471] How effectively it can do this depends, however, on the context, and drafters sometimes use it even if they do not intend to use the exclusive *or*.[472]

Instead of agonizing over ways of making it clear that any given *or* is inclusive or exclusive, you could provide in a section stating drafting conventions that *or* is inclusive and not exclusive unless the context clearly requires.[473] I have yet to use such a provision, since I am not sure that its rigidity is a lesser evil than the ambiguity it aims to eliminate.

Ambiguity similar to that inherent in *or* also infects *and*, in that there is the "several"[474] *and* (A and B, jointly or severally, meaning A separately, B separately, or A and B together) and the "joint" *and* (A and B, jointly but not severally, meaning A and B together and not A separately or B separately),[475] although Dickerson suggests that in legal contexts *and* is normally used in the former sense.[476] In contract drafting it is often advisable to be explicit as to which sense you intend. How to achieve this depends upon the context. I would, for example, rephrase *Acme and Widgetco may transfer their Shares* to read *each of Acme and Widgetco may transfer its Shares*, so as to preclude any inference that Acme and Widgetco must both transfer their Shares. In a phrase such as *Smith and Jones are liable for Widget's failure to perform its obligations*, you should specify whether liability is "joint and several"[477] or "joint but not several."[478]

The ambiguity inherent in *or* and *and* is sufficiently complex that it would take several more pages to tackle the subject comprehensively. Furthermore, corporate agreements exhibit a relatively restricted range of language and many of the nuances involving *and* and *or* rarely arise. Consequently, I have only scratched the surface of this topic.[479]

Using (s) *to Denote Singular and Plural Simultaneously*

Some drafters tack (*s*) onto the singular form of a noun when they wish to convey that a given situation may involve one or more than one of a given item. Two examples: *Parent shall cause to be filed a registration statement(s) on Form S-3 . . .* ; and *upon the surrender of the certificate(s) previously representing those shares . . . .*

It is best to steer clear of (*s*), since more straightforward alternatives are always available. In the above examples, I would use the plural noun preceded by "one or more."

When the noun receiving the (*s*) treatment is the subject of the sentence, some drafters attempt to cover the bases by offering the verb in both singular and plural form: *The following individual(s) is (are) key personnel for performance of the research.* If you insist on using (*s*), use just the plural form of the verb.

Using That Certain *When Referring to an Agreement*

Drafters quite often use *that certain* when introducing a given agreement, perhaps because, consciously or not, they find appealing the note of bureaucratic pomp that it adds: *Acme and Widgetco are party to that certain Management Agreement dated April 12, 2000. That certain* is analogous to using *one* as an adjective before a proper name (*one* Edward Smith),[480] and like that usage it is best avoided. In the preceding example, refer simply to *a Management Agreement.*

The Earlier *[or* Later, Greater, *or* Lesser] of X and Y

In drafting contracts you often need to provide for selection of the earlier or later, or greater or lesser, of two alternatives. (When three or more items are involved, you would refer to the earliest or latest, or greatest or least, of those alternatives.) One example: *Acme shall retain any records of the Business transferred to Acme pursuant to this Agreement until the later of (1) expiration of the applicable tax statute of limitations, including extensions thereof, and (2) the seventh anniversary of the Closing Date.* A second example: *"Aggregate Net Proceeds" means the greater of (1) any Aggregate Gross Proceeds minus that portion of the aggregate Capital Contributions attributable to the Axion Internet Shares to which those Aggregate Gross Proceeds relate, and (2) zero.*

In the preceding examples, I use *and* as the conjunction. Most lawyers, however, use *or*,[481] presumably on the grounds that when you select one item from a group, *or* is the usually appropriate conjunction to use, as in *You may select A, B, or C.*

While it may be contrarian of me,[482] in my own drafting I will for the time being continue to use *and* when selecting among alternatives by means of *the earlier* [or *later, greater,* or *lesser*] *of. And* "has logic on its side," in that one is selecting one item from a group of two or more.[483] Using *or* is harmless, but requires that one select, say, the greater of each item considered individually, which does not make sense. In order to use *or* in the preceding examples, you would need to rephrase them using *whichever is.* The first example so rephrased: *Acme shall retain any business records of the Business transferred to Acme pursuant to this Agreement until (1) expiration of the applicable tax statute of limitations, including extensions thereof, or (2) the seventh anniversary of the Closing Date, whichever is later.* Because it places at the end of the sentence the basis for selecting between the items being compared, I generally use the formula *whichever is* only when the description of those items is relatively brief.

Mutual *and* Mutually

The principal meaning of the adjective *mutual* is "reciprocal" or "directed by each toward the other or others," as in *Smith and Jones regarded each other with mutual mistrust.*[484] When in a corporate agreement *mutual* is used to convey this meaning, it often modifies *agreement,* as in *"Product" means any product whose promotion and detailing is assigned to Acme by mutual agreement with Pharmaco.* In this case *mutual* is redundant, as reciprocity is inherent in the notion of agreement.[485]

One also encounters references to *mutual consent,* as in *This Agreement may be terminated at any time by mutual written consent duly authorized by the boards of directors of Parent and Acme.* It would be preferable to use *by the mutual exchange of written consents,*[486] but better yet would be *by written agreement of Parent and Acme,* as *mutual exchange of consents* is the long-winded functional equivalent of *agreement.*

Another meaning of *mutual* is "pertaining to both parties."[487] Consequently, one could refer in a set of recitals to the parties wanting to take a given action *for their mutual benefit.* An alternative would be *for the benefit of each of them.* Combining the two, as in *for the mutual benefit of each of them,* would result in redundancy.[488]

In corporate agreements, the adverb *mutually* is often used with the verb *agree*, as in *such other date as the parties mutually agree*. It is also used to modify the adjective *agreeable*, as in *Any public announcement must be in a form mutually agreeable to the Company and Parent*. In each such instance, *mutually* is redundant, for the same reason that *mutual* is superfluous in *mutual agreement*.

Mutually is sometimes mistakenly used instead of *jointly*, as in *such bank or trust company as shall be mutually designated by the Company and Parent*. Here is an example of *mutually* used appropriately to convey reciprocity: *Merger Sub and the Company shall issue mutually acceptable public announcements regarding execution of this Agreement.*

CHAPTER 6

Specifying Drafting Conventions

L ONGER CONTRACTS OFTEN INCLUDE a section, generally entitled "Construction" or "Interpretation," that provides for shortcuts and seeks to eliminate ambiguities. In this chapter I provide a selection, with commentary, of the sort of provisions included in such sections; I have, to varying degrees, tidied them up. None of them is essential. If you elect to use any of them, I would preface them with the statement that *The parties shall interpret this Agreement in accordance with the following* and list them as tabulated enumerated clauses. I also include provisions specifying drafting conventions to use with respect to language of obligation and references to time. I do so, however, to supplement earlier discussion of these issues; I do not expect you to use those provisions.

USEFUL PROVISIONS

I have on occasion found useful the following provisions:

- *Any reference in this Agreement to a section, article, schedule, or exhibit is to a section, article, schedule, or exhibit of this Agreement, unless otherwise stated*: This is a useful tool in the battle against *hereof* and *attached hereto*.[489]

- *The words "include," includes," and "including" are to be read as if they were followed by the phrase "without limitation" [or "but not limited to"]*: To ensure that courts interpret the word *including* as introducing an illustrative rather than exhaustive list, drafters generally tack on each time the rather ponderous *without limitation* or *but not limited to*.[490] This provision is one relatively painless way to accomplish that.

- *A pronoun used in reference to any member of a class of persons, or persons and things, applies to each member of that class, whether of the masculine, feminine, or neuter gender*: If I am drafting, say, a stockholder agreement and need a pronoun to refer to "any Stockholder," no one pronoun will do, strictly speaking, if the stockholders consist of men, women, and entities. In that context, this provision would make it impossible to argue, however implausibly, that if, for example, I use "it," I intend to exclude those Stockholders who are natural persons. This provision represents my reworking of the usual forms, such as *"it" or "its" or words denoting any gender include all genders*.

- *The headings in this Agreement are provided for convenience only and do not affect its meaning*: I have difficulty imagining a court, in the context of a contract between ostensibly sophisticated parties represented by counsel, accepting the argument of one of the parties that it was misled by a section heading. This provision is nonetheless standard; it is often placed in a section on its own.

- *Unless specified otherwise, any reference to a statute means that statute and any successor statute and any regulations thereunder, all as amended or supplemented from time to time*: This provision is intended to ensure that if a contract requires ongoing compliance with a given statute, compliance is measured against the statute as amended, rather than against the statute as it was at the closing date, without your having to tack "as amended" onto each statute reference.

LESS-USEFUL PROVISIONS

I prefer not to use the following provisions. They range from the harmless to the pointless.

- *The words "hereof," "herein," "hereunder," and "hereby" refer to this Agreement as a whole and not to any particular provision of this Agreement*: I suggest that you dispense with the majority of here- words[491] instead of concerning yourself with their meaning. Also, this provision does not take into account that anomaly, *hereby* used in language of performance.[492]

- *Unless the context clearly requires, "or" is not exclusive*: This provision would spare drafters having to ensure, by means of *and/or* or otherwise, that a given *or* is inclusive rather than exclusive. There is little risk that it could render inclusive an *or* that a drafter had intended to be exclusive; given that in legal contexts *or* tends to be inclusive, a drafter intending to use a given *or* exclusively would in any event be advised to make sure that the meaning is clear, whether from the context, by using *either . . . or*, or otherwise.[493] By the same token, however, what it seeks to prevent—a court holding that a given *or* is exclusive though the drafter intended it to be inclusive—might be sufficiently unlikely that this provision would serve little purpose. More generally, I am reluctant to use a rigid provision of this sort to address the ambiguity inherent in *or*, which I prefer to handle on a case-by-case basis.

- *The definitions in this Agreement apply equally to both singular and plural forms of the terms defined*: This is intended to ensure, for example, that the definition of "Permit" applies to any reference to "the Permits," or that the definition of "Employee Benefit Plans" applies to a reference to "an Employee Benefit Plan." I am comfortable that this would be the case even without this provision. A common variant on this provision is *words denoting the singular include the plural and vice-versa*. This suggests that every noun in the contract could be either singular or plural, and as such makes no sense.

In addition, I recommend that you steer clear of the following:

- *Any reference to an agreement means that agreement as amended or supplemented from time to time, including by waiver or consent, unless otherwise provided*: When requiring that a party comply with a given agreement, you normally specify that compliance is measured against that agreement as it may be amended. This provision would allow you to state this once. That said, I have yet to feel it necessary to abandon the case-by-case approach in favor of this provision.

- *All exhibits and schedules attached to this Agreement are hereby incorporated in and made part of this Agreement as if set forth in full herein*: By referring in the body of a contract to the exhibits and schedules to that contract, you automatically make them a part of the contract, so a statement to that effect is unnecessary. It also follows that no purpose is served by stating that the exhibits and schedules are incorporated in the contract, whatever that means.[494]

PROVISIONS TO THINK ABOUT

Two of the issues discussed in this book could be addressed by means of the following provisions specifying drafting conventions.

- *The word "shall" means "has a duty to," "must" means "is required to," and "may" means "is permitted to"*: This provision could be used to address the issue that underlies most litigation regarding use of the word *shall*, namely whether or not it is mandatory.[495] It would help prevent a court from rendering your *shalls* anything less than mandatory.[496] You should not, however, think of using this provision unless in using *shall* you follow rigorously the "strict American rule."[497] I suspect that very few corporate lawyers do.

I have occasionally encountered provisions specifying drafting conventions that govern references to time. I have also seen such provisions offered in form books[498] and by commentators.[499] Invariably, these provisions address only a fraction of the ambiguities lurking in references to time,[500] and in doing so ignore many of the nuances. A provision that addresses these issues anywhere near comprehensively would have to be long and involved; below is my attempt at such a provision. Needless to say, I do not recommend that you actually incorporate it in a contract; I only include it in this book to caution against easy solutions and to suggest that rooting out every last ambiguity can be a complex and perhaps ultimately self-defeating task.

- *This Agreement may refer to one or more points in time that mark a change in a party's rights or obligations. Here is an example of this usage: "This Agreement terminates on August 12, 2005." If it is not* specified that any such point in time is to occur at a specified time of day, or if it is not indicated by means of "inclusive" or "exclusive" which day that point in time relates to, the following rules apply for purposes of determining when any such point in time occurs:

(1) if the relation of a point of time to a specified day is stated by means of "after," "following" or "through," that point in time occurs at midnight at the end of that day;

(2) if the relation of a point of time to a specified day is stated by means of "from," that point in time occurs at midnight at the end of that day, unless the specified day is the date of this Agreement, in which case that point in time occurs at midnight at the beginning of that day;

(3) if the relation of a point of time to a specified day is stated by means of "on," "starting," "by," "before," "ending," "to," or "until," that point in time occurs at midnight at the beginning of that day; and

(4) if two points in time are linked by "between," the earlier point in time occurs at midnight at the end of the specified day and the later point in time occurs at midnight at the beginning of the specified day.

- This Agreement may refer to one or more periods of time, measured in a given unit of time (days, weeks, months, or years) in relation to a specified day, during which a party's rights or obligations will be as specified. Here is an example of this usage: "Doe may exercise the Option any time during the 30 days from the day she receives the Option Notice." The following rules apply for purposes of determining the beginning or end of any such period of time:

(1) when counting forward a number of units of time "from," "after," or "following" a specified day, that day is not counted, except that if that day is the date of this Agreement, that day is counted;

(2) when counting back a number of units of time "before" or "prior" to a specified day, that day is not counted;

(3) if a party must not or may not take or cease taking a given action until a forward-running period of time lapses, and that period consists of a stated number of "entire," "clear," or "complete" units of time, the day the party takes or ceases

taking that action is not counted for purposes of determining whether the period of time has lapsed;

(4) if a party must or may take or cease taking a given action at least a stated number of entire units of time before a specified date, as is the case when a party is required to give notice a stated number of units of time before a specified date, the day the party takes or ceases taking that action is not counted for purposes of determining whether there remains the required number of entire units of time before the specified date;

(5) a "day" means any period of 24 hours measured from one midnight to the next;

(6) for purposes of determining the duration of a period of time measured in one or more weeks, a "week" means a period of any seven consecutive days beginning any day of the week;

(7) for purposes of determining the duration of a period of time measured in one or more years, a "year" means a period of any 365 consecutive days beginning any day of the year (with an additional day added if those 365 days include February 29); and

(8) for purposes of determining the duration of a period of time measured in one or more months, a "month" means a period that starts any specified day of any month and runs (A) in the case of a forward-running period, to midnight at the end of the day of the following month that corresponds to the day before that specified day or, if there is no corresponding day, the last day of the following month, or (B) in the case of a backward-running period, to midnight at the beginning of the day of the preceding month that corresponds to the day after that specified day or, if there is no corresponding day, the last day of the preceding month.

• This Agreement may refer to one or more periods of time, measured in a given unit of time (days, weeks, months, or years), for purposes of setting a limit, per unit of time, to any given obligation or right of a party. Here is an example of this usage: "Roe shall pay Doe $10,000 a month." The following rules apply for purposes of determining the beginning or ending of any such period of time:

(1) a "day" means a period of 24 hours measured from one midnight to the next;

(2)   a *"week"* means a period of seven consecutive days starting any Monday;

(3)   a *"month"* means one of the 12 months of the year starting the first day of that month and running through the last day of that month; and

(4)   a *"year"* means a period starting January 1 and running through the following December 31.

• If a party must or may take or cease taking a given action on a given day, or on or prior to a given day, and that day is not a business day, that party will have complied with the terms of this Agreement if it takes or ceases taking that action on the next day that is a business day. For purposes of this provision, a *"business day"* means any day other than Saturday, Sunday, or a day on which banks are closed in the jurisdiction whose law governs this Agreement.

CHAPTER 7

Drafting as Writing

WHILE THE CLARITY AND EFFICIENCY of a contract depend largely on how the drafter addresses the issues of language and structure I discuss in the previous chapters, other considerations come into play. Contract drafting is just one form of writing, albeit a specialized one, so that to draft effectively it is not enough that you master legal usage; you must also bring to bear general principles of good writing. In this chapter I indicate which of those principles I think most relevant for purposes of contract drafting.

DO NOT MAKE SENTENCES TOO LONG

Contracts generally contain sentences that wander on for much longer than the 20 or 25 words recommended for general legal writing[501] or the 30 words recommended for drafting.[502] In general, long sentences are harder to read than short ones.

Often, overlong sentences are the result of the drafter attempting to address, in one fell swoop, all facets of a given provision by stringing together clauses that could constitute sentences in their own right and piling on exceptions, qualifications, and conditions. Breaking such sentences down into their constituent components often makes them easier to read and does not affect meaning.

If a sentence needs to contain several enumerated clauses,[503] there is generally no way to avoid making it lengthy, but tabulating the enumerated clauses would serve to break it down into manageable portions.

AVOID WIDE GAPS BETWEEN THE SUBJECT, THE VERB, AND THE OBJECT

A sentence is easier to understand if the subject, the verb, and the object (if any) are close together.[504] Drafters often test a reader's stamina by creating unnecessary gaps between subject and verb or between verb and object. In the first example below, the gap is between the subject and the verb; in the second, it is between the verb and the object. Sometimes fixing this requires turning the intervening words into a separate sentence; at other times, as in the examples below, the offending words can be shunted to the beginning or end of the sentence.[505] (In the examples below, the underlining denotes the offending text and shows where it was moved.)

Gap

Acme may not <u>without the prior written consent of Excelsior, which Excelsior may not unreasonably withhold,</u> transfer the Shares to any Person.

No Gap

Acme may not transfer the Shares to any Person <u>without the prior written consent of Excelsior, which Excelsior may not unreasonably withhold</u>.

Gap

Acme shall deliver to Widgetco<u>, within 15 days after any given Quarterly Period, unless the Gross Revenue for that Quarterly Period is less than $1,000,000,</u> a stock certificate representing those shares of Acme common stock that Acme is required to issue with respect to that Quarterly Period.

No Gap

<u>Within 15 days after any given Quarterly Period, unless the Gross Revenue for that Quarterly Period is less than $1,000,000,</u> Acme shall deliver to Widgetco a stock certificate representing those shares of Acme common stock that Acme is required to issue with respect to that Quarterly Period.

FAVOR VERBS OVER NOUNS

Drafters often use abstract nouns when verbs would serve them better; in other words, they use "nominalizations," also referred to as "buried verbs";[506] this is demonstrated in the first five examples below. Adjectives too can act as buried verbs; see the last of the examples below. (Note that it is an example of a passive-type policy, a variety of language of policy that I discuss above.)[507]

Using Buried Verbs	*Using Strong Verbs*
Immediately following issuance of the Shares, ...	Immediately after Acme issues the Shares, ...
. . . all expenses the Bank incurs in connection with establishment and maintenance of the Deposit Account.	. . . all expenses the Bank incurs in establishing and maintaining the Deposit Account.
Upon the failure of Smith to timely make the payment of the Purchase Price, ...	If Smith fails to timely pay the Purchase Price, ...
If at any time there is a merger or consolidation of Acme	If at any time Acme merges or consolidates . . . .
Jones shall promptly give notice to the other parties	Jones shall promptly notify the other parties . . . .
The Warrants are not redeemable by Acme at any time.	Acme may not at any time redeem the Warrants.

I think it only slight hyperbole to describe the use of buried verbs as "one of the most serious afflictions of legal prose, draining a sentence of vitality."[508] Avoiding buried verbs provides the following significant benefits:

- first, it allows you to use "strong" or "action" verbs rather than "weaker" verbs, including *is* and *has*;

- second, it permits you to avoid the prepositions and other surplusage inherent in using abstract nouns; and

- third, you make it clear who is doing what, which will not always be clear when you use buried verbs (see the first two of the above examples).

But do not get carried away, since buried verbs are not always the inferior option. For instance, if a number of different parties could exercise a particular option, you might want to stick with *Upon exercise of the Option* rather than use a strong verb. Before replacing a buried verb with a strong verb, make sure it represents an improvement.[509]

Avoid Wordy Phrases

You might want to steer clear of phrases that do not rise to the level of legalese, but are nonetheless unduly formal or wordy. For example, I use *if* rather than *in the event that*;[510] I avoid *subsequent to* in favor of *after*;[511] and use *per year, each year*, or *annually* rather than *per annum*.[512] For lists of such phrases, I leave you to consult other authorities.[513]

Use Possessives

One simple way of making contract prose less wooden is to not stint on using possessives. Refer to *Acme's board of directors* rather than *the board of directors of Acme*, and to *Smith's shares* rather than *the shares held by Smith*.

Do Not Overuse Initial Capitals

I discuss above the way drafters unnecessarily give initial capitals to references to agreements.[514] That is one example of a broader overuse of initial capitals; here are some further examples:

- Drafters generally refer to "the Board of Directors" of a given corporation, but the term is sufficiently generic to warrant using lowercase letters.[515]

- One often sees "director" with a capital "D," but that is inconsistent with good usage in general writing because professional titles are not capitalized unless they are accompanied by a personal name.[516] Similarly, drafters invariably use initial capitals when referring to officer titles (*The certificate must be signed by the President of Acme*), but it is only appropriate to do so when the title is followed by a name (*President Jane Doe*), which is never the case in corporate agreements.

- It is standard practice to use initial capitals when referring to a corporation's organizational documents (*Acme's Restated*

Certificate of Incorporation and Bylaws). Again, this is contrary to normal usage: One is referring not to the title of a work but to a category of document.

- Many drafters also use, for no apparent reason, initial capitals when referring to a company's capital stock (*the Common Stock, par value $0.01 per share, of Widgetco*).

Such use of initial capitals seems to be prompted by the notion that if something is important, it is best to give it initial capitals. This sort of overuse is essentially trivial, but not without cost: initial capitals can be distracting, and what with names and defined terms, corporate agreements are not wanting for initial capitals used appropriately. It does not follow, however, that you should immediately start using lowercase letters. Some of the above usages are sufficiently ingrained—particularly the use of initial capitals in officer titles—that using lowercase letters could appear awkward, at least initially, to you and your readers. If you are inclined to shift to lowercase letters, be flexible.

I myself indulge in one form of overuse of initial capitals. When in a contract you refer to one or more articles or sections of that or another contract, you do not need to use initial capitals.[517] Nevertheless, most drafters do, and this usage is harmless enough that I see little point in resisting it.

CHAPTER 8

Some Thoughts on the Drafting Process

A S THIS IS A BOOK ON LEGAL USAGE in the drafting of corporate agreements rather than a more general how-to book, I do not address many of the issues that can arise in the drafting process, such as who should do the drafting or how you go about determining your client's needs.[518] Instead, I focus on those aspects of the process that have the greatest impact on the quality of the drafting.

USING MODEL CONTRACTS

You have just been asked to draft a contract, say a merger agreement. You could conceivably draft it from scratch. Alternatively, you may have at hand a contract that fits the deal perfectly, requiring that you simply change the party details and other incidental information. More often than not, however, you will find yourself between these extremes, but in order to avoid needlessly reinventing the wheel will nevertheless base your contract on models prepared by others. Consequently, it is likely that the most important step toward allowing you to draft that agreement effectively and efficiently would be for you to secure one or more suitable models to base it on.

The first question is, what should you look for? The key terms of your deal may have already been decided and are perhaps reflected in a letter of intent or term sheet. Alternatively, your client may have decided to move discussions along by presenting the other side with a draft. Either way, you know that your client, Parent, is a public company that is acquiring Target, a privately held company, in a stock-for-stock reverse subsidiary merger, with the stock being issued pursuant to an exemption from registration under the Securities Act of 1933.

You could seek out a suitable model based on that information alone, but you would also need to know whether there will be a simultaneous or deferred closing; with a deferred closing, you would need to incorporate conditions to closing and termination provisions. And it transpires that there are a number of other aspects to the deal that you need to incorporate in your draft, including the following:

- It is a fixed-price, floating-exchange-ratio deal, with a collar that limits any increase or decrease in the number of shares to be issued by Parent due to a change in Parent's stock price between signing and closing.

- Target stockholders have agreed to put into escrow a portion of the shares they are to receive in the merger, and Parent's sole recourse for any inaccurate representations or breached obligations will be against those shares.

- Target has a stock option plan, and options for Target stock will be converted into options to acquire Parent stock.

- The Nasdaq rules require that your client seek stockholder approval of the merger because it will be issuing a number of shares in excess of 20 percent of the number of shares currently outstanding.

- You have advised your client that it also needs to ensure that Target's stockholders and any purchaser's representatives of Target's stockholders were, for purposes of the exemption under the Securities Act, provided with sufficient information to allow them to assess their investment decision.

- Because Target is an insurance company, you will likely want to have Target make some industry-specific representations.

The odds of your finding a satisfactory model contract that addresses all these points is slim; if you are lucky, you will find a model for a deal with the same basic structure and perhaps one or more other aspects of your deal, and will rely on a range of other models that you can judiciously copy from.

If you have previously drafted a superior merger agreement for another very similar deal, you will want to use that as your principal model. It may be, however, that you do not have such a model at hand, in which case you will need to seek out suitable contracts prepared by others.

Where should you look for model contracts? The instinct of most lawyers is to look to their colleagues. Some firms institutionalize this process to a greater or lesser extent by maintaining files of vetted contracts that are periodically updated. At many firms, one can word-search the documents on the computer system; this allows lawyers to trawl for contracts that might serve as models. I suspect, however, that more often than not a lawyer in need of a model contract simply wanders down the hall, picks up the phone, or sends an all-hands e-mail, and in response colleagues scan their deal closing binders, root in their form files, or check the word-processing system and perhaps find something they think fits the bill.

If I want to supplement the models that my colleagues and I are able to come up with or need precedent for a particular provision, my next stop is generally EDGAR, the electronic system that public companies use to file documents with the Securities and Exchange Commission. Public companies are required to attach as exhibits to certain filings, under the category "Exhibit 10, Material Contracts," any significant agreements to which they are party. You can access EDGAR free of charge through the SEC's web site, among others, but if you are looking for forms you need to use a service that allows you to word-search the EDGAR exhibit filings. In addition to the standard search features, you can limit your search by date and also by Standard Industrial Classification, or "SIC," code number, which is helpful if you are looking for a type of contract or provision relating to a particular industry.

You should, however, be cautious when using as a model the final version of any agreement, whatever the source, since it likely will reflect the give-and-take of negotiation.[519] You could end up unwittingly incorporating from the form any number of provisions—such as "knowledge" or "materiality" qualifications to the seller's representations, more-extensive purchaser representations, or less-advantageous indemnification provisions—that your counterpart on that deal fought against and only ended up including because the client had little bargaining power or because the other party made suitable concessions elsewhere in the document.

The perils of using as a model the final version of a document has led to the recommendation that you use, whenever possible, the first draft of any agreement.[520] One would need to determine, however, what constitutes the first draft of an agreement. If it is the first version saved on your computer system, that could well represent a valiant first effort by someone two weeks out of law school, with the subsequent three versions representing changes wrought by more senior lawyers and the four versions after that reflecting further changes after input from the client. The best document to work from would be the first version that is submitted to the other side, since it presumably represents the drafting side's most coherent statement of its position, before the waters were muddied by negotiations. Establishing which version that was might prove difficult.

While I think it generally best to use the last pre-negotiation draft of any contract that you are using as a model, comments by the other side to a transaction have often allowed me to significantly improve a draft. Consequently, sometimes when I use as a model an early draft of a contract that is on my firm's computer system, I prepare a computer-generated comparison of the early draft against the final version and add to a copy of the early draft any of the later changes that I regard as improvements.

If you use as a model a contract from a deal that you did not work on, you would probably benefit from consulting with someone who is familiar with that deal. He or she should be able to tell you which side your firm represented, who drafted the document, and what the balance of bargaining power was.

Furthermore, there are benefits to using a contract that was drafted by someone at your firm or your legal department. For one thing, it will likely be on your computer system, and you and your support staff will be spared having to scan or input the document and then proofread it. More importantly, however, you (and, if you are a law firm associate, the partner on the deal) will probably feel more comfortable working with a document produced by one of your colleagues, particularly one who is known to be a reliable drafter, rather than one drafted by the lawyer on the other side of a previous deal or, in the case of a document retrieved from EDGAR, a complete stranger.

Finally, a further source of models is form contracts contained in books and articles. I have on occasion referred to forms included in publications of the Practicing Law Institute; they have the advantage of being up to date, often specify whether they favor one side of the deal or the other, are prepared by mainstream corporate lawyers, and can be retrieved in electronic format. The quality varies, however, and in any event I never use them as my principal model. One source I consult only rarely is form books such as *West's Legal Forms* or *Warren's Forms of Agreements.*[521] They can be unwieldy, are usually unavailable in electronic format, and their coverage tends to be vast but not very deep.

REVISING AND EDITING

After sufficient rummaging, you have assembled one principal model and a stack of secondary models. Then begins the process of revising and editing. This can be a significant undertaking. I have a rule of thumb that when I am preparing anything other than a routine draft and am using contracts prepared by others, a good first draft takes me about an hour a page to prepare; when I use my own forms, it can take me about a quarter of that time.

Revising involves cutting away irrelevant provisions, reordering those that remain, inserting pertinent provisions from other forms, drafting from scratch those you have not found forms for, and making global changes of party names and the like. You will then need to edit, in other words apply to the whole your own house style. My system is rather rudimentary: I start from the top and slowly churn my way through the document, applying in one fell swoop the usages I recommend in this book; the text that emerges is, I hope, leaner and infinitely more digestible. Then I go over it again, and probably a third time, to catch whatever I missed the first time around.

It is for the most part at the editing stage that you would go about adopting the usages I recommend in this book. If you are responsible for drafting a given contract, have some time to devote to the task, and are not committed to following any given precedent, by all means incorporate wholesale my recommendations. Often, however, you will find yourself operating under severe time constraints or you will be asked to base your draft on the rather clunky contract your client used in its previous deal. In such circumstances your task will be to prepare a document that might not represent an exemplary piece of drafting but basically accomplishes the client's goals.

REVIEWING YOUR DRAFTS

Every draft contract would benefit from being reviewed by someone other than the drafter. An astute colleague might suggest a more efficient structure for your transaction, spot a potential hazard that you had not noticed, or recommend any number of other improvements. On a more mundane level, no drafter can be expected to catch all typographic errors or internal inconsistencies.

The extent to which one of your drafts would benefit from being reviewed depends on a number of factors. How complex or unusual is the transaction? How frenetic is the pace? Do you have the luxury of being able to set the document aside for a day or two and return to it refreshed? Do you have someone else do the word processing, or do you do it yourself? (You are not the best proofreader of your own typing.) There are times when, due to a particularly inauspicious interplay of these factors, I simply cannot bring myself to read a given draft yet another time, but you should not wait for such dire circumstances before bringing in a fresh pair of eyes.

There is now available software that assists in the checking process. Deal Proof, a software tool developed by Expert Ease Software, uses artificial intelligence to scan legal documents and highlight errors and inconsistencies. It flags, for example, cross-references to sections or exhibits that do not exist; defined terms that are not defined, that are defined more than once, or that are not used; blanks and other indicia of terms that have yet to be finalized; and variations in the wording of any recurring phrase. A number of major law firms have purchased licenses to Deal Proof.

COMMENTING ON
THE OTHER SIDE'S DRAFTS

Scrutinizing a draft proposed by the other side in a transaction is obviously not the same thing as editing one of your own drafts, and you should avoid recommending, for example, that the drafter adopt a more principled use of *shall* or remove archaisms such as *WITNESSETH*. Such changes are unlikely to significantly advance your client's interests and could earn you a reputation for being a pedant.

DOCUMENT-ASSEMBLY SYSTEMS

There should be little call for originality in most contract drafting. Whatever the transaction, the odds are that the constituent components of the deal documents have featured in countless other transactions, and those aspects of a transaction that are truly distinctive—assuming that there are any—likely represent a very modest proportion of a given draft. Consequently, most contracts could in theory be successfully drafted using a suitably sophisticated document-assembly system.

A document-assembly system is a software program integrated with one or more template documents and a text editor or word-processing software. To create a document from a template, the user answers a series of questions; based upon the responses, the program inserts text into the document, selects clauses from various alternatives, and generates a first draft that can then be revised using a word-processing program.[522]

Document-assembly systems have been available to the legal profession for over 20 years.[523] Originally, they were typically used to generate a large quantity of simple documents, the aim being to automate repetitive processes that did not require much legal expertise.[524] As the technology developed, some law firms made efforts to use document-assembly systems to generate more complex transaction documents.[525]

What is now limiting adoption of document-assembly systems is less the technology than the significant investment required to develop and keep current a large library of template documents.[526] To date, perhaps the most ambitious effort by a law firm toward implementing a document-assembly system is London-based Allen & Overy's "new-change documents" system, which constitutes part of that firm's "new-change" series of Internet and technology-driven services.[527] This system, which was announced in January 2000, is in its early stages, but the aim is that it ultimately encompass the drafting of documents in a wide range of practice areas by both the firm and its clients.[528] If any other law firm has implemented a similar document-assembly system, it is keeping quiet about it.[529]

The primary benefit of a sophisticated document-assembly system is the speed with which high-quality drafts of complex documents can be assembled. This would be a significant advantage for clients, such as banks, that can win or lose business depending on how quickly they are able to put deals together. It would also allow a law firm to handle more matters simultaneously.[530]

There are other benefits. A document-assembly system would allow a law firm to ensure that the contracts it prepares for its clients are of a consistent quality, more so than if they were based on model contracts scavenged from who-knows-where or even firm-sanctioned templates. And a document prepared using a document-assembly system would likely contain fewer mistakes—such as incorrect cross-references, pronouns of the wrong gender, defined terms that are used but not defined—than one drafted using a number of model contracts.[531]

The notion of document-assembly systems being widely adopted by laws firms raises various client-relations and marketing issues. But in terms of legal usage in drafting corporate agreements, two thoughts come to mind. First, those responsible for preparing the template documents should adopt a house style that addresses comprehensively the issues of language and structure that arise in drafting corporate agreements, as any drafting flaws in the template documents would be replicated in any offspring. Second, if in the future corporate lawyers are able to generate contract drafts by answering a list of questions, and their drafting is limited to fine-tuning the initial document and further revising it to reflect negotiations, I could imagine the ability to draft becoming an esoteric skill practiced by a minority of corporate lawyers. For better or worse, we are a long way from that.

NOTES

The citations in these notes follow the *Bluebook*[532] system, except in one respect. Because this book uses endnotes rather than footnotes, I have added to each reference to text accompanying one or more specified notes the page or range of pages on which the note reference number or numbers occur. This should make it easier for readers to find the text in question.

[1] *See* BRYAN A. GARNER, A DICTIONARY OF MODERN LEGAL USAGE 519, 950 (2d ed. 1995) [hereinafter DMLU] (listing works on general legal writing).

[2] *E.g.,* ELMER A. DRIEDGER, THE COMPOSITION OF LEGISLATION (2d ed. 1976) (published in Canada); GARTH C. THORNTON, LEGISLATIVE DRAFTING (4th ed. 1996) (published in the U.K.).

[3] *E.g.,* BARBARA CHILD, DRAFTING LEGAL DOCUMENTS: PRINCIPLES AND PRACTICES (2d ed. 1992) (intended for law students); ROBERT C. DICK, LEGAL DRAFTING IN PLAIN LANGUAGE (3d ed. 1995) (published in Canada); F. REED DICKERSON, THE FUNDAMENTALS OF LEGAL DRAFTING (2d ed. 1986); ELMER DOONAN, DRAFTING (1995) (published in the U.K.); THOMAS R. HAGGARD, LEGAL DRAFTING IN A NUTSHELL (1996); E. L. PIESSE, THE ELEMENTS OF DRAFTING (J.K. Aitken ed., 9th ed. 1995) (published in Australia).

[4] *E.g.,* SCOTT J. BURNHAM (2d ed. 1993) (primarily addressing principles of contract law); CARL FELSENFELD & ALAN SIEGEL, WRITING CONTRACTS IN PLAIN ENGLISH (1981) (principally concerned with the drafting of consumer contracts).

[5] DMLU, *supra* note 1.

[6] *See* DAVID MELLINKOFF, THE LANGUAGE OF THE LAW 286 (1963); Robert W. Benson, *The End of Legalese: The Game is Over*, XIII N.Y.U. REV. L. & SOC. CHANGE 519, 520–22, 527–29 (1984–85).

[7] For bibliographies of works on legal writing, see MELLINKOFF, *supra* note 6, at 455–78; George D. Gopen, *The State of Legal Writing: Res Ipsa Loquitur*, 86 MICH L. REV. 333, 366–80 (1987); Joseph Kimble, *Plain English: A Charter for Clear Writing*, 9 T.M. COOLEY L. REV. 1, 28–30 (1992).

[8] TOM GOLDSTEIN & JETHRO K. LIEBERMAN, THE LAWYER'S GUIDE TO WRITING WELL 3 (1989).

[9] *See* DICKERSON, *supra* note 3, at 3; DMLU, *supra* note 1, at 297.

[10] *See, e.g.*, DICKERSON, *supra* note 3, at 2 (referring to "the confusions, turgidities, circumlocutions, and expressions of downright gobbledygook that infect so many definitive legal instruments"); DMLU, *supra* note 1, at 297 (stating that "many of the worst mannerisms of legalese pervade legal drafting"); Kirk, *Legal Drafting: Curing Unexpressive Language*, 3 TEX. TECH. L. REV. 23, 24 (1971) (stating that "most legal drafting, legislative or otherwise, is not well done").

[11] *See* VII THE OXFORD ENGLISH DICTIONARY 804 (2d ed. 1989) [hereinafter OED] (defining legalese as "[t]he complicated technical language of legal documents").

[12] *See, e.g.*, Kimble, *supra* note 7, at 8 ("Legalese is unnecessary and no more precise than plain English.").

[13] *See* Benson, *supra* note 6, at 533; Joseph Kimble, *Answering the Critics of Plain Language*, 5 SCRIBES J. LEGAL WRITING 51, 78–82 (1994–95).

[14] *See* Benson, *supra* note 6, at 527–30 (discussing how legalese "alienates the public").

[15] *See, e.g.*, GOLDSTEIN & LIEBERMAN, *supra* note 8, at 18–33 (discussing the "fourteen causes of bad legal writing"); Benson, *supra* note 6, at 569–71 (suggesting reasons for the continued dominance of legalese).

[16] *See* DMLU, *supra* note 1, at 518 ("As a whole, the profession disdains literary accomplishment within law—it believes in a sharp (and illusory) split between style and substance.").

[17] *See* DICKERSON, *supra* note 3, at 2 ("Unfortunately, many lawyers have tended not only to downgrade important aspects of drafting but to think of themselves as individually accomplished in this respect. It is hard to sell people new clothes if they consider themselves already well accoutered.").

[18] See *infra* Chapter 1—*The Introductory Clause.*

[19] See *infra* Chapter 5—*Defined Terms and Definitions*.

[20] Regarding this distinction, see 1 RICHARD A. LORD, WILLISTON ON CONTRACTS §§ 1:7, 1:16 (4th ed. 1990) [hereinafter WILLISTON].

[21] 1 ARTHUR L. CORBIN, CORBIN ON CONTRACTS § 1.5 (revised ed., Joseph M. Perillo ed. 1993) ("Today, the distinction [between formal and informal contracts] is only rarely noted and is not of great importance.").

[22] See *infra* Chapter 2—*Language of Representation—The Distinction Between* Representations *and* Warranties.

[23] See *infra* Chapter 1—*The Introductory Clause—Verbs*.

[24] See *infra* Chapter 2.

[25] See *infra* Chapter 1—*The Introductory Clause—Reference to the Type of Agreement*.

[26] *See* Kimble, *supra* note 13, at 51–52; Benson, *supra* note 6, at 558–68.

[27] *See, e.g.*, MELLINKOFF, *supra* note 6, at 290–398 (demonstrating the lack of precision in traditional legal language); Benson, *supra* note 6, at 558–68 (rebutting arguments in defense of legalese).

[28] *See* BLACK'S LAW DICTIONARY 1170 (Bryan A. Garner ed. in chief, 7th ed. 1999) [hereinafter BLACK'S] (defining the plain-language movement as "1. The loosely organized campaign to encourage legal writers and business writers to write clearly and concisely—without legalese—while preserving accuracy and precision. 2. The body of persons involved in this campaign").

[29] For an introduction to "plain English," see DMLU, *supra* note 1, at 661–65; Kimble, *supra* note 7.

[30] *See* Plain English Disclosure, Securities Act Release No. 7497, [1997 Transfer Binder] Fed. Sec. L. Rep. (CCH) ¶ 86,003, at 80,125 (Jan. 28, 1998); SECURITIES AND EXCHANGE COMMISSION, A PLAIN ENGLISH HANDBOOK (1998) [hereinafter SEC PLAIN ENGLISH HANDBOOK] (a handbook prepared by the SEC to help speed and smooth the transition to plain English).

[31] *See, e.g.*, BRYAN A. GARNER, THE ELEMENTS OF LEGAL STYLE 7 (1991) (defining plain language as "the idiomatic and grammatical use of language that most effectively presents ideas to the reader"); DMLU, *supra note* 1, at 663–64 (stating the "chief guidelines" of plain language).

[32] FELSENFELD & SIEGEL, *supra* note 4, at 27.

[33] See *infra* Chapter 1—*The Recitals*—WITNESSETH, WHEREAS, *and* NOW, THEREFORE.

[34] See *infra* Chapter 2—*Expressing Conditions*.

[35] See *infra* Chapter 5—*Defined Terms and Definitions*.

[36] *See, e.g.,* H. W. FOWLER, A DICTIONARY OF MODERN ENGLISH USAGE (1926) (being perhaps the best-known example); *see also* BRYAN A. GARNER, A DICTIONARY OF MODERN AMERICAN USAGE 672 (1998) ("*usage* generally refers to an idiom or form of speech, an occurrence of one, or forms of speech in general.").

[37] *See* DMLU, *supra* note 1 (using the term "legal usage" in the title); DAVID MELLINKOFF, MELLINKOFF'S DICTIONARY OF AMERICAN LEGAL USAGE (1992) (same).

[38] *See* DMLU, *supra* note 1, at 664 ("And even simple documents should have descriptive titles (not *Agreement*, but *Agreement Restricting Stock Transfers*).").

[39] *See id.* at 40. *But see* MELLINKOFF, *supra* note 37, at 116 ("For general reference, *agreement* and *contract* (n.) are synonyms, with definitions chasing each other into oblivion.").

[40] *Id.* ("As the title of a document, either word [*agreement* or *contract*] will do.").

[41] *See* DMLU, *supra* note 1, at 466 ("[*Introductory clause, commencement*, and *exordium*] are the three names given to the paragraph, placed at the outset of a contract, that gives introductory material. The best of the three phrases is *introductory clause*, and the worst *exordium*."); *see also* BURNHAM, *supra* note 4, at 221 (referring to the introductory clause as the "caption"); 1 MODEL AGREEMENTS FOR CORPORATE COUNSEL 100.001 (1998) (referring to the introductory clause as the "heading").

[42] DMLU, *supra* note 1, at 160.

[43] *See id.*

[44] See *infra* Chapter 1—*The Recitals*.

[45] *See* XII OED, *supra* note 11, at 305 (defining *preamble* as "[a]n introductory paragraph or part in a statute, deed or other formal document, setting forth the grounds and intention of it"); BLACK'S, *supra* note 28, at 1194 (defining *preamble* as "[a]n introductory statement

in a constitution, statute, or other document explaining the document's basis and objective; esp., a statutory recital of the inconveniences for which the statute is designed to provide a remedy").

[46] See *supra* text accompanying note 30, at page xviii.

[47] See *infra* text accompanying notes 121–24, at page 22.

[48] See *infra* text accompanying note 106, at page 19.

[49] See *infra* text accompanying note 108, at page 20.

[50] See *infra* text accompanying note 110, at page 20.

[51] *See* RANDOLPH QUIRK, SIDNEY GREENBAUM, GEOFFREY LEECH & JAN SVARTVIK, A COMPREHENSIVE GRAMMAR OF THE ENGLISH LANGUAGE § 4.25 (1985) [hereinafter QUIRK].

[52] THE CHICAGO MANUAL OF STYLE § 8.43 (14th ed. 1993).

[53] *See* DMLU, *supra* note 1, at 80 ("[T]he phrase frequently signifies the effective legal date of a document, as when the document is backdated or when the parties sign at different times. When such a nuance is not intended, *as of* is the wrong phrase.").

[54] *See* BLACK'S, *supra* note 28, at 589 (providing as one of the definitions of *execute* "[t]o make (a legal document) valid by signing; to bring (a legal document) into its final, legally enforceable form"); DMLU, *supra* note 1, at 337 (noting that "the word *sign* is often preferable" to the word *execute*, "especially when communicating with non-lawyers"); MELLINKOFF, *supra* note 37, at 220 (defining *execute* as "to do what is required to bring an instrument to life, the formalities varying according to the instrument and local law, e.g., signing, signing and delivery, acknowledgment, witnessing, etc.").

[55] See *infra* text accompanying note 300, at page 64.

[56] *See* WORDS AND PHRASES (1971 & Supp. 2000).

[57] DMLU, *supra* note 1, at 80.

[58] Regarding the concluding clause, see *infra* Chapter 4—*The Concluding Clause.*

[59] *See, e.g.,* DICK, *supra* note 3, at 147 (referring to "the ordinary grammatical rule that *between* must only be used where there are two things or persons and *among* where there are more than two").

[60] II OED, *supra* note 11, at 154; *see also* THE NEW FOWLER'S MODERN ENGLISH USAGE 10 (R.W. Burchfield ed., 3d ed. 1996) [hereinafter NEW FOWLER'S MODERN ENGLISH USAGE] (quoting *The Oxford*

English Dictionary, and citing as a recent example of a "somewhat forced" use of *among* "a conversation among Richard Smith, Sir Anthony Grabham, and Professor Cyril Chantler").

[61] II OED, *supra* note 11, at 155; *see also* Michael Swan, Practical English Usage 95 (2d ed. 1995) ("We say that somebody or something is *between* two or more clearly separate people or things. We use *among* when somebody or something is in a group, a crowd or a mass of people or things which we do not see separately.").

[62] II OED, *supra* note 11, at 155.

[63] *See* Dickerson, *supra* note 3, at 210 (recommending one use "New Jersey corporation" instead of "corporation organized and existing under the laws of New Jersey").

[64] As to why it serves no purpose to state that a party intends to be legally bound, see *infra* notes 296–97 and accompanying text, at page 64.

[65] See *infra* Chapter 5—*Defined Terms and Definitions*.

[66] *See* DMLU, *supra* note 1, at 182 (recommending this practice).

[67] Use of such pared-down parenthetical information is appropriate when providing a defined term for any integrated definition, not just party names. See *infra* text accompanying note 361, at page 78.

[68] See *infra* Chapter 5—*Defined Terms and Definitions—Types of Definitions—Integrated Definitions*.

[69] *See* Bryan A. Garner, Advanced Legal Drafting G-13 to G-14 (1997) (seminar materials) (recommending, by means of an example, that one place the definition [*read* defined term] after the party name to which it relates, rather than after "descriptive information," including the jurisdiction of organization).

[70] *See* Quirk, *supra* note 51, at § 17.65.

[71] See *infra* Chapter 5—*Defined Terms and Definitions—Types of Definitions—Integrated Definitions*.

[72] *See* DMLU, *supra* note 1, at 19 ("An *acronym* is made from the initial letters or parts of a phrase or compound term. One ordinarily reads or speaks it as a single word, not letter by letter (e.g., *radar* = radio detection and ranging). An *initialism*, by contrast, is made from the initial letters or parts of a phrase or compound term, but is usually pronounced letter by letter, not as a single word (e.g., *r.p.m.* = revolutions per minute).").

[73] *See id.* at 447 (bemoaning the trend to "initialese," namely the overuse of acronyms and abbreviations, and noting the adverse effect that it has on readability).

[74] *See* Barry Graynor, *Swat Out Those Nits*, BUS. LAW TODAY, Sept.–Oct. 1996, at 2 (recommending that one dispense with the definite article on the grounds that doing so results in shorter contracts).

[75] For a discussion of emphasis and capitalization, see *infra* Chapter 5—*Typography—Appearance.*

[76] See *supra* Chapter 1—*Reference to the Type of Agreement.*

[77] See *infra* Chapter 5—*Defined Terms and Definitions—Types of Definitions—Integrated Definitions.*

[78] *See* II E. ALLAN FARNSWORTH, FARNSWORTH ON CONTRACTS 279 (2d ed. 1998).

[79] *Cf.* Maurice B. Kirk, *Legal Drafting: Some Elements of Technique*, 4 TEX. TECH L. REV. 297, 304 (1973) ("It is sometimes desirable to prepare a record of the 'context' in which . . . a consensual bargain was created. . . . A preamble or recital attempts to preserve for future use those circumstances—facts or interpretations of facts—which 'caused' the action.").

[80] *See id.* ("[A] policy or purpose section is a statement of the factual (or legal?) result that one hopes to produce by the . . . agreement . . . .").

[81] *See* DMLU, *supra* note 1, at 942.

[82] *See* II FARNSWORTH, *supra* note 78, at 279 ("No experienced drafter will make the mistake of using such clauses to bear the burden of substantive provisions of the agreement, for courts regard recitals as subordinate to the operative part of the contract."); Kirk, *supra* note 79, at 304 ("To avoid becoming an unintended limitation on the operation of the document, the policy or purpose section should be very broad in concept and ordinarily should be more general, in terms of the facts it covers, than any command or authorization within the document.").

[83] *See* II FARNSWORTH, *supra* note 78, at 279–80.

[84] *See* MARTIN D. FERN & DANIELLE F. FERN, 1 WARREN'S FORMS OF AGREEMENTS § 1.1.03 (2000) [hereinafter WARREN].

[85] DMLU, *supra* note 1, at 938.

[86] *See* XX OED, *supra* note 11, at 213 ("In view or consideration

of the fact that; seeing that, considering that, forasmuch as, inasmuch as. (Chiefly, now only, introducing a preamble or recital in a legal or other formal document)"). This can be contrasted with the modern meaning. *See id.* ("Introducing a statement of fact in contrast or opposition to that expressed by the principal clause.").

[87] *See* DMLU, *supra* note 1, at 929 ("*[W]hereas* is the archetypal legalism—it was formerly every lawyer's idea of how to begin a recital in a contract. The more modern drafting style is to use a heading such as *Recitals* or *Background*, followed by short declarative sentences, as opposed to the sometimes unceasing stream of independent clauses linked by semicolons and *whereases.*"); MELLINKOFF, LEGAL WRITING: SENSE & NONSENSE 134 (1982) ("*Whereas*—When used for anything but to express a contrary . . . , *whereas* is worthless . . . . Delete."); MELLINKOFF, *supra* note 6, at 324 ("Because *whereas* so frequently introduces recitals, its effect is confused with the effect of the recital. That effect varies from state to state, and does not depend on the word *whereas.*").

[88] *See* DMLU, *supra* note 1, at 929 (proposing *RECITALS* or *BACK-GROUND*).

[89] *See id.* at 434 (recommending that one use *therefore* instead of *in consideration of the premises*).

[90] *Id.* at 234 ("*covenant and agree* is a needless doublet common in drafting. *Agree* suffices in virtually every context in which the phrase appears."); MELLINKOFF, *supra* note 37, at 135 ("The formula expression *covenant and agree* is a worthless redundancy."). Regarding the meaning of *covenant*, see *infra* text accompanying notes 159–60, at page 27.

[91] DMLU, *supra* note 1, at 434 ("[T]his hoary old phrase [*in consideration of the mutual covenants herein contained*] supposedly makes clear that the contract cannot fail for lack of consideration. In fact, though, the phrase is deadwood: courts look to the mutual promises to ascertain whether consideration exists, and if one side has promised nothing, vague recitals of consideration will not suffice to save the contract."); I FARNSWORTH, *supra* note 78, at 150 ("[I]t is not within the drafter's power to transform something that *cannot* be consideration into consideration by reciting that it is given 'in consideration.'").

[92] *See id.* at 150–51; *see also* 3 WILLISTON, *supra* note 20, at § 7:23 ("It would destroy the requirement of consideration to hold that an

admission of consideration in an unsealed writing prevented the promisor from showing that no consideration existed . . . . [T]he solution of the law has been generally to entitle the recital to some weight but to permit the introduction of contrary evidence except in a few narrowly defined areas" (footnotes omitted)); HOWARD O. HUNTER, MODERN LAW OF CONTRACTS § 5.03[3] (1993) (stating that the more common rule is that recitals of consideration simply create a rebuttable presumption of adequate and sufficient consideration).

[93] *See* 3 WILLISTON, *supra* note 20, at §§ 7:22, 7:23 (stating that in sealed instruments and, among unsealed agreements, contracts of insurance or guaranty and option contracts, a sham recital of consideration is effective to prevent the introduction of extrinsic evidence to show its falsity).

[94] *See, e.g.,* AMERICAN BAR ASSOCIATION SECTION OF BUSINESS LAW, MODEL STOCK PURCHASE AGREEMENT WITH COMMENTARY 4 (1995) [hereinafter ABA MODEL STOCK PURCHASE AGREEMENT] (offering as the lead-in to a model stock purchase agreement *The parties, intending to be legally bound, agree as follows* . . .). Regarding the redundancy of statements of intent to be legally bound, see *infra* text accompanying note 297, at page 64.

[95] See *infra* text accompanying note 126, at page 22.

[96] For a discussion of the index of defined terms, see *infra* Chapter 5—*Defined Terms and Definitions—The Definition Section.*

[97] *See, e.g.,* SUSAN L. BRODY, JANE RUTHERFORD, LAUREL A. VIETZEN & JOHN C. RUTHERFORD, LEGAL DRAFTING 206 (1994) [hereinafter BRODY] (using the term "the body of the contract"); CHILD, *supra* note 3, at 127 (same).

[98] *See* DMLU, *supra* note 1, at 620 ("*Operative* = (1) having effect; in operation; efficacious <the statute is now operative>; or (2) having principal relevance <*may* is the operative word of the statute>.").

[99] *See, e.g.,* BURNHAM, *supra* note 4, at 229 (using the term "operative provisions").

[100] *Cf.* BLACK'S, *supra* note 28, at 1221 (defining procedural law as "[t]he rules that prescribe the steps for having a right or duty judicially enforced, as opposed to the law that defines the specific rights or duties themselves. . . . Cf. SUBSTANTIVE LAW.").

[101] *See* QUIRK, *supra* note 51, at 198.

[102] *See id.* at § 3.37 n.[e] ("In some legal documents in archaic style, the auxiliary DO construction is used merely as an alternative to the simple present or past tense: I, the undersigned, being of sound mind, *do* this day hereby *bequeath . . .*").

[103] See *infra* Chapter 5—*Miscellaneous Other Issues—Here- and There- Words*.

[104] *See, e.g.*, BRODY, *supra* note 97, at 114 (including *hereby* in a list of archaic words to be avoided); MELLINKOFF, *supra* note 37, at 283 ("*Hereby* is superfluous."); Kimble, *supra* note 7, at 21 ("The word *hereby* does not add an iota of precision."); Maryann A. Waryjas, *Universal Issues in Drafting Corporate Agreements*, in DRAFTING CORPORATE AGREEMENTS 2001 53, 56 (Practicing Law Institute Corporate Law and Practice Handbook Series No. B-1219) (recommending that one avoid "lawyerisms" such as *hereby*).

[105] See *infra* Chapter 5—*Miscellaneous Other Issues—Here- and There- Words*.

[106] *See* QUIRK, *supra* note 51, at §§ 4.6–4.7.

[107] *See id.* at § 4.6.

[108] *See id.* at § 4.7.

[109] *See id.*

[110] *See id.*

[111] *See id.*

[112] See *supra* text accompanying note 81, at page 12.

[113] *See* QUIRK, *supra* note 51, at § 4.7.

[114] *See id.* at § 11.3 n.[a] (noting that "[t]he possible insertion of *hereby* is an indication of the performative use of the verb").

[115] *See, e.g.*, DMLU, *supra* note 1, at 402 ("Sometimes the word is (correctly) omitted where you might expect to find it—e.g.: 'The writs of scire facias and mandamus are abolished.' Fed. R. Civ. P. 81(b). The less-polished drafter would have written *are hereby abolished.*"); THORNTON, *supra* note 2, at 93 (stating that in the examples provided, which constitute language of performance, *hereby* "is unnecessary," and that "[i]t adds nothing and it is fusty").

[116] MELLINKOFF, *supra* note 87, at 3 (suggesting that in the phrase *I hereby resign the Office of President of the United States*, "*hereby* is pure legal kneejerk," and that "[i]t adds nothing to 'I resign,' except to tell us that a lawyer had a hand in the writing").

[117] *See* DOONAN, *supra* note 3, at 114 (indicating that *hereby*, among other words, is superfluous in the phrase *It is hereby expressly declared and agreed that*); DMLU, *supra* note 1, at 402 (stating that *hereby* can often "be excised with no loss of meaning: *I hereby declare* has no advantages over *I declare*").

[118] *But see* QUIRK, *supra* note 51, at § 11.3 n.[a] (providing *I hereby name this ship Dreadnought* as an example of the possible use of *hereby* as an indication of performative use of the verb).

[119] See *supra* text accompanying note 81, at page 12.

[120] *But see* MELLINKOFF, *supra* note 6, at 314 (stating that it is inherently unclear whether *hereby* "refers to the entire document or only part of it").

[121] *See, e.g.,* GARNER, *supra* note 36, at 483–84; WILLIAM STRUNK, JR. & E.B. WHITE, THE ELEMENTS OF STYLE 18 (3d ed. 1979).

[122] *See, e.g.,* DICK, *supra* note 3, at 91–92; DOONAN, *supra* note 3, at 120–22; DMLU, *supra* note 1, at 643–45; PIESSE, *supra* note 3, at 92; SEC PLAIN ENGLISH HANDBOOK, *supra* note 30, at 19–21; RICHARD C. WYDICK, PLAIN ENGLISH FOR LAWYERS 29–34 (4th ed. 1998).

[123] NEW FOWLER'S MODERN ENGLISH USAGE, *supra* note 60, at 576.

[124] DMLU, *supra* note 1, at 643.

[125] See *infra* Chapter 2—*Language of Obligation*.

[126] DICKERSON, *supra* note 3, at 185. Regarding language of policy, see *infra* Chapter 2—*Language of Policy*.

[127] *See, e.g.,* DICK, *supra* note 3, at 93 (stating that one should "[u]se 'shall' to impose a duty"); DICKERSON, *supra* note 3, at 214 ("To create a duty, say 'shall.'"); DOONAN, *supra* note 3, at 171 ("'Shall' should be used only . . . to impose a duty or obligation on the legal subject to whom it refers."); *see also* GEORGE COODE, ON LEGISLATIVE EXPRESSION (2d ed. 1852), *reprinted in* DRIEDGER, *supra* note 2, app. I at 371 (stating that *shall* "denotes the compulsion, the obligation to act").

[128] The description of the grammar of *shall* contained in this paragraph is derived from Joseph Kimble, *The Many Misuses of* Shall, 3 SCRIBES J. LEGAL WRITING 61, 61–64 (1992), as supplemented by the other authorities cited.

[129] NEW FOWLER'S MODERN ENGLISH USAGE, *supra* note 60, at 706–07.

[130] *See* QUIRK, *supra* note 51, at § 4.58; GARNER, *supra* note 36, at 597–98.

[131] *See* QUIRK, *supra* note 51, at § 4.58 n.[c] ("A further restricted use of *shall* with a 3d person subject occurs in legal or quasi-legal discourse, in stipulating regulations or legal requirements. Here *shall* is close in meaning to *must*: The vendor *shall* maintain the equipment in good repair.").

[132] DMLU, *supra* note 1, at 939 (noting that use of *shall* runs afoul of the principle that "a word used repeatedly in a given context is presumed to bear the same meaning throughout"). For a general statement of this principle, see DICK, *supra* note 3, at 86–87; DICKERSON, *supra* note 3, at 15–16 ("Consistency of expression has appropriately become the 'Golden Rule' of drafting."); DOONAN, *supra* note 3, at 108; PIESSE, *supra* note 3, at 18–19.

[133] *See* DMLU, *supra* note 1, at 940–41; MELLINKOFF, *supra* note 37, at 402–03; WYDICK, *supra* note 122, at 66–67.

[134] DMLU, *supra* note 1, at 940.

[135] *Id.*

[136] *Id.*

[137] *See id.*

[138] *See id.* at 106–07.

[139] QUIRK, *supra* note 51, at § 4.58 n.[c] (noting that for purposes of stipulating legal requirements, *shall* is close in meaning to *must*).

[140] DRIEDGER, *supra* note 2, at 10.

[141] *See* Kimble, *supra* note 128, at 76.

[142] *Id.* at 70.

[143] *Id.* at 73.

[144] *Id.* at 73–74.

[145] *Id.* at 74–75.

[146] DMLU, *supra* note 1, at 941 (observing that "[i]n private drafting—contracts as opposed to statutes, rules, and regulations—some drafters consider *must* inappropriately bossy").

[147] *Id.* at 940.

[148] See *infra* Chapter 2—*Expressing Conditions—Language of Obligation Used to Express Conditions.*

[149] DMLU, *supra* note 1, at 941 (suggesting that *will* "is probably the best solution" for expressing obligations when the relationship is a delicate one, as in a corporate joint venture); WYDICK, *supra* note

122, at 67 (stating that one should use *will* to express both parties' obligations in a delicate contract between equals).

[150] CHILD, *supra* note 3, at 383–84 ("'Shall' expresses orders. . . . 'Will' expresses agreement."); PIESSE, *supra* note 3, at 69 (stating that "[w]here the obligation is created by the opening words of an instrument, or a clause, it is unnecessary and inelegant to repeat words of obligation in passages governed by those opening words," and using the sentence *The parties agree that each of them will pay an equal proportion of the stamp duty on this deed* as an example of how *shall* can thus be rendered superfluous); *Cf.* Howard M. Darmstadter, *Shall? Will? Who Makes the Rules?*, BUS. LAW TODAY, May–June 1998, at 10 ("Micawber isn't legally bound to do something because the document says 'Micawber shall' rather than 'Micawber will.' Micawber is bound because the document says that 'the parties agree that' Micawber shall or will perform its humble tasks.").

[151] See *supra* text following note 131, at page 23.

[152] *See* PIESSE, *supra* note 3, at 69 (treating *The parties agree* as constituting language of obligation).

[153] See *supra* text accompanying note 112, at page 20.

[154] See *infra* text accompanying note 175, at page 31.

[155] See *supra* note 132 and accompanying text, at page 24.

[156] See *supra* text accompanying notes 133–36, at page 24.

[157] See *supra* text accompanying note 81, at page 12.

[158] *See* DMLU, *supra* note 1, at 234 (stating that the strict sense of *covenant* is "a promise made in a deed"); MELLINKOFF, *supra* note 37, at 135 (stating that *covenant* "[o]nce, but no longer, referred only to a *contract under seal*").

[159] *See id.* (referring to *covenant* as an old synonym for *contract* and *agreement* that is still used in this sense, usually as a variant of *agreement* and the verb form *agree*); BLACK'S, *supra* note 28, at 369 (defining *covenant* as "[a] formal agreement or promise, usu. in a contract").

[160] *See* DMLU, *supra* note 1, at 234 (stating that "ordinarily, in modern contexts, the better practice is to write *agree*" rather than the verb *to covenant*).

[161] See *supra* text accompanying note 90, at page 14.

[162] DMLU, *supra* note 1, at 942; *see also* DICKERSON, *supra* note 3, at 214 ("To create a right, say 'is entitled to.'"); BLACK'S, *supra* note 28, at

553 (providing as one definition of *entitle* "[t]o grant a legal right to or to qualify for").

[163] Regarding use of *is entitled to* in language of discretion, see *infra* text accompanying notes 188–89, see pages 34–35.

[164] *See* Garner, *supra* note 69, at 20.

[165] *See, e.g.*, Del. Code Ann. tit. 8, § 103 (1999) ("The certificate of incorporation . . . shall be signed by the incorporator or incorporators.").

[166] *See, e.g.*, 15 U.S.C. § 77j(c) ("Any prospectus shall contain such other information as the Commission may by rule or regulation require . . . .").

[167] F. Reed Dickerson, *Choosing Between* Shall *and* Must *in Legal Drafting*, 1 Scribes J. Legal Writing 144, 145–46 (1990).

[168] *See id.* at 146.

[169] *Id.*

[170] See *supra* text accompanying note 138, at page 24.

[171] *See* Garner, *supra* note 69, at 20.

[172] See *supra* text accompanying note 135, at page 24.

[173] *See* DMLU, *supra* note 1, at 941 ("Under the ABC rule . . . , *must* denotes all required actions, whether or not the subject of the clause performs the action of the verb . . . ."); Wydick, *supra* note 122, at 67.

[174] See *supra* text accompanying note 149, at page 26.

[175] *See* DMLU, *supra* note 1, at 941.

[176] See *supra* text accompanying notes 151–55, at page 26.

[177] See *supra* text accompanying notes 121–24, at page 22.

[178] *See* Wydick, *supra* note 122, at 33.

[179] See *infra* text accompanying notes 212–14, at page 39.

[180] See *supra* text accompanying notes 121–24, at page 22.

[181] See *infra* Chapter 2—*Expressing Conditions—Language of Obligation Used to Express Conditions*.

[182] IX OED, *supra* note 11, at 501 ("4. Expressing permission or sanction: To be allowed (to do something) by authority, law, rule, morality, reason, etc.").

[183] DMLU, *supra* note 1, at 942; *see also* Dickerson, *supra* note 3, at 214 ("To create discretionary authority, say 'may.'").

[184] Kirk, *supra* note 79, at 303.

[185] Regarding *be*-verb circumlocution in the context of language of obligation, see *supra* text accompanying note 138, at page 24.

[186] See *supra* text accompanying notes 121–24, at page 22.

[187] *See* IX OED, *supra* note, at 501 ("5. Expressing subjective possibility, i.e. the admissibility of a supposition. a. (with [present infinitive]) In relation to the future (*may* = 'perhaps will')."); Kirk, *supra* note 79, at 302 (referring to "the potential ambiguity of 'may' as authorization and as possibility").

[188] See *supra* text accompanying notes 162–63, at page 29.

[189] See *infra* text accompanying note 235, at page 43.

[190] See *supra* text accompanying note 138, at page 24.

[191] See *infra* text accompanying notes 197–201, at page 36.

[192] See *infra* note 208 and accompanying text, at page 37.

[193] See *infra* Chapter 7—*Favor Verbs Over Nouns*.

[194] DMLU, *supra* note 1, at 941.

[195] *Id.* at 942.

[196] See *supra* text accompanying notes 151–55, at page 26.

[197] DMLU, *supra* note 1, at 942.

[198] *See* DICKERSON, *supra* note 3, at 216 (noting that "A person may not" "is an acceptable substitute for 'A person shall not'"); DMLU, *supra* note 1, at 942 (noting that *must not* and *may not* "are nearly synonymous").

[199] *See, e.g.*, DICKERSON, *supra* note 3, at 216 (stating that "[i]n case of doubt, it is probably safer to use ['A person shall not']"); DMLU, *supra* note 1, at 942 (suggesting that "the phrase *must not* is usually the more appropriate wording").

[200] See *supra* text accompanying note 187, at page 34.

[201] *See* Kirk, *supra* note 79, at 303.

[202] *See* DRIEDGER, *supra* note 2, at 10–11.

[203] *See* Kirk, *supra* note 10, at 28.

[204] *See* DICKERSON, *supra* note 3, at 215; Kirk, *supra* note 10, at 28 ("[Effectiveness of the phrase 'no person shall'] depends upon a meaning which the words do not in fact convey. The phrase 'no person' negates the existence of the person rather than the occurrence of con-

duct. . . . Technically speaking, there is 'no person' to whom the duty is applicable.").

[205] *See* DICKERSON, *supra* note 3, at 215 (stating that "No person may" probably constitutes a "stronger prohibition" than "No person shall"); DOONAN, *supra* note 3, at 177 (advocating that one use "No Employee may" rather than "No employee shall"). *But see* Kirk, *supra* note 10, at 28 n.15 (objecting to the usage *no person may* on the grounds that it "is an artificial duty, regardless of whether it is [used] with 'shall' or with 'may,'" and disagreeing with the proposition that "'No person may . . .' is an effective denial of permission or authority").

[206] *See* CHILD, *supra* note 3, at 127 (using the term "policy"); *see also* Kirk, *supra* note 79, at 309 (using the term "declaration").

[207] For a discussion of autonomous definitions, see *infra* Chapter 5—*Defined Terms and Definitions—Types of Definitions—Autonomous Definitions*.

[208] *See* SIDNEY GREENBAUM, THE OXFORD ENGLISH GRAMMAR 255 (1996) (noting that the state present is primarily used for situations that include the time of speaking or writing and involve a state that remains unaltered for the duration of the situation); QUIRK, *supra* note 51, at § 4.5 (noting that in the state present, "there is no inherent limitation on the extension of the state into the past and future (unless such a limitation is indicated by adverbials or other elements of the clause)").

[209] *Id.* at § 4.45 ("In main clauses, the future use of the simple present may be said to represent a marked future of unusual definiteness, attributing to the future the degree of certainty one normally associates with the present and the past. It is used, for example, for statements about the calendar . . . .").

[210] CHILD, *supra* note 3, at 127; *see also* Kirk, *supra* note 79, at 309 (stating that "conduct that can be stated as a major duty . . . can also be handled in the declaratory form").

[211] QUIRK, *supra* note 51, at § I.40, at 1555.

[212] Kimble, *supra* note 128, at 64.

[213] *See id.* at 61 (stating that "*shall* is the most important word in the world of legal drafting").

[214] *Cf.* Kirk, *supra* note 79, at 302 ("[I]t now appears to be part of the language to use 'shall' whenever it is desirable to have the assurance that law stands behind the declaration.").

[215] *See* 3A Arthur L. Corbin, Corbin on Contracts § 627 (1960) ("Like all other words, the term 'condition' is used in a variety of senses. There is no law against this; and there is no single 'correct' definition.").

[216] Restatement (Second) of Contracts § 224 (1981).

[217] 3A Corbin, *supra* note 215, at § 627.

[218] Quirk, *supra* note 51, at § 15.33.

[219] *Id.* at 1089.

[220] *Id.*

[221] *See* Coode, *supra* note 127, at 322, 332–43.

[222] *See* Driedger, *supra* note 2, at 3; Thornton, *supra* note 2, at 21.

[223] *See, e.g.,* Dick, *supra* note 3, at 60–65; Doonan, *supra* note 3, at 139–47; Piesse, *supra* note 3, at 30–37.

[224] *See* Driedger, *supra* note 2, at 3 ("Grammatically, there is no distinction between Coode's case and condition. . . . It is frequently impossible to identify a particular phrase or clause as a case or a condition under Coode's definitions."); Thornton, *supra* note 2, at 22 ("Coode's 'case' and 'condition' are not distinguishable in any meaningful way so far as syntax is concerned.").

[225] *See* Coode, *supra* note 127, at 372–73.

[226] DMLU, *supra* note 1, at 831.

[227] See *supra* text accompany notes 221–24, at page 40.

[228] *See, e.g.,* DMLU, *supra* note 1, at 830–31 (citing as "poor drafting language" examples of conditional clauses using *shall*); Driedger, *supra* note 2, at 12–13 ("[*Shall*] was frequently used in conditional clauses . . . , as in . . . If a fire *shall be* caused . . . . Here, the *shall* is a future auxiliary, and while this style was common in old literature it is now regarded as archaic and has given way to the simple present tense, which is also better suited to modern drafting style."); *see also* Dick, *supra* note 3, at 93 (providing an example of a conditional clause incorrectly using *shall* and correctly using the present tense); Doonan, *supra* note 3, at 174 (providing similar examples); Piesse, *supra* note 3, at 65 (same).

[229] *See* DMLU, *supra* note 1, at 831.

[230] See *supra* text accompanying note 106, at page 19.

[231] *See* Quirk, *supra* note 51, at § 14.22 (stating that "[t]he simple present is commonly used in certain types of adverbial clauses to ex-

press future meaning," and citing as an example "If he *arrives*, the bank will play the National Anthem").

[232] See *supra* text accompanying note 106, at page 19.

[233] Quirk, *supra* note 51, at § 15.36.

[234] *See id.* (giving as an example "If any vehicle *be* parked on these premises without written permission, it shall be towed away at the expense of the vehicle's owner"); *see also* Coode, *supra* note 127, at 334–35 (discussing use of the subjunctive in conditional clauses).

[235] *See* Quirk, *supra* note 51, at 228 (using the example "If litmus paper is dipped in acid, it *will* turn red").

[236] *See* Garner, *supra* note 69, at 42 (using as an example the sentence "If [or As long as] the borrower timely makes all the scheduled payments, the interest rate *is* 15 percent" (emphasis in original removed and emphasis added)).

[237] *See* Coode, *supra* note 127, at 344; Dick, *supra* note 3, at 62; Piesse, *supra* note 3, at 32.

[238] *See* Driedger, *supra* note 2, at 3 (stating that the position of conditional clauses cannot be prescribed in the abstract in advance but depends entirely on the nature of the sentence and the nature of the conditional clauses); Piesse, *supra* note 3, at 33 (suggesting that improving the readability of a sentence or its impact on the reader may warrant nontraditional ordering).

[239] *See* Garner, *supra* note 69, at 59–67 (demonstrating the effect of shifting complex conditional clauses from the front of a sentence to the back).

[240] SEC Plain English Handbook, *supra* note 30, at 33 ("When there is more than one *if* and more than one *then*, you'll probably need to break it down into more than one sentence, taking care to specify which *ifs* apply to which *thens*.").

[241] See *infra* Chapter 3—*The Format of the Body of the Contract— Enumerated Clauses*.

[242] *See* ABA Model Stock Purchase Agreement, *supra* note 94, at 158–78 (using *must* and *must have* to express closing conditions).

[243] *See* Quirk, *supra* note 51, at § 3.59.

[244] *See id.*

[245] *See* Dickerson, *supra* note 3, at 214 ("To create a mere condition precedent, say 'must' (e.g., 'To be eligible to occupy the office of

mayor, a person must . . .')")"; *cf.* DRIEDGER, *supra* note 2, at 14 ("To say . . . that an *owner shall sign the application* may not express the exact sense intended; the owner is not being compelled to sign, but his application will not be considered unless he does sign.").

[246] *See* Kimble, *supra* note 128, at 67 ("Unfortunately, reserving *must* for conditions has not caught on, at least not yet. No matter which term is used, the drafter must add words to make a condition explicit: 'As a condition precedent to the corporation's paying for a loss, the insured must not destroy the tobacco stalks until the corporation inspects them.'").

[247] I BUSINESS ACQUISITIONS 170 (2d ed. John W. Herz & Charles H. Baller 1981); *see* JAMES C. FREUND, ANATOMY OF A MERGER 153 n.33 (1975).

[248] BLACK'S, *supra* note 28, at 1303–04.

[249] *See* I FARNSWORTH, *supra* note 78, at 448.

[250] *See, e.g.,* Cohen v. Koenig, 25 F.3d 1168, 1172 (2d Cir. 1994) ("Nonetheless, a relatively concrete representation as to a company's future performance . . . may ground a claim of fraud."); 37 AM. JUR. 2D FRAUD & DECEIT § 57 (1999) (referring to "the proper test to determine whether a representation is of an existing fact or of a futurity"); LOU R. KLING & EILEEN NUGENT SIMON, NEGOTIATED ACQUISITIONS OF COMPANIES, SUBSIDIARIES AND DIVISIONS § 11.01[3] (1997) (indicating that an acquisition agreement could require the Seller to represent on the date of signing, January 1, that on March 1 the Company will be in compliance with applicable law).

[251] *See* BLACK'S, *supra* note 28, at 1581–83.

[252] *Id.* at 1581.

[253] U.C.C. § 2-313(1)(a).

[254] *See* 1 WILLIAM D. HAWKLAND, UNIFORM COMMERCIAL CODE SERIES § 2-313:3 (1999) (noting that at common law, "an affirmation was more or less equated with the word 'representation'").

[255] *Id.* at § 2-313:2.

[256] *See* BURNHAM, *supra* note 4, at 237–38 ("The drafter should not rely on a particular word such as *representation* or *warranty* to convey a precise meaning, but should identify the legal consequences that attach to each operative part of a contract. When drafters sloppily employ legal terms, courts interpreting agreements look to the intentions of the parties."); *see also* U.C.C. § 2-313(2) ("It is not necessary

to the creation of an express warranty that the seller use formal words such as 'warrant' or 'guarantee' or that he have a special intention to make a warranty.").

[257] See *supra* text accompanying note 256, at page 48.

[258] *See* I FARNSWORTH, *supra* note 78, at 448 ("An assertion limited to a future event may be a promise that imposes liability for breach of contract or a mere prediction that does not, but it is not a misrepresentation as to that event."); *see, e.g.*, Bass v. Coupel, 671 So. 2d 344, 355 (La. Ct. App. 1995) ("In addition to not constituting fraud, the future promises made by [the plaintiff] do not form the basis of a breach of contract. The alleged representations were future promises of acts to be performed by others. One party's statement regarding the future actions of third parties, which may affect the enjoyment and value of the thing sold, is not compensable under a breach of contract theory if those things do not occur.").

[259] *See* BLACK'S, *supra* note 28, at 183 (defining "breach of covenant" as "The violation of an express or implied promise, usu. in a contract, either to do or not to do an act.").

[260] *See id.* (defining "breach of warranty" as "[a] breach of an express or implied warranty relating to the title, quality, content, or condition of goods sold. U.C.C. § 2-313."); *see, e.g.*, 1 HAWKLAND, *supra* note 254, at § 2-312:8 (referring to "breach of warranty of title").

[261] See *supra* text accompanying notes 251–55, at page 47.

[262] See *supra* text following note 250, at page 47.

[263] See *supra* text accompanying note 212, at page 39.

[264] See *supra* text accompanying note 106, at page 19.

[265] See *infra* Chapter 3—*The Format of the Body of the Contract—Enumerated Clauses*.

[266] Regarding the heading to give such sections, see *infra* text accompanying note 273, at page 54.

[267] "Multiple-numeration system" is the term preferred by THE CHICAGO MANUAL OF STYLE, *supra* note 52, at § 1.77.

[268] *See* BLACK'S, *supra* note 28, at 106 (providing as a definition of *article* "[a] separate and distinct part . . . of a writing, esp. in a contract, statute, or constitution").

[269] For further discussion of the merits and demerits of first-line

indents and hanging indents in the context of subsections and enumerated clauses, see *infra* text accompanying note 275, at page 55, and note 286, at page 60.

[270] Regarding use of emphasis, see *infra* Chapter 5—*Typography—Appearance*.

[271] *See* CHILD, *supra* note 3, at 132–33.

[272] For an example of such a provision, see *infra* Chapter 6—*Useful Provisions*.

[273] See *supra* text accompanying note 266, at page 52.

[274] *See* THORNTON, *supra* note 2, at 81.

[275] See *supra* text accompanying note 269, at page 54.

[276] *But see* DMLU, *supra* note 1, at 290 ("Artfully employed, headings and subheadings make a document much easier to follow."); Howard M. Darmstadter, *Using New Technology—and Good Sense—to Clarify Documents*, BUS. LAW TODAY, July–Aug. 1993, at 6.

[277] *See* THE CHICAGO MANUAL OF STYLE, *supra* note 52, at § 5.100 ("A colon should not be used to introduce a list that is the complement or object of an element in the introductory statement . . . ."); THE NEW YORK PUBLIC LIBRARY WRITER'S GUIDE TO STYLE AND USAGE 262 (1994) ("A colon is always correct after a complete sentence that introduces a list. . . . If the introduction is not a complete sentence, the colon should not be used—a dash or no punctuation at all is preferred. . . . A colon is incorrect after words like *such as*, between a verb and the rest of the sentence, and between a preposition and its object."). *But see* MERRIAM-WEBSTER'S STANDARD AMERICAN STYLE MANUAL 1010 (1985) ("Although most style manuals and composition handbooks . . . recommend that a full independent clause precede the colon, the interrupting colon is common.").

[278] *See* THE CHICAGO MANUAL OF STYLE, *supra* note 52, at § 5.94.

[279] *See* DICK, *supra* note 3, at 118; DICKERSON, *supra* note 3, at 115; DMLU, *supra* note 1, at 290.

[280] *See* DICK, *supra* note 3, at 118; DRIEDGER, *supra* note 2, at 53.

[281] *See* DICKERSON, *supra* note 3, at 197; DONALD HIRSCH, DRAFTING FEDERAL LAW 27 (1989).

[282] *See* DICKERSON, *supra* note 3, at 197 (advocating that one not use to designate clauses the series used to designate subsections).

283 See *supra* text accompanying note 30, at page xviii.

284 *See* GARNER, *supra* note 69, at G-22.

285 *See id.*

286 See *supra* text accompanying note 269, at page 54, and note 275, at page 55.

287 See *supra* text accompanying note 275, at page 55.

288 DICKERSON, *supra* note 3, at 81–84; *see also* CHILD, *supra* note 3, at 131–34 (paraphrasing Dickerson's approach).

289 See *supra* text accompanying note 159, at page 27.

290 See *infra* text accompanying notes 364–66, at page 82.

291 DICKERSON, *supra* note 3, at 89–90.

292 *But see* Howard M. Darmstadter, *Chickens and Eggs*, BUS. LAW TODAY, May–June 1996, at 47 (recommending that one order contract provisions according to their significance in the deal at hand rather than according to tradition).

293 *See* BURNHAM, *supra* note 4, at 229 (using the term "closing"); MODEL AGREEMENTS FOR CORPORATE COUNSEL, *supra* note 41, at 100.004 (same).

294 *See* 2A FLETCHER CORPORATION FORMS ANNOTATED § 2161 (4th ed. 1998) (referring to the concluding clause as the "conclusion").

295 *See* DMLU, *supra* note 1, at 875.

296 *See* 1 WARREN, *supra* note 84, at § 1.1.04 ("A simple, more modern ending is 'THE PARTIES, INTENDING TO BE LEGALLY BOUND, have executed this agreement as of the date first set forth above.' . . . .").

297 *See* I FARNSWORTH, *supra* note 78, at 197 ("[O]ne who signs a writing may be bound by it, even though one neither reads it nor considers the legal consequences of signing it. This rule, making a party's intention to be bound legally irrelevant, has the salutary effects of generally relieving each party to a dispute of the burden of showing the other's state of mind in that regard and of helping to uphold routine agreements.").

298 *See* MELLINKOFF, *supra* note 87, at 191 (including "In Witness Whereof" among old formalisms that "can be dropped from the legal vocabulary without any loss of precision, and with gains in brevity and clarity").

299 *See* XII OED, *supra* note 11, at 396 ("[T]he present document

or writing; these words or statements: used in a document to denote the document itself . . . . Chiefly, now only, in legal use.").

[300] See *supra* text accompanying note 53, at page 5.

[301] See *supra* text accompanying note 110, at page 20.

[302] *See* QUIRK, *supra* note 51, at § 4.35.

[303] 1 CORBIN, *supra* note 21, at § 2.11 ("All that is necessary to the creation of an informal contract . . . is an expression of assent in any form. The writing itself is not necessary, if put in writing, a signature is not necessary. Even if in writing and signed, a delivery is not necessary. It is an expression of assent that is required. Delivery of a writing may be sufficient evidence of such an assent. Words of assent are sufficient, conduct other than delivery may also be sufficient" (footnotes omitted)).

[304] *See, e.g.,* CHILD, *supra* note 3, at 122 (including a sample contract that does not have the signatures preceded by a concluding clause); ROBERT A. FELDMAN & RAYMOND T. NIMMER, DRAFTING EFFECTIVE CONTRACTS: A PRACTITIONER'S GUIDE 2-58 (2d ed. 1999) (same).

[305] *See* DMLU, *supra* note 1, at 89 (stating that an *attestation clause* appears at the end of a will and is signed by witnesses to the will); *see also* BLACK'S, *supra* note 28, at 124 (providing as a definition for *attest* "To affirm to be true or genuine; to authenticate by signing as a witness").

[306] *See* 1 WARREN, *supra* note 84, at § 1.1.04.

[307] GARNER, *supra* note 69, at G-16 ("Use the term 'exhibit' for a complete document that has an independent existence apart from the contract to which it is attached."); Howard M. Darmstadter, *About Those Boys in the Back Room: Schedules and Exhibits*, BUS. LAW TODAY, July–Aug. 1998, at 29 ("An exhibit, to any way of thinking, is a standalone document that is relevant to, but not properly part of, the main agreement.").

[308] See *infra* Chapter 5—*Miscellaneous Other Issues*—Here- *and* There- *Words*. For a provision that would permit you to dispense with *hereto* with confidence, see *infra* Chapter 6—*Useful Provisions*.

[309] Darmstadter, *supra* note 307, at 29 ("A schedule . . . contains information that is properly part of the main agreement but that . . . has been moved to the back.").

[310] KLING & NUGENT SIMON, *supra* note 250, at § 10.2 n.2.

[311] *See* DMLU, *supra* note 1, at 606.

[312] *See, e.g.*, Dickerson, *supra* note 3, at 125; DMLU, *supra* note 1, at 606 ("The noxious habit of spelling out words and putting numbers in parentheses decreases the readability of much legal writing . . . .").

[313] *Cf.* Dickerson, *supra* note 3, at 125 ("Why should we take this precaution in some instances ('ten (10) days') and not in others ('329 Mass. 453' or 'chapter X')?").

[314] *See, e.g.*, David Margolick, *How Three Missing Zeros Brought Red Faces and Cost Millions of Dollars*, N.Y. Times, Oct. 4, 1991, at B16 (due to a typing error in a mortgage, indebtedness to the lender was recorded as $92,855 rather than $92,855,000; this error "generated a spate of litigation, hundreds of thousands of dollars in legal fees, millions of dollars in damages and an untold fortune in embarrassment").

[315] Dickerson, *supra* note 3, at 125.

[316] *See* Graynor, *supra* note 74, at 3 (recommending that one retain the dual approach for the principal amount of promissory notes); *see also* DMLU, *supra* note 1, at 606 ("If, on the other hand, clarity and readability are not one's primary goals as a drafter—if one is more concerned with unmistakable meaning, however hard a reader might have to work to get at it—then the belt-and-suspenders approach makes perfect sense.").

[317] *See id.* at 605. *But see* The Chicago Manual of Style, *supra* note 52, at § 8.3 (recommending that one write out numbers one through 100 and use numerals thereafter); Merriam-Webster's Standard American Style Manual, *supra* note 277, at 1010 (recommending that one write out numbers one through nine or one through 99, and use numerals thereafter).

[318] *See* DMLU, *supra* note 1, at 605–06.

[319] *See id.*

[320] *See, e.g.*, Child, *supra* note 3, at 376 (referring to "defined terms"); DMLU, *supra* note 1, at 258 (same). *But see, e.g.*, Doonan, *supra* note 3, at 79 (incorrectly referring to defined terms as "definitions").

[321] Dickerson, *supra* note 3, at 137.

[322] *See* Child, *supra* note 3, at 356–60; DMLU, *supra* note 1, at 257–58; Dickerson, *supra* note 3, at 138–40; Dick, *supra* note 3, at 77–80; Piesse, *supra* note 3, at 45–48.

323 See *infra* text accompanying notes 331–32, at page 74.

324 DICKERSON, *supra* note 3, at 138.

325 *See* CHILD, *supra* note 3, at 356–57; DICK, *supra* note 3, at 77–78.

326 *Id.* at 77.

327 *See* DMLU, *supra* note 1, at 257 ("Lexical definitions are like dictionary definitions; they purport to give the entire meaning of a word ('"Litigation" means . . .'). Stipulative definitions, by contrast, rely on the ordinary meaning of the word and merely expand a word's meaning ('"Litigation" includes mediation') or contract a word's meaning ('"Litigation" does not include prefiling investigations').").

328 See *infra* text accompanying notes 345–49, at page 76.

329 See *supra* note 72, at page 9.

330 See *supra* note 72, at page 9.

331 *See* GARNER, *supra* note 69, at 83 (citing *American Depository Receipt* as a lexical definition of *ADR*).

332 *See* CHILD, *supra* note 3, at 357 (citing *the Department of Natural Resources* as a stipulative definition of *Department*).

333 *See id.* at 367 ("It is conventional to define words in the singular, not in the plural.").

334 *See* DMLU, *supra* note 1, at 258 (noting that most legal readers find it unacceptable to not signal which words are defined terms).

335 *See* DOONAN, *supra* note 3, at 79 ("For example, if a particular company was defined throughout an agreement as 'the company,' it should be cited as 'the Company' to distinguish it from other companies[,] which may be referred to as 'the company'.").

336 *See* DMLU, *supra* note 1, at 258 ("The most common way to tell the reader that a term is defined is by using initial capitals . . . .").

337 *See id.* (noting that boldfacing or italicizing defined terms whenever they appear "can lead to unsightly text").

338 *See* Darmstadter, *supra* note 292, at 46 ("Terms whose meanings are obvious (such as 'subsidiary') . . . should usually not be capitalized.").

339 See *supra* Chapter 1—*The Introductory Clause—Defined Terms in the Introductory Clause.*

340 *See* DICK, *supra* note 3, at 81–82 (describing such definitions as "forced definitions"); DICKERSON, *supra* note 3, at 141–44 (referring to

such definitions as "Humpty Dumpty definitions"); Doonan, *supra* note 3, at 82–83; DMLU, *supra* note 1, at 257–58 ("[O]ne must be careful not to use counterintuitive definitions, as by saying that the word *dog* is deemed to include all horses.").

[341] *See* Kenneth P. Kopelman, *Some Thoughts Re: Drafting Corporate Agreements—A Step by Step Approach, in* Drafting Corporate Agreements 1997–1998 17, 26 (Practicing Law Institute Corporate Law and Practice Handbook Series No. B-1025).

[342] Garner, *supra* note 69, at G-14.

[343] *Cf.* Driedger, *supra* note 2, at 48–49 ("Normally a definition should not use the word defined. But use of the defined word in the definition causes no difficulty where the definition merely particularizes a general description as in *"contract" means a contract made under this Act* or in some *including* definitions, as in *"child" includes adopted child*, where the purpose is to settle doubts.").

[344] *See* Child, *supra* note 3, at 367 ("It is important to make a defined term stand out as such in the sentence giving its definition. The most common convention for doing this is to put a defined term in quotation marks.").

[345] *See id.* at 356 (using the term "full definition"); DMLU, *supra* note 1, at 258 (using the term "complete definition").

[346] *See id.* (recommending that one use *means* for a complete definition).

[347] *See* Child, *supra* note 3, at 361 (using the term "enlarging definition"); Thornton, *supra* note 2, at 146 (using the term "extending definition"); *see also* Dick, *supra* note 3, at 81; DMLU, *supra* note 1, at 258; Doonan, *supra* note 3, at 82; Piesse, *supra* note 3, at 46.

[348] *See* Child, *supra* note 3, at 364 (using the term "confining definition"); Dick, *supra* note 3, at 80 (same); Thornton, *supra* note 2, at 146–47 (using the term "narrowing definition").

[349] See *supra* text accompanying note 328, at page 73.

[350] Dickerson, *supra* note 3, at 147; Garner, *supra* note 69, at 86, G-14.

[351] Dickerson, *supra* note 3, at 147.

[352] *See, e.g.,* ABA Model Stock Purchase Agreement, *supra* note 94, at 4–30 (in the definition section, using a dash to replace *means*).

For a discussion of the definition section, see *infra* Chapter 5—*Defined Terms and Definitions—The Definition Section.*

[353] See *supra* text accompanying note 208, at page 37.

[354] *See* CHILD, *supra* note 3, at 367 ("Avoid the falsely imperative statement that terms 'shall mean.'"); *see also* DICK, *supra* note 3, at 94; DMLU, *supra* note 1, at 258. Regarding the meaning of *shall*, see *supra* text accompanying note 127, at page 22.

[355] THORNTON, *supra* note 2, at 149; *see* CHILD, *supra* note 3, at 365; DICK, *supra* note 3, at 79; DMLU, *supra* note 1, at 258.

[356] *See* CHILD, *supra* note 3, at 364–65; THORNTON, *supra* note 2, at 149.

[357] *Id.*

[358] *See* DICKERSON, *supra* note 3, at 151–52 (referring to "stuffed definitions"); DMLU, *supra* note 1, at 258 (same); DICK, *supra* note 3, at 84–85 (referring to "loaded definitions"); DOONAN, *supra* note 3, at 86–87 (same); *see also* CHILD, *supra* note 3, at 367–68 (discussing "rules buried in definitions").

[359] *See* HAGGARD, *supra* note 3, at 214–15.

[360] *See, e.g.,* CHILD, *supra* note 3, at 355–74; DICK, *supra* note 3, at 77–86; DICKERSON, *supra* note 3, at 137–52.

[361] *See* HAGGARD, *supra* note 3, at 214 (recommending that one avoid using *hereinafter referred to as* in integrated definitions); PIESSE, *supra* note 3, at 42 (noting that it has become common to omit phrases such as *hereinafter called* when defining terms).

[362] GARNER, *supra* note 69, at 88.

[363] *See* Darmstadter, *supra* note 276, at 5. My views on the definition section were heavily influenced by this article. To spare the reader, rather than cite this article every other sentence, I will only cite it this once, except where I quote it.

[364] *See, e.g.,* CHILD, *supra* note 3, at 355 ("If you are using defined terms in more than one section, then it is appropriate to gather definitions together in a section at the beginning of the document. . . . [I]f a definition is to aid a user of the document, it needs to appear before rather than after the user encounters the defined term.").

[365] GARNER, *supra* note 69, at 87.

[366] Darmstadter, *supra* note 276, at 5.

[367] See *supra* text following note 310, at page 69.

[368] *But see* GARNER, *supra* note 69, at 87 (suggesting that one consider placing the definition section in a schedule or appendix).

[369] See *infra* Chapter 5—*Cross-References*.

[370] See *supra* text accompanying note 291, at page 61.

[371] *See* DMLU, *supra* note 1, at 257 ("The best legal writers and drafters use definitions only when they are necessary—i.e., where there is a gain in clarity and precision. Poor writers and drafters frequently define terms that they either never use again or use perhaps once or twice after the definition.").

[372] VI OED, *supra* note 11, at 211.

[373] *See* 74 AM. JUR. 2D *Time* § 21.

[374] *See* CHILD, *supra* note 3, at 321 (recommending *after*); DICKERSON, *supra* note 3 , at 127 (same).

[375] *See* 74 AM. JUR. 2D *Time* § 25 ("The word 'after' has been given a variety of meanings and applications by the courts, although generally, time 'after' an act is computed by excluding the day on which the event took place."); BLACK'S LAW DICTIONARY 668 (6th ed. 1990) [hereinafter BLACK'S SIXTH EDITION] ("Word 'from' or 'after' an event or day does not have an absolute and invariable meaning, but each should receive an inclusion or exclusion construction according to intention with which such word is used.").

[376] *See* MELLINKOFF, *supra* note 87, at 41 (recommending *starting*).

[377] *See* PIESSE, *supra* note 3, at 113 ("If a period of time is stated to begin on a named day, that day is included.").

[378] *See* CHILD, *supra* note 3 at 320 (noting the ambiguity inherent in *to* and *until*); 74 AM. JUR. 2D *Time* § 23 (stating that *to* and *until* may be either inclusive or exclusive of the date or event that follows it).

[379] *See id.* at § 27 (noting that in some cases *by* has been defined as meaning, in relation to a specified day, "on or before" that day, while in other cases it has been defined as excluding that day).

[380] *See* CHILD, *supra* note 3, at 321 (recommending *before*); MELLINKOFF, *supra* note 87, at 42 (same).

[381] *See* XVIII OED, *supra* note 11, at 11 (providing as one definition of *through* "*U.S.* Up to (a date, a number, a specified item, etc.) inclusively, up the end of, up to and including, to, until; often correlative to *from*.").

382 *See* J. A. Bock, Annotation, *Inclusion or Exclusion of First and Last Days in Computing the Time for Performance of an Act or Event Which Must Take Place a Certain Number of Days Before a Known Future Event*, 98 A.L.R.2D 1331 § 9 (1999) [hereinafter Bock Annotation] (stating that the word *between* has "been considered intermediate and as implying an exclusion of both first and last terminating days"); BLACK'S SIXTH EDITION, *supra* note 375, at 161 ("If an act is to be done 'between' two certain days, it must be performed before commencement of the latter day. In computing the time in such a case, both the days named are to be excluded.").

383 *See* CHILD, *supra* note 3, at 320.

384 See *infra* text accompanying note 400, at page 89.

385 See *infra* Chapter 6—*Provisions to Think About*.

386 *See* 74 AM. JUR. 2D *Time* § 11; DMLU, *supra* note 1, at 247.

387 *See* 74 AM. JUR. 2D *Time* § 15.

388 *See, e.g., id.* at § 21 (stating that when a period of time is to be reckoned "from" a certain day, the day from which the time is to be reckoned is excluded "unless there is something in the context or circumstances to indicate a different intention").

389 *See* MELLINKOFF, *supra* note 37, at 645 (suggesting that if a 10-day lease is made on July 10, "the first day of the lease is July 10, the last day July 19 (unless otherwise provided)").

390 *See* Bock Annotation, *supra* note 382, at § 3 ("[I]t is generally held that in computing the time for performance of an act or event which must take place a certain number of days before a known future day, one of the terminal days is included in the count and the other is excluded.").

391 *See id.* at § 4(b).

392 *See id.* at § 4(a) ("Where an intention to count only 'clear' or 'entire' days is expressed or implied by reason of the facts in the particular case, the courts have, as a limitation of or an exception to the general rule, reckoned time by excluding both first and last days from the count."); DMLU, *supra* note 1, at 247.

393 *See* Bock Annotation, *supra* note 382, at § 8(b).

394 *See id.* at § 8(a).

395 See *supra* text accompanying note 386, at page 86.

396 *See* 74 AM. JUR. 2D *Time* § 10.

[397] *See id.* at § 9.

[398] *See* E. L. Strobin, Annotation, *What 12-Month Period Constitutes "Year" or "Calendar Year" As Used in Public Enactment, Contract, or Other Written Instrument,* 5 A.L.R.3D 584 § 2 (1996) [hereinafter Strobin Annotation] ("In the cases involving questions of the measurement of a specific number of years before or after a given date or event, the decisions tend to go on an anniversary-to-anniversary date theory.").

[399] *See, e.g.,* CHILD, *supra* note 3, at 120–21 (noting in annotations to a sample employment contract that the contract states a period of time as "730 days" in an attempt to avoid the ambiguity inherent in "two years").

[400] *See* DMLU, *supra* note 1, at 247. Regarding that ambiguity inherent in identifying points in time solely by reference to their dates, see *infra* Chapter 5—*References to Time—For Specifying the Term of a Contract or Stating When a Party May or Must Take a Particular Action—Points in Time.*

[401] *See* 28 THE NEW ENCYCLOPAEDIA BRITANNICA 670 (15th ed. 1997).

[402] *See id.*

[403] *See* THE ASSOCIATED PRESS STYLEBOOK AND BRIEFING ON MEDIA LAW 160 (Norm Goldstein ed. 2000) (stating that midnight "is part of the day that is ending, not the one that is beginning").

[404] *See* 28 THE NEW ENCYCLOPAEDIA BRITANNICA, *supra* note 401, at 670.

[405] *See id.*

[406] *See* CHILD, *supra* note 3, at 321 (citing *11:59 P.M.* as an improvement upon *midnight*).

[407] *See* Strobin Annotation, *supra* note 398, at § 2 ("[W]here the term 'year' or one of its variations was used to effect merely the identification of a period of time, the cases tend to a January 1 to December 31 theory when the added word 'preceding' does not appear . . . .").

[408] *See id.* at § 4(d).

[409] *See, e.g.,* BLACK'S, *supra* note 28, at 1024 (stating that both *month* and *calendar month* mean "[o]ne of the twelve periods of time in which the calendar is divided").

[410] *See* 74 AM. JUR. 2D *Time* § 9.

[411] See *infra* Chapter 6—*Less-Useful Provisions.*

[412] *See* SEC PLAIN ENGLISH HANDBOOK, *supra* note 30, at 46 (suggesting that you may want to add more leading for an "airier" document); Howard M. Darmstadter, *Two-and-a-Half Rules for Type*, BUS. LAW TODAY, Sept.–Oct. 1995, at 62–63 (suggesting that "little changes in line spacing make a big difference in readability).

[413] *See, e.g.*, DMLU, *supra* note 1, at 290 ("Many readability specialists insist that unjustified right margins are more readable than justified ones. In letters, contracts, briefs, and the like, an unjustified right margin is often desirable."); SEC PLAIN ENGLISH HANDBOOK, *supra* note 30, at 44 ("Research shows that the easiest text to read is left justified, ragged right text.").

[414] *See* DMLU, *supra* note 1, at 290 ("The one typeface to avoid at all costs still predominated in American legal writing in the mid-1990s: Courier. It is an eyesore."); Darmstadter, *supra* note 412, at 62 ("Courier is easy to spot—it looks like it came out of a typewriter. Send it back.").

[415] *See* THE NEW YORK PUBLIC LIBRARY WRITER'S GUIDE TO STYLE AND USAGE, *supra* note 277, at 73 (1994) ("*Serif* faces are characterized by finishing strokes on letter forms. Faces lacking these finishing strokes are called *sans serif* (*sans* is French for 'without').").

[416] *See id.* ("A time-honored rule dictates the use of serif types for body text, especially in longer works, because in certain studies subjects have found serif type easier to read than sans serif. . . . On the other hand, it has been found that people find most readable the typestyle they're most used to seeing. . . . Custom, too, plays a role in decisions about typefaces. . . . A general rule is that serif faces are perceived as more formal and traditional than sans serif. Sans serif body text is found more frequently in scientific and technical works; serif, in the humanities and works of fiction.").

[417] *See* DMLU, *supra* note 1, at 290; SEC PLAIN ENGLISH HANDBOOK, *supra* note 30, at 40; Darmstadter, *supra* note 412, at 62.

[418] DMLU, *supra* note 1, at 130; SEC PLAIN ENGLISH HANDBOOK, *supra* note 30, at 43.

[419] *See* DMLU, *supra* note 1, at 130 ("The effect of underlining is to take up white space between lines and therefore to make the lines harder for readers to discern.").

[420] *But see* Darmstadter, *supra* note 276, at 8 (recommending that

one emphasize words in the body of enumerated clauses to highlight the differences between them, and emphasize connectors such as *if*, *then*, *and*, *or*, *but*, and *unless* to guide a reader through a long sentence).

[421] *See* U.C.C. § 2-316(2); *see also* U.C.C. § 1-201(10) ("A term or clause is conspicuous when it is so written that a reasonable person against whom it is to operate ought to have noticed it.").

[422] *See* Barclays Bank of New York, N.A. v. Heady Electric Co., 571 N.Y.S.2d 650 (N.Y. App. Div. 1991).

[423] *See* Bonfield v. Aamco Transmissions, Inc., 717 F. Supp. 589 (N.D. Ill. 1989); Phoenix Leasing v. Sure Broadcasting, Inc., 843 F. Supp. 1379 (D.C. Nev. 1994), *aff'd*, 89 F.3d 846 (9th Cir. 1996).

[424] *See* U.C.C. § 1-201(10) ("Language in the body of a form is 'conspicuous' if it is in larger or other contrasting type or color."); William H. Danne, Jr., Annotation, *Construction and Effect of UCC § 2-316(2) Providing that Implied Warranty Disclaimer Must Be "Conspicuous,"* 73 A.L.R.3D 248.

[425] *But see* Darmstadter, *supra* note 276, at 9 (stating that 12-point type is "too large for document work").

[426] *See* THE CHICAGO MANUAL OF STYLE, *supra* note 52, at § 18.17 ("As a rule, text matter intended for continuous reading (as opposed to reference material) should be set in lines neither too wide nor too narrow for comfortable reading. Ideally the line should accommodate 65 to 70 characters."); DMLU, *supra* note 1, at 290 ("Ideally, a line of type should accommodate 45 to 70 characters . . . ."). *But see* SEC PLAIN ENGLISH HANDBOOK, *supra* note 30, at 47 ("A comfortable line length for most readers is 32 to 64 characters.").

[427] *See* MELLINKOFF, *supra* note 6, at 120–22 (discussing the origins of the practice of using strings of synonyms); *see also* DICKERSON, *supra* note 3, at 163–64; DMLU, *supra* note 1, at 292–93.

[428] *See id.* at 293–94 (providing a list of common "doublets, triplets, and synonym-strings"); MELLINKOFF, *supra* note 87, at 189–90 (providing a list of common "coupled synonyms").

[429] *See* DMLU, *supra* note 1, at 773–74 (suggesting that the more modern drafting style is to replace this triplet with the broadest of the three words, *interest*).

[430] *Cf.* SCOTT FITZGIBBON & DONALD W. GLAZER, FITZGIBBON AND GLAZER ON LEGAL OPINIONS 148 (1992) (stating that for purposes of

legal opinions, "corporate power" and "corporate authority" have customarily been interpreted to mean the same thing, and suggesting that it is best to use only the term "power").

431 DMLU, *supra* note 1, at 294.

432 *See* XII OED, *supra* note 11, at 720 ("2. A clause inserted in a legal or formal document, making some condition, stipulation, exception, or limitation, or upon the observance of which the operation or validity of the instrument depends . . . .").

433 Regarding language of performance, see *supra* Chapter 2—*Language of Performance.*

434 *See* DRIEDGER, *supra* note 2, at 93–95.

435 Regarding the lead-in, see *supra* text accompanying note 81, at page 12.

436 *Cf.* DRIEDGER, *supra* note 2, at 95 (stating that since statutes are preceded by an enacting clause, it is arbitrary to thereafter use an enacting formula such as *provided that* for one sentence but not others). Regarding the redundancy of having parties state in the body of the contract that they agree to any given provision, see *supra* text accompanying note 157, at page 27.

437 *See* DRIEDGER, *supra* note 2, at 95–96.

438 DMLU, *supra* note 1, at 710; *see also* DRIEDGER, *supra* note 2, at 96.

439 *Id.*

440 *See id.* ("Notwithstanding its frequency or antiquity, the proviso is hardly more than a legal incantation. The best that can be said for it is that it is an all-purpose conjunction, invented by lawyers but not known or understood by grammarians."); DMLU, *supra* note 1, at 710 (stating that "the words *provided that* are a reliable signal that the draft is not going well"); MELLINKOFF, *supra* note 37, at 520 (describing the proviso as "one of the horrors of legal writing"); THORNTON, *supra* note 2, at 80 ("The case against the lawyer's proviso is overwhelming.").

441 *See* DMLU, *supra* note 1, at 849 (stating that "*such* = of this kind").

442 *See* QUIRK, *supra* note 51, at § 5.14 (using the term "demonstrative determiners"); GARNER, *supra* note 36, at 505 (referring to "pointing words").

[443] *See* Dick, *supra* note 3, at 138 (noting that this usage is contrary to normal English usage); Dickerson, *supra* note 3, at 217 (same); DMLU, *supra* note 1, at 849 (suggesting that this use of *such* "typifies legalese as much as *aforesaid* and *same*"); Eric Partridge, Usage and Abusage 329 (Janet Whitcut ed. 1994) (describing this usage as "pompous").

[444] DMLU, *supra* note 1, at 600.

[445] Mellinkoff, *supra* note 37, at 432.

[446] *See* Thornton, *supra* note 2, at 101 (recommending that one use *subject to* when drafting a provision intended to be subservient to another).

[447] DMLU, *supra* note 1, at 254; *see* Thornton, *supra* note 2, at 99.

[448] See *supra* text accompanying notes 208–09, at page 37.

[449] *See* DMLU, *supra* note 1, at 401 (referring to "*here-* and *there-*words").

[450] See *supra* text accompanying notes 103–20, at pages 19–21.

[451] DMLU, *supra* note 1, at 401.

[452] *But see* Mellinkoff, *supra* note 37, at 283 ("herein: in this. Where? This sentence, this paragraph, this contract, this statute? . . . *Herein* is the start of a treasure hunt rather than a helpful reference.").

[453] DMLU, *supra* note 1, at 401; *see* Mellinkoff, *supra* note 37, at 283 (referring to "the common *here-*compounds of Old and Middle English" as being "unfit for anything other than a touch of nostalgia").

[454] See *infra* Chapter 6—*Useful Provisions.*

[455] *See* Wydick, *supra* note 122, at 49–50, 54–55; DMLU, *supra* note 1, at 48–49; Thornton, *supra* note 2, at 22–28.

[456] See *supra* text accompanying note 187, at page 34, regarding the ambiguity inherent in *may*; also see *supra* Chapter 5—*References to Time* and Chapter 5—*Miscellaneous Other Issues—The Ambiguous* Or *and* And.

[457] DMLU, *supra* note 1, at 49.

[458] *See* Thornton, *supra* note 2, at 22 ("A modifier is a word or group of words that makes the meaning of other words more exact by limiting, restricting or describing them.").

[459] *See* Wydick, *supra* note 122, at 54–55; Garner, *supra* note 69, at 107–09.

[460] *See id.* at 107; *see also* HAGGARD, *supra* note 3, at 266 (referring to "the Rule of Last Modification").

[461] DICKERSON, *supra* note 3, at 105; DMLU, *supra* note 1, at 624.

[462] DICKERSON, *supra* note 3, at 106.

[463] *See* QUIRK, *supra* note 51, at § 13.28 ("Typically *or* is EXCLUSIVE; that is, it excludes the possibility that both conjoins are true, or are to be fulfilled . . . . But even when both alternatives are clearly possible, . . . *or* is normally interpreted as exclusive . . . .").

[464] *See* DICKERSON, *supra* note 3, at 104.

[465] *See, e.g.,* 11 WILLISTON, *supra* note 20, at § 30:12 ("[R]egardless of how purists may feel about the term, it is fairly clear and certain that where the term 'and/or' is used in a contract, the intention is that the one word or the other may be taken accordingly as the one or the other will best effect the purposes of the parties as gathered from the contract as a whole."); *see also* QUIRK, *supra* note 51, at § 13.28 (noting that *and/or* can be used "where precision is required").

[466] *See, e.g.,* DICK, *supra* note 3, at 107 (referring to *and/or* as a "linguistic aberration"); MELLINKOFF, *supra* note 37, at 28 ("Where precision is called for, *and/or* is a disaster."); *see also* DMLU, *supra* note 1, at 56 (quoting the views of some "ardent haters" of *and/or*); 11 WILLISTON, *supra* note 20, at § 30:12 (noting that *and/or* "has provoked outbursts of invective which are somewhat disproportionate to the amount of harm it causes").

[467] DMLU, *supra* note 1, at 56.

[468] *See* DICK, *supra* note 3, at 110; DOONAN, *supra* note 3, at 189.

[469] MELLINKOFF, *supra* note 37, at 28.

[470] NEW FOWLER'S MODERN ENGLISH USAGE, *supra* note 60 (stating that "*and/or* verges on the inelegant when used in general writing"), at 53; *see* PARTRIDGE, *supra* note 443, at 27 (suggesting that despite its utility in legal and official contexts, *and/or* should not be "allowed to infect general writing").

[471] QUIRK, *supra* note 51, at § 13.34 ("*Either* . . . *or* emphasizes the EXCLUSIVE meaning of *or* . . . .").

[472] *See* Maurice B. Kirk, *Legal Drafting: The Ambiguity of "And" and "Or,"* 2 TEX. TECH L. REV. 235, 245 (1971) (stating that the *either* . . . *or* structure "usually does not solve the question whether 'but not both' is to be inferred").

473 See *infra* Chapter 6—*Less-Useful Provisions.*

474 *See* BLACK'S, *supra* note 28, at 1378 ("several, *adj.* . . . 2. (Of liability, etc.) separate; particular; distinct, but not necessarily independent <a several obligation>.").

475 *See* DICKERSON, *supra* note 3, at 105; DMLU, *supra* note 1, at 624.

476 DICKERSON, *supra* note 3, at 106.

477 *See* BLACK'S *supra* note 28, at 926 (defining "joint and several liability" as "[l]iability that may be apportioned either among two or more parties or to only one or a few select members of the group, at the adversary's direction").

478 *See id.* (defining "joint liability" as "[l]iability shared by two or more parties").

479 For further discussion of *and* and *or*, see DICKERSON, *supra* note 3, at 104–14; MELLINKOFF, *supra* note 6, at 306–10; Kirk, *supra* note 115.

480 *See* DMLU, *supra* note 1, at 618.

481 *See id.* at 501.

482 *See id.* ("But the wording with *and* sounds as pedantic—and as wrong—as *a number of people was there.*"); Richard H. Miller, *A Drafting Dilemma,* 4 SCRIBES J. LEGAL WRITING 127 (1993) (opting for *or*).

483 DMLU, *supra* note 1, at 501.

484 *See* BLACK'S, *supra* note 28, at 1039; DMLU, *supra* note 28, at 578.

485 *See id.* at 578–79.

486 *See id.* at 578 (recommending "by the mutual exchange of letters" rather than "by mutual letters").

487 *See* NEW FOWLER'S MODERN ENGLISH USAGE, *supra* note 60, at 509.

488 *See* DMLU, *supra* note 1, at 579.

489 See *supra* Chapter 5—*Miscellaneous Other Issues*—Here- *and* There- *Words.*

490 *See* DMLU, *supra* note 1, at 432 ("Even though the word *including* itself means that the list is merely exemplary and not exhaustive, the courts have not invariably so held. So the longer, more explicit variations may be considered necessary by some drafters.").

[491] See *supra* Chapter 5—*Miscellaneous Other Issues*—*Here- and There- Words*.

[492] See *supra* text accompanying notes 103–20, at pages 19–21.

[493] See *supra* Chapter 5—*Miscellaneous Other Issues*—*The Ambiguous Or and And*.

[494] *See* Darmstadter, *supra* note 307, at 31 (expressing doubt as to whether incorporation by reference is an appropriate way of linking a contract and its exhibits and schedules).

[495] See *supra* text accompanying note 144, at page 25.

[496] *See* Kimble, *supra* note 128, at 76–77 (suggesting that defining terms of authority is "the neatest way" to make the distinction between *shall, must,* and *may*).

[497] See *supra* text accompanying note 171, at page 31.

[498] *See, e.g.,* AM. JUR. LEGAL FORMS § 68:242 (2d ed. 1997) (providing a section defining "words denoting time").

[499] *See, e.g.,* THORNTON, *supra* note 2, at 122–23 (suggesting that it is not difficult to achieve certainty and clarity in provisions relating to time and the computation of periods of time, and providing an example of the sort of provision that would facilitate this).

[500] See *supra* Chapter 5—*References to Time*.

[501] *See* DMLU, *supra* note 1, at 793 (stating that in technical writing, the average sentence length should be 20 words or fewer); WYDICK, *supra* note 122, at 38 (recommending that one keep the average sentence length below 25 words).

[502] *See* GARNER, *supra* note 69, at 45 (suggesting that for most drafted documents, an average sentence length of 30 words is a more realistic goal than 20 words).

[503] See *supra* Chapter 3—*The Format of the Body of the Contract*—*Enumerated Clauses*.

[504] *See* WYDICK, *supra* note 122, at 43–45.

[505] *See id.* at 44.

[506] *See* DMLU, *supra* note 1, at 122–23 (using the term "buried verb"); GOLDSTEIN & LIEBERMAN, *supra* note 8, at 137–40 (using the term "nominalization"); WYDICK, *supra* note 122, at 25 (same).

[507] See *supra* text accompanying notes 210–11, at pages 37–38.

[508] GOLDSTEIN & LIEBERMAN, *supra* note 8, at 138.

509 *See id.* at 140; WYDICK, *supra* note 122, at 26.

510 *See* GARNER, *supra* note 36, at 267.

511 *See id.* at 627.

512 *See id.* at 488.

513 *See* DMLU, *supra* note 1, at 517 (listing "legalisms and lawyer-isms"); WYDICK, *supra* note 122, at 13 (stating that "compound constructions use three or four words to do the work of one or two words," and providing a list of examples).

514 See *supra* Chapter 1—*The Introductory Clause—Reference to the Type of Agreement.*

515 *See* THE ASSOCIATED PRESS STYLEBOOK AND BRIEFING ON MEDIA LAW, *supra* note 403, at 31 (stating that "board of directors" should always be lowercase).

516 *See* THE CHICAGO MANUAL OF STYLE, *supra* note 52, at § 7.22; *see also* THE NEW YORK TIMES MANUAL OF STYLE AND USAGE 108 (Allan M. Siegal & William G. Connolly eds., rev. and expanded ed. 1999) (stating under the entry for "director" "[d]o not capitalize: . . . *Stacy W. Daan, a director of General Motors"*).

517 *Cf.* THE CHICAGO MANUAL OF STYLE, *supra* note 52, at § 7.141 (noting that in text references in a book, "the word *chapter* is lowercased").

518 FREUND, *supra* note 247, remains a useful source of guidance on such issues.

519 *See id.* at 142.

520 *See id.*; Kopelman, *supra* note 341, at 21–22; Ronald B. Risdon, *Universal Issues, in* DRAFTING CORPORATE AGREEMENTS 2001 9, 13 (Practicing Law Institute Corporate Law and Practice Handbook Series No. B-1219).

521 *See* WARREN, *supra* note 84.

522 *See* Gregory P. Pressman, *In Search of Perfect Document Assembly,* N.Y.L.J., Aug. 11, 1997, at S6.

523 *See* Clifford P. Jones & David W. Johnson, *Document Assembly Can Help Alleviate Drafting Nightmares,* N.Y.L.J., Oct. 28, 1996, at S4; Pressman, *supra* note 522.

524 *See* Steven Moore & Gretta Rusanow, *E-Business Solutions for the Global Practice,* N.Y.L.J., Mar. 7, 2000, at 5.

[525] *See, e.g.,* Pressman, *supra* note 522 (noting that Schulte Roth & Zable LLP has found document-assembly systems to be extremely useful in its investment fund practice).

[526] *See* Moore & Rusanow, *supra* note 524 ("Document assembly systems and sophisticated template document libraries require a large initial investment in lawyer time to develop the documents, and an ongoing investment to keep those documents current. Consequently, most law firms and law departments have not traditionally dedicated significant resources to these initiatives.").

[527] See information available at http:/www.newchange.com.

[528] Telephone interview with Carl Sheldon, Partner, Allen & Overy (Feb. 14, 2001).

[529] *See* Richard Susskind, *Online*, TIMES (London), Feb. 8, 2000 (referring, in the context of a discussion of Allen & Overy's "newchange documents" system, to "strong rumours of other, similar systems coming to market").

[530] *See* Jones & Johnson, *supra* note 523.

[531] *See id.*

[532] THE BLUEBOOK: A UNIFORM SYSTEM OF CITATION (Columbia Law Review Ass'n et al. eds., 17th ed. 2000).

APPENDIX

A Sample Contract, "Before" and "After"

In order to give a sense of the overall effect of the approaches I recommend in this book, I have included below two versions of a simple contract. The first version incorporates many widely accepted usages; the second version reflects how I would revise the first. I have annotated, by means of footnotes, both versions to explain changes I made or did not make; page references in the footnotes are to the main part of the book.

These "before" and "after" contracts are not illustrative of how one would go about revising and editing a contract. For one thing, I have assumed that apart from issues of legal usage, the text of the "before" contract is entirely adequate; in practice, it is unlikely that you would happen upon a model contract that covers all aspects of your transaction. (Given this assumption, I do not recommend that you use either of these contracts as precedent for a specific transaction.) Also, if when revising a standard contract provision I encounter text that I am not happy with, often I will not attempt to revise it but will instead copy a tried-and-true alternative from a contract I drafted.

A. "Before" Version of Sample Contract

OPTION AGREEMENT[1]

This OPTION AGREEMENT[2] (this "**Agreement**")[3] is made and entered into as of the 22nd day of January, 2001,[4] by and between[5] SARGASSO HOLDINGS, INC., a corporation duly organized and validly existing under the laws of the State of Delaware[6] with its principal offices at 38th Floor, 909 Sixth Avenue, New York, NY 10022[7] (hereinafter referred to as[8] the "**Stockholder**"),[9] and NEIL J. PROCTOR, an individual residing at 2265 Atlantic Street, Stamford, CT 06902 (hereinafter referred to as the "**Optionholder**").[10]

WITNESSETH: [11]

WHEREAS,[12] since April 1999 the Optionholder has been acting as intellectual property licensing consultant to Jorvik Research, Inc., a Delaware corporation (the "**Company**"), and since July 1999 has been a member of the board of business advisers of the Company;[13]

---

[1] Do not use boldface in the title, or anywhere else for that matter. See pages 98–100.

[2] Since the title occurs immediately above the introductory clause, there is no need to emphasize with full capitals the reference in the introductory clause to the type of agreement involved. See page 3.

[3] Emphasize with underlining, rather than boldface, each defined term where it is defined. See pages 8, 97.

[4] This date format is archaic; use instead *January 22, 2001*. See page 4.

[5] Use instead the formula *is dated . . . and is between*. See pages 3–4.

[6] Rephrase this as *a Delaware corporation*. See page 7.

[7] Do not include party addresses in the introductory clause. See page 7.

[8] Do not introduce defined terms in this manner. See pages 8, 78.

[9] Base the defined term for an entity's name on that name rather than on a common noun. See page 9.

[10] Use as the defined term for an individual's name that individual's last name preceded by an appropriate honorific. See page 9.

[11] *WITNESSETH* is archaic, and in any event recitals do not need a heading. See pages 12, 13.

[12] Do not use *WHEREAS*, and organize the recitals as conventional paragraphs rather than as single-sentence paragraphs separated by semicolons. See page 13.

[13] Use the possessive. See page 126.

WHEREAS, the Stockholder is the principal stockholder of the Company;[13]

WHEREAS, in April 2000 the Stockholder and the Optionholder agreed orally that Optionholder[14] shall be entitled to[15] compensation equivalent to five percent (5%)[16] of any financing the Optionholder was instrumental in securing for the Company;

WHEREAS, in September 2000, the Optionholder introduced the Company to Whitney Technology Ventures, Inc., a New York corporation ("**Whitney**");[17]

WHEREAS, Whitney has decided to invest in the Company, and as of the date hereof[18] shall be[19] purchasing two thousand eight hundred (2,800)[16] shares of Series A Preferred Stock,[20] par value $.001 per share, of the Company ("**Preferred Stock**") representing a thirty-five percent (35%)[16] ownership interest in the Company; and

WHEREAS, as compensation for the Optionholder's role in securing such[21] financing, the Stockholder wishes to grant the Optionholder an option to purchase a number of shares of common stock, par value $.001 per share ("**Common Stock**")[22] of the Company held by the Stockholder.

---

[14] When using a noun or noun phrase as the defined term for a party, be consistent in using or not using the definite article *the*. See page 9.

[15] This is not language of obligation, as the Optionholder is not under a duty. See page 22. Use *would be entitled to* instead of *shall be entitled to*.

[16] Except in particularly sensitive contexts, do not express numbers in both words and numerals. Use words for whole numbers up to ten; use numerals for 11 and upwards. See page 72.

[17] It would be preferable to do without this defined term, as "Whitney" is used only once thereafter, in the next recital.

[18] Use *of this Agreement* rather than *hereof*. See page 107.

[19] *Shall be* is inappropriate, as this is not language of obligation. Use *is*. See page 22.

[20] There is no need for initial capitals in *Preferred Stock*. See page 127.

[21] Use *that* instead of *such*. See pages 103–4.

[22] The defined-term parenthetical is inappropriately placed in the middle of the noun phrase that constitutes the definition. See pages 78–79.

NOW, THEREFORE,[23] in consideration of the promises and mutual covenants and agreements hereinafter contained,[24] the parties hereto,[25] intending to be legally bound,[26] hereby agree[27] as follows:

1.   **Grant of Option.**[28]

(a)[29]   Subject to the terms of this Agreement,[30] the Stockholder hereby grants the Optionholder an irrevocable option (the "**Option**")[22] to purchase up to one hundred forty (140)[16] shares (the "**Shares**")[31] of Common Stock for a purchase price of Two Thousand Five Hundred Dollars ($2,500)[16] per share.

(b)   The Option may be exercised[32] from time to time with respect to twenty (20)[16] or more shares in any one instance.

(c)   The Option expires on the tenth (10th)[16] anniversary of the date of this Agreement[33] (that date, the "**Termination Date**").[34]

---

[23] *NOW, THEREFORE* is archaic. See page 13.

[24] Recitals of consideration are ineffectual. See pages 14–15.

[25] Dispense with *hereto*. See page 10.

[26] It serves no purpose to have parties express their intent to be legally bound. See pages 14–15, 64.

[27] It is preferable to not use *hereby* in performatives using verbs of speaking. See page 21.

[28] Use underlining rather than boldface to emphasize section headings. See pages 54, 97.

[29] Place immediately after the heading and on the same line the *(a)* designating the first subsection of a section, rather than placing it on a new line. See page 55. Be consistent (compare Section 1(a) to Section 4(a)).

[30] This phrase is superfluous. See page 106.

[31] The defined term "the Shares" is unnecessary; note that the defined term parenthetical should be placed at the end of the noun phrase constituting the definition, rather than in the middle. See pages 78–79.

[32] This is better phrased in the active voice, to make it clear who may exercise the option. See page 22.

[33] Expressing points in time by reference to only a given day can result in ambiguity. See pages 85, 89.

[34] The defined term "Termination Date" is unnecessary, as one can express the concept efficiently without the need for a defined term. See Section 4(a) of the "after" version, which uses *Before the Option expires* instead of *Prior to the Termination Date.*

2.   **Method of Exercise.** The parties agree[35] that the Option or any part thereof may be exercised[36] by the giving of a written notice to the Stockholder (each an "**Exercise Notice**")[37] executed by or on behalf of the Optionholder, which Exercise Notice shall[38] state the election to exercise the Option,[39] the number of whole Shares with respect to which the Option is being exercised, and the date for the closing of the purchase;[40] provided, however,[41] that such date shall[42] be not earlier than three (3)[16] business days nor later than fifteen (15)[16] business days after the date such[43] notice is given.[44] Each closing of a purchase of Shares pursuant hereto shall[45] be held at the principal offices of Jorvik.[13]

3.   **Payment and Delivery of Shares.** At any closing hereunder, (a)[46] the Optionholder shall pay the aggregate purchase price for the Shares to be purchased, which shall be payable by bank check or by wire transfer to an account designated by Stockholder,[47] and (b) the

---

[35] Since in the lead-in the parties state that they agree to that which follows, there is no need for them to state in the body of the contract that they agree to any given provision. See page 27.

[36] This would be better phrased in the active voice rather than the passive. See page 22.

[37] This defined term is unnecessary.

[38] Use *must* instead of *shall*. See pages 45–46. Even better, rephrase this provision using *stating*.

[39] Use a verb instead of a "buried verb." See pages 125–26.

[40] The defined term *the Closing* would be helpful.

[41] This proviso is better stated as a separate sentence. See pages 102–3.

[42] At a minimum, replace *shall be* with *must be*. See pages 30–31. The better option, though, would be to rephrase this as an obligation of the parties. See pages 31–32.

[43] Use *any* rather than *such*. See pages 103–4.

[44] Instead of using the passive voice with a silent *by*-agent, use the active voice. See page 22.

[45] At least use *must* rather than *shall*, as the obligation is not imposed on the subject of the sentence, *Each closing*, but on the parties. See pages 30–31. Even better, rephrase the sentence with the parties as the subject. See page 31.

[46] Use the *(1)* hierarchy, rather than the *(a)* hierarchy, for enumerated clauses, see page 59, but enumeration is unnecessary here.

[47] This nonrestrictive clause is a "passive-type policy," so it should use *will* rather than *shall*. See pages 37–39. More to the point, it would be better phrased as language of obligation. See page 39.

Stockholder shall deliver to the Optionholder certificate(s)[48] representing the Shares so purchased (i)[49] registered in the name of the Optionholder or his designee or (ii) duly endorsed in blank for transfer or accompanied by appropriate stock powers duly executed in blank.

4. **Ownership of Shares.** (a) Prior to the Termination Date,[34] the Stockholder will not[50] take, and will not[50] permit anyone else to take, any action that might have the effect of preventing the Stockholder from delivering the Shares free of any liens, claims, security interests, or encumbrances whatsoever[51] (other than pursuant to the stockholders agreements dated February 28, 1998 and May 12, 2000, between the Company and certain stockholders of the Company (collectively, the **"Stockholders Agreements"**)) to the Optionholder upon exercise of the Option, or from otherwise performing his obligations under this Agreement.

(b) In the event that[52] at any time the Stockholder shall agree[53] to transfer to any individual, corporation (including any non-profit corporation), general or limited partnership, limited liability company, joint venture, estate, trust, association, organization, labor union, governmental authority or other entity (**"Person"**)[54] other than pursuant hereto[55] a number of its shares of Common Stock so that it shall be[56] left with a number of shares of Common Stock that is less

---

[48] Use instead *one or more certificates*. See page 111.

[49] Use the *(A)* hierarchy for the second level of enumerated clauses, see page 59, but in this instance eliminating the first level of enumerated clause will result in this becoming the first level.

[50] Use instead *shall not*, as this represents language of obligation rather than a representation as to the future. See pages 36, 49.

[51] Create a defined term "Lien," and define it in a definition section, since one can deduce its general meaning without needing to refer to the definition. See page 81. Use it wherever appropriate.

[52] Use *if* instead. See page 126.

[53] Use the present tense, *agrees*, in this conditional clause rather than *shall be*. See page 42.

[54] Place in a definition section any definitions whose exact or general meaning can be deduced from the defined term. See page 81.

[55] Use *to this Agreement*. See page 107.

[56] Use the present tense, *is*, rather than *shall be*.

than the number of shares the Optionholder shall be entitled to[57] purchase upon exercise of[58] the Option, that transfer may only be effected[59] if the transferee shall agree in writing to be subject to the Option and bound by the terms of this Agreement with respect to the number of shares that would, when added to the remaining shares held by the Stockholder, equal the number of shares that the Optionholder shall be entitled to[57] purchase upon exercising the Option, and the Stockholder shall remain liable[60] for breach by such[21] transferee of the terms of this Agreement with respect to such[21] shares.[61]

5.   **Adjustments.**

(a)[62]   In case at any time after the date of this Agreement[63] the following occurs:

(i)[64]   declaration by the Company of[39] a dividend or the making by the Company of a distribution on the Common Stock in shares of its capital stock;

(ii)   subdivision of[39] the outstanding Common Stock;

(iii)   combination of[39] the outstanding Common Stock into a smaller number of shares;

(iv)   issuance of[39] any shares of the Company's capital stock by reclassification of the Common Stock (including any

---

[57] Use *is entitled to*. See pages 34–35.

[58] Use *exercising* rather than *upon the exercise of*, which constitutes a "buried verb." See pages 125–26.

[59] Use the active voice rather than the passive with an absent *by*-agent. See page 22.

[60] Since this is a matrix clause following a conditional clause, use the simple future. See page 43.

[61] To make this one-sentence subsection rather more manageable, turn the last clause into a separate sentence.

[62] Rather than begin this section with a multi-part conditional clause, use a defined term encompassing each of the events described in the five enumerated clauses and define that term in a separate subsection. See page 43.

[63] The phrase *after the date of this Agreement* is unnecessary; since the provision relates to the future, by definition it applies after the date of the agreement.

[64] Use the *(1)* hierarchy for enumerated clauses; for tabulated enumerated clauses, place the subsection designation flush left and use the hanging-indent format. See pages 59–60.

such reclassification in connection with a consolidation or merger in which the Company is the continuing corporation);

(v) the taking of[39] any action by the Company similar to (i) through (iv);

[65]then the number and kind of shares of capital stock purchasable upon exercise of this[66] Option immediately after the happening[39] of such[21] event[67] shall[68] be adjusted so that, after giving effect to such[21] adjustment, the Optionholder shall[69] be entitled to purchase the number and kind of shares of capital stock upon exercise that such holder[70] would have been entitled to purchase had such Option[71] been exercised[36] immediately prior to the happening of the events described above (or in the case of clause (i) above, immediately prior to the record date therefor).

(b) In case of any consolidation or merger of the Company with or into another corporation[39] (other than a merger with a subsidiary in which the Company is the continuing corporation and which does not result in any reclassification, capital reorganization or other change of the outstanding Shares issuable upon exercise of the Option) or in case of the sale, transfer or other disposition of all or substantially all of the assets of the Company,[39] then the Optionholder shall[69] be entitled to purchase upon exercise of the Option such[72] number and kind of shares of capital stock or other securities or

---

[65] This text is "dangling text," in other words section or subsection text that follows tabulated enumerated clauses constituting the front part of a sentence. See page 60. It is best to avoid dangling text, but in this instance the problem is solved by moving the tabulated enumerated clauses to a separate subsection and using instead a defined term.

[66] Do not use *this*, as it suggests that there is more than one Option (with a capital "O").

[67] It is preferable that *immediately after the happening of such event* relate to the adjustment rather than exercise of the Option.

[68] Use *will*: since the adjustment would be automatic, this is a policy rather than language of obligation. See page 37.

[69] Because of the preceding conditional clause, use *will* rather than *is*. See page 43. Do not use *shall*, as the Optionholder is not under a duty. See pages 34–35.

[70] Use either the defined term *Optionholder* or *he*.

[71] Do not use *such Option*, as it suggests that there is more than one Option.

[72] Use *the* instead of *such*.

property distributable upon, or as a result of, such[21] transaction that the Optionholder would have been entitled to purchase had the Option been exercised[36] immediately prior to such[21] transaction.

6. **Representations and Warranties**[73] **of the Stockholder.** The Stockholder represents and warrants[74] to the Optionholder as follows:

(a)   The Stockholder is a corporation validly existing and in good standing under the laws of the State of Delaware with power and authority[75] to own all of its properties and assets and to carry on its business as it is currently being conducted.

(b)   The Stockholder has all requisite[76] power and authority[75] to execute and deliver this Agreement and to perform its obligations hereunder. Execution and delivery of this Agreement and performance by the Stockholder of its obligations under this Agreement[39] have been duly authorized by the Board of Directors[77] of the Stockholder[36] and no other corporate proceedings of the Stockholder are necessary with respect thereto.

(c)   This Agreement constitutes the valid and binding obligation of the Stockholder, enforceable in accordance with its terms, except as the same[78] may be[79] limited by (i)[80] any applicable bankruptcy, insolvency, reorganization, moratorium or similar law affecting creditors' rights generally, or (ii) general principles of equity, whether considered in a proceeding in equity or at law.

(d)   The Stockholder is not required to obtain any approval, consent, waiver, or other authorization of any Person, including

---

[73] Refer only to *representations* rather than *representations and warranties*. See page 47.

[74] Have the parties *represent* rather than *represent and warrant*. See page 47.

[75] It is sufficient to refer to *power* rather than *power and authority*. See page 100.

[76] *All requisite* is redundant, as it is sufficient to say that someone *has the power* to do something.

[77] Omit the initial capitals in *Board of Directors*. See page 126.

[78] Do not use *same* as a pronoun.

[79] Use *is* rather than *may be*, as the *except as* clause is best considered a conditional clause taking the present tense; the exception applies in the event of actual, rather than potential, limitations.

[80] Use the *(1)* hierarchy for enumerated clauses. See page 59.

any party to any contract to which the Stockholder is a party, in connection with execution and delivery of this Agreement and performance of its obligations under this Agreement.

(e)   Execution and delivery of this Agreement by the Stockholder and performance of its obligations under this Agreement do not (i)[80] violate any provision of the articles of incorporation or by-laws of the Stockholder as currently in effect, (ii) conflict with, result in a breach of, constitute a default under (or an event which, with notice or lapse of time or both, would constitute a default under), accelerate the performance required by, result in the creation of any liens, charges, pledges, deeds of trust,[81] security interests, or encumbrances whatsoever[51] upon any of the properties or assets of the Stockholder[13] under, or create in any party the right to terminate, modify, or cancel, or require any notice under, any contract to which the Stockholder is a party or by which any properties or assets of the Stockholder[13] are bound, or (iii) violate any federal, state or local law, ordinance or regulation, or any court order, judgement, or injunction, currently in effect to which the Stockholder is subject.

(f)   The Stockholder is the record and beneficial owner and holder of 1,350 shares of Common Stock, free of any liens, claims, security interests, or encumbrances whatsoever other than pursuant to the Stockholders Agreements, and other than the Stockholders Agreements, there are no voting trusts, proxies, or other contracts to which the Stockholder is a party relating to the transfer, voting, or registration of its shares of Common Stock.

7.   **Representations and Warranties[73] of the Optionholder.** The Optionholder represents and warrants[74] to the Stockholder as follows:

(a)   The Optionholder has full legal capacity to execute and deliver this Agreement and to perform his obligations under this Agreement.

(b)   This Agreement constitutes the valid and binding obligation of the Optionholder, enforceable in accordance with its terms, except as enforceability is limited by (i) any applicable bankruptcy, insolvency, reorganization, moratorium or similar law affecting

---

[81] The preceding three items are not included in the otherwise identical list used several times in this agreement. Such inconsistency can cause problems; that is one reason for using a defined term (in this case, "Lien") instead of repeating such lists. See page 101.

creditors' rights generally, or (ii) general principles of equity, whether considered in a proceeding in equity or at law.

(c) The Optionholder is not required to obtain any approval, consent, waiver, or other authorization of any Person, including any party to any contract to which the Optionholder is a party, in connection with execution and delivery of this Agreement and performance of his obligations under this Agreement.

(d) The Optionholder's execution and delivery of this Agreement and performance of his obligations under this Agreement do not and will not (i)[80] conflict with, result in a breach of, constitute a default under (or an event which, with notice or lapse of time or both, would constitute a default under), accelerate the performance required by, result in the creation of any liens, claims, security interests, or encumbrances whatsoever[51] upon any of the properties or assets of the Optionholder[13] under, or create in any party the right to accelerate, terminate, modify, or cancel, or require any notice under, any contract to which the Optionholder is a party or by which any properties or assets of the Optionholder[13] are bound, or (ii) violate any federal, state or local law, ordinance or regulation, or any court order, judgement, or injunction, currently in effect to which the Optionholder is subject.

8. **Specific Performance.** The Stockholder acknowledges and agrees[82] that its breach or threatened breach of this Agreement would cause irreparable damage to the Optionholder and that the Optionholder will not[83] have an adequate remedy at law. Accordingly, the Stockholder expressly acknowledges[84] that the Optionholder shall[85] be entitled to specific performance, injunctive relief or any other equitable remedy against the Stockholder in the event of any breach or threatened breach of any provision of this Agreement by the Stockholder.[39] The rights and remedies of the parties hereto[25] are cumulative and shall not be[86] exclusive, and

---

[82] *And agrees* is superfluous.

[83] Use *would not*.

[84] *Expressly* is redundant.

[85] Use *will*, as this is a policy rather than language of obligation and relates to an event that may or may not occur. See page 37.

[86] Use *are not* rather than *shall not be*, as this is a policy rather than language of obligation. See page 37.

each such[87] party shall be entitled to[88] pursue all legal and equitable rights[89] and remedies to secure performance by the other party of its obligations under this Agreement, and enforcement of one or more such[90] rights and remedies by a party shall in no way preclude such[21] party from pursuing, at the same time or subsequently, any and all other rights and remedies available to it.

9.   **Further Assurances.** The Stockholder and the Optionholder each agree to[35] execute and deliver such other reasonable documents or agreements[91] as may be necessary or desirable for consummation of the transactions contemplated by this Agreement.

10.   **Governing Law.** This Agreement shall be[92] governed by and construed in accordance with[93] the laws of the State of New York without giving effect to principles of conflict of laws.

11.   **Jurisdiction; Service of Process.** Any proceeding seeking to enforce any provision of this Agreement may be brought against any of the parties hereto[25] in the courts of the State of New York, County of New York, or, if it has or can acquire jurisdiction, in the United States District Court for the Southern District of New York,[36] and each of the parties consents to the jurisdiction of those courts (and of the appropriate appellate courts) in any such action or proceeding and waives any objection to venue laid therein. Process in any such action or proceeding may be served by delivering a copy of the process to the party to be served at the address and in the manner provided for the giving of notices in Section 12 hereof.[94] Nothing in this Section 11, however, shall affect[95] the right of any party hereto[25] to serve legal process in any other manner permitted by law.

---

[87] *Such* is superfluous.

[88] Use *may* rather than *shall be entitled to*. See pages 33–35.

[89] Delete *rights and*, as it does not make sense to refer to pursuing rights.

[90] Use *of those* rather than *such*. See pages 103–4.

[91] Delete *reasonable* and insert *reasonably* before *necessary* so as to focus on the reasonableness of a need rather than of a document.

[92] Use *is*, as this is a policy rather than language of obligation. See page 37.

[93] *Governed by* is sufficient. See page 101.

[94] *Hereof* is superfluous. See pages 107–8.

[95] Use *affects* rather than *shall affect*, as this is a policy rather than language of obligation. See page 37.

12. **Notices.** Every notice or other communication required or contemplated by this Agreement shall[96] be in writing and sent by (a)[97] personal delivery, in which case delivery shall[92] be deemed to occur the day of delivery, unless it is delivered after 5:00 p.m., in which case delivery shall[92] be deemed to occur the following day, (b) certified or registered mail, postage prepaid, return receipt requested, in which case delivery shall[92] be deemed to occur the day it is officially recorded by the U.S. Postal Service as delivered to the intended recipient, or (c) next-day delivery to a U.S. address by recognized overnight delivery service such as Federal Express, in which case delivery shall[92] be deemed to occur upon receipt. In each case, a notice or other communication sent to a party shall[96] be directed to the address for that party set forth below, or to another address designated by such[21] party by written notice:

If to the Stockholder, to:

Sargasso Holdings, Inc.
38th Floor
909 Sixth Avenue
New York, NY 10022

If to the Optionholder, to:

Mr. Neil J. Proctor
Proctor Investments, Inc.
2265 Atlantic Street
Stamford, CT 06902

13. **Severability.** If any term, provision, covenant, or condition[98] hereof,[18] or the application thereof to any Person, place or circumstance,[99] shall be[100] held to be invalid, unenforceable, or void[98] by any court of competent jurisdiction, all other conditions and

---

[96] Use *must*, as the obligation is not imposed on the subject of the sentence. See pages 30–31.

[97] These enumerated clauses would be more readable if they were tabulated. Also, use the *(1)* hierarchy for enumerated clauses. See page 59.

[98] Eliminate redundant synonyms or near-synonyms. See pages 100–102.

[99] This clause is redundant.

[100] Since this is a conditional clause, use *is* rather than *shall be*. See page 42.

provisions[98] hereof[18] shall[85] remain in full force and effect.[101] In the event that[52] any term, provision, covenant, or condition[98] hereof[18] shall be[100] held to be invalid, unenforceable, or void[98] only in part or degree, it shall[85] remain in full force and effect to the extent not held invalid, unenforceable, or void.[98]

14. **Entire Agreement.** This Agreement constitutes the entire agreement between the parties pertaining to the subject matter hereof[18] and supersedes all prior agreements, understandings, negotiations and discussions,[98] whether oral or written, of the parties hereto[25] relating to such[21] subject matter.[102]

15. **Amendment.** This Agreement can[103] only be amended by a writing signed by the parties.

16. **Counterparts.** This Agreement may be executed in counterparts, each of which is an original and all of which together shall be deemed to[104] constitute one and the same instrument.

IN WITNESS WHEREOF,[105] the parties hereto[25] have duly executed[106] and delivered[107] this Agreement as of the date first above written.[108]

SARGASSO HOLDINGS, INC.

By: _____

   Name:
   Title:

_____

Neil J. Proctor[109]

---

[101] If a provision is in full force it must also be in full effect. Avoid this redundancy by using *effective* instead.

[102] Dividing this section into two sentences would make it slightly more readable. See pages 123–24.

[103] Use *may*. See page 33.

[104] Dispense with *shall be deemed to*, as it would be a stretch to describe this as establishing a legal fiction. See page 107.

[105] *IN WITNESS WHEREOF* is an archaism. See page 64.

[106] Use instead the present progressive (*are executing*). See page 65.

[107] Omit any reference to delivery of the agreement. See page 65.

[108] Refer to the date stated in the introductory clause. See page 66.

[109] Use all capital letters rather than initial capital letters to state in a signature block the name of a party that is an individual. See page 66.

B. "A<small>FTER</small>" V<small>ERSION OF</small> S<small>AMPLE</small> C<small>ONTRACT</small>

OPTION AGREEMENT

This Option Agreement[1] (this "<u>Agreement</u>")[2] is dated January 22, 2001, and is between SARGASSO HOLDINGS, INC., a Delaware corporation ("<u>Sargasso</u>"), and NEIL J. PROCTOR, an individual ("<u>Mr. Proctor</u>").

Since April 1999, Mr. Proctor has been acting as intellectual property licensing consultant to Jorvik Research, Inc., a Delaware corporation ("<u>Jorvik</u>"). Since July 1999, Mr. Proctor has been a member of Jorvik's board of business advisers. Sargasso is Jorvik's principal stockholder.

In April 2000, Sargasso and Mr. Proctor agreed orally that Mr. Proctor would be entitled to compensation equivalent to 5% of any financing Mr. Proctor was instrumental in securing for Jorvik.

In September 2000, Mr. Proctor introduced Jorvik to Whitney Technology Ventures, Inc., a New York corporation, which has decided to invest in Jorvik and as of the date of this Agreement is purchasing 1,400 shares of Jorvik Series A preferred stock representing a 35% ownership interest in Jorvik.

As compensation for Mr. Proctor's role in securing this financing, Sargasso wishes to grant Mr. Proctor an option to purchase a number of shares of Jorvik common stock, par value $.001 per share[3] ("<u>Common Stock</u>"), held by Sargasso.

Sargasso and Mr. Proctor therefore agree as follows:

1.   <u>Grant of Option</u>. (a) Subject to the term of this Agreement, Sargasso hereby grants Mr. Proctor an irrevocable option to purchase

---

[1] You need not use initial capitals when referring to this or any other agreement, but since drafters invariably do, I have retained the initial capitals in *This Option Agreement*. See page 3.

[2] The defined term *this Agreement* is unnecessary, but since most drafters use it, and since it is harmless, I have retained it. See page 10.

[3] Referring to par value serves little purpose, since Jorvik could only have one class of common stock. But including par value in the definition of a class of capital stock is standard practice, and a harmless one at that, so I am willing to retain this reference.

up to 70 shares of Common Stock for a purchase price of $2,500 per share (that option, the "Option").

(b)   Mr. Proctor may exercise the Option from time to time with respect to 10 or more shares in any one instance.

(c)   The Option expires at midnight at the beginning of the tenth anniversary of the date of this Agreement.

2.   Method of Exercise. To exercise the Option, in whole or in part, Mr. Proctor must[4] provide Sargasso with a written notice stating that Mr. Proctor is exercising the Option and stating the number of shares with respect to which he is exercising the Option and the date for closing the purchase of those shares (each closing of a purchase of shares pursuant to Mr. Proctor's exercising the Option, a "Closing"). The parties shall not[5] hold any Closing sooner than three business days, or later than 15 business days, after the date of any notice delivered by Mr. Proctor pursuant to this Section 2. The parties shall hold each Closing at Jorvik's principal offices.

3.   Payment and Delivery of Shares. At any Closing, Mr. Proctor shall pay by bank check or by wire transfer to an account designated by Sargasso the aggregate purchase price for the shares to be purchased, and Sargasso shall deliver to Mr. Proctor one or more certificates representing the shares so purchased (1) registered in the name of Mr. Proctor or his designee or (2) duly endorsed in blank for transfer or accompanied by appropriate stock powers duly executed in blank.

4.   Ownership of Shares. (a) Before the Option expires, Sargasso shall not[5] take, and shall not permit anyone else to take, any action that might have the effect of preventing Sargasso from delivering to Mr. Proctor, upon his exercising the Option, shares free of any Liens (other than pursuant to the stockholders agreements dated February 28, 1998 and May 12, 2000, between Jorvik and certain Jorvik stockholders (collectively, the "Stockholders Agreements")), or from otherwise performing his obligations under this Agreement.

(b)   If at any time Sargasso agrees to transfer to any Person other than pursuant to this Agreement a number of its shares of Common Stock so that it is left with a number of shares of Common

---

[4] Since this is a condition rather than language of obligation, it is appropriate to use *must* rather than *shall*. See pages 45–46.

[5] Note that I do not use *may not*. See page 36.

Stock that is less than the number of shares Mr. Proctor is then entitled to purchase upon exercising the Option, Sargasso may effect that transfer only if the transferee agrees in writing to be subject to the Option and bound by the terms of this Agreement with respect to the number of shares that would, when added to the remaining shares held by Sargasso, equal the number of shares Mr. Proctor is entitled to purchase upon exercising the Option, and Sargasso will remain liable for breach by any such transferee of the terms of this Agreement with respect to those shares.

5.   Adjustments. (a) If an Adjustment Event occurs, the number and kind of shares of capital stock purchasable upon exercise of the Option will immediately be automatically adjusted so that, after giving effect to that adjustment, upon his exercising the Option Mr. Proctor will be entitled to purchase the number and kind of shares of capital stock that he would have been entitled to purchase had he exercised the Option immediately prior to effectiveness of that Adjustment Event (or in the case of an Adjustment Event of the sort described in Section 5(b)(1), immediately prior to the record date for that Adjustment Event).

(b)   An "Adjustment Event" will occur any time after the date of this Agreement that Jorvik does any of the following:

(1)   declares a stock dividend upon shares of Common Stock or distributes any shares of its capital stock to holders of shares of Common Stock;

(2)   subdivides the outstanding shares of Common Stock;

(3)   combines the outstanding shares of Common Stock into a smaller number of shares;

(4)   issues any shares of its capital stock by reclassification of the Common Stock (including any reclassification in connection with a consolidation or merger in which Jorvik is the continuing corporation); or

(5)   takes any action similar to those listed in clauses (1) through (4) above.

(c)   If Jorvik merges or consolidates with another corporation (other than pursuant to a merger in which Jorvik is the continuing corporation and that does not result in any reclassification, capital reorganization or other change in the shares issuable upon exercise of the Option) or Jorvik sells, transfers, or otherwise disposes of all or substantially all of its assets, then upon his exercising the Option

Mr. Proctor will be entitled to purchase the number and kind of shares of capital stock or other securities or property distributable upon, or as a result of, that transaction that he would have been entitled to purchase had he exercised the Option immediately prior to that transaction.

6. <u>Representations of Sargasso</u>. Sargasso represents to Mr. Proctor as follows:

(1)[6] Sargasso is a corporation validly existing and in good standing under the laws of the State of Delaware with the power to own all of its properties and assets and to carry on its business as it is currently being conducted;

(2) Sargasso has the power to execute and deliver this Agreement and to perform its obligations under this Agreement;

(3) Sargasso's board of directors has duly authorized Sargasso to execute and deliver this Agreement and perform its obligations under this Agreement, and no other corporate proceedings of Sargasso are necessary with respect thereto;[7]

(4) this Agreement constitutes the valid and binding obligation of Sargasso, enforceable in accordance with its terms, except as enforceability is limited by (A) any applicable bankruptcy, insolvency, reorganization, moratorium or similar law affecting creditors' rights generally, or (B) general principles of equity, whether considered in a proceeding in equity or at law;

(5) Sargasso is not required to obtain the Consent of any Person, including the Consent of any party to any Contract to which Sargasso is a party, in connection with execution and delivery of this Agreement and performance of its obligations under this Agreement;

(6) Sargasso's execution and delivery of this Agreement and performance of its obligations under this Agreement do not (A) violate any provision of Sargasso's articles of incorporation or by-laws as currently in effect, (B) conflict with, result in a breach of, constitute a default under (or an event which, with notice or lapse of time or both, would constitute a default under), accelerate the performance required by, result in the creation of any Lien

---

[6] These representations could equally well have been presented as subsections rather than tabulated enumerated clauses.

[7] In this instance I am willing to use *thereto*, as the alternatives are too wordy.

upon any of Sargasso's properties or assets under, or create in any party the right to accelerate, terminate, modify, or cancel, or require any notice under, any Contract to which Sargasso is a party or by which any of Sargasso's properties or assets are bound, or (C) violate any Law or Order currently in effect to which Sargasso is subject; and

(7) Sargasso is the record and beneficial owner and holder of 1,350 shares of Common Stock, free of any Liens other than pursuant to the Stockholders Agreements, and other than the Stockholders Agreements, there are no voting trusts, proxies, or other Contracts to which Sargasso is a party relating to the transfer, voting, or registration of its shares of Common Stock.

7. <u>Representations of Mr. Proctor</u>. Mr. Proctor represents to Sargasso as follows:

(1)[6] Mr. Proctor has full legal capacity to execute and deliver this Agreement and to perform his obligations under this Agreement;

(2) this Agreement constitutes the valid and binding obligation of Mr. Proctor, enforceable in accordance with its terms, except as enforceability is limited by (A) any applicable bankruptcy, insolvency, reorganization, moratorium or similar law affecting creditors' rights generally, or (B) general principles of equity, whether considered in a proceeding in equity or at law;

(3) Mr. Proctor is not required to obtain the Consent of any Person, including the Consent of any party to any Contract to which Mr. Proctor is a party, in connection with execution and delivery of this Agreement and performance of his obligations under this Agreement; and

(4) Mr. Proctor's execution and delivery of this Agreement and performance of his obligations under this Agreement do not (A) conflict with, result in a breach of, constitute a default under (or an event which, with notice or lapse of time or both, would constitute a default under), accelerate the performance required by, result in the creation of any Lien upon any of Mr. Proctor's properties or assets under, or create in any party the right to accelerate, terminate, modify, or cancel, or require any notice under, any Contract to which Mr. Proctor is a party or by which any of Mr. Proctor's properties or assets are bound, or (B) violate any Law or Order currently in effect to which Mr. Proctor is subject.

8.   Specific Performance. Sargasso acknowledges that its breach or threatened breach of this Agreement would cause irreparable damage to Mr. Proctor and that Mr. Proctor would not have an adequate remedy at law. Accordingly, Sargasso acknowledges that Mr. Proctor will be entitled to specific performance, injunctive relief or any other equitable remedy against Sargasso if Sargasso breaches or threatens to breach any provision of this Agreement. The rights and remedies of the parties are cumulative and not exclusive, and each party may pursue all legal and equitable remedies to secure performance by the other party of its obligations under this Agreement, and enforcement of one or more of those rights and remedies by a party will in no way preclude that party from pursuing, at the same time or subsequently, any and all other rights and remedies available to it.

9.   Definitions.[8] When used in this Agreement, the following terms have the following meanings:

"Consent" means any approval, consent, ratification, filing, declaration, registration, waiver, or other authorization.

"Contract" means any oral or written agreement, contract, obligation, promise, arrangement, or undertaking that is legally binding.

"Governmental Body" means any (1) nation, state, county, city, town, village, district, or other jurisdiction of any nature, (2) federal, state, local, municipal, foreign, or other government, (3) governmental or quasi-governmental authority of any nature (including any governmental agency, branch, department, official, or entity and any court or other tribunal, including an arbitral tribunal), (4) multi-national organization or body, or (5) body exercising, or entitled to exercise, any administrative, executive, judicial, legislative, police, regulatory, or taxing power of any nature.

"Law" means any federal, state, local, municipal, foreign, international, multinational, or other administrative order, constitution, law, ordinance, principle of common law, regulation, statute, or treaty.

---

[8] This definition section is perhaps longer than is strictly necessary, but I regard that as a tolerable consequence of my using for many different contracts, in the interest of efficiency, the same set of representations and a definition section that lists the defined terms contained in those representations. See page 83.

"Lien" means any charge, claim, community property interest, condition, equitable interest, lien, option, pledge, security interest, right of first refusal, or restriction of any kind, including any restriction on use, voting, transfer, receipt of income, or exercise of any other attribute of ownership.

"Order" means any award, decision, injunction, judgment, order, ruling, subpoena, or verdict of any court, arbitral tribunal, administrative agency, or other Governmental Body.

"Person" means any individual, corporation (including any non-profit corporation), general or limited partnership, limited liability company, joint venture, estate, trust, association, organization, labor union, Governmental Body or other entity.

10.   Further Assurances. Both parties shall execute and deliver such other documents or agreements as may reasonably be necessary or desirable for consummation of the transactions contemplated by this Agreement.

11.   Governing Law. This Agreement is governed by the laws of the State of New York without giving effect to principles of conflict of laws.

12.   Jurisdiction; Service of Process. A party may initiate in the courts of the State of New York, County of New York, or, if it has or can acquire jurisdiction, in the United States District Court for the Southern District of New York, any proceeding seeking to enforce any provision of this Agreement. Each of the parties consents to the jurisdiction of those courts (and of the appropriate appellate courts) in any such action or proceeding and waives any objection to venue laid therein. Process in any such action or proceeding may be served by delivering a copy of the process to the party to be served at the address and in the manner provided for the giving of notices in Section 13. Nothing in this Section 12, however, affects the right of any party to serve legal process in any other manner permitted by law.

13.   Notices. (a) Every notice or other communication required or contemplated by this Agreement must be in writing and sent by one of the following methods:

(1)   personal delivery, in which case delivery will be deemed to occur the day of delivery;

(2) certified or registered mail, postage prepaid, return receipt requested, in which case delivery will be deemed to occur the day it is officially recorded by the U.S. Postal Service as delivered to the intended recipient; or

(3) next-day delivery to a U.S. address by recognized overnight delivery service such as Federal Express, in which case delivery will be deemed to occur upon receipt.

(b) In each case, a notice or other communication sent to a party must be directed to the address for that party set forth below, or to another address designated by that party by written notice:

If to Sargasso, to:

Sargasso Holdings, Inc.
38th Floor
909 Sixth Avenue
New York, NY 10022

If to Mr. Proctor, to:

Mr. Neil J. Proctor
Proctor Investments, Inc.
2265 Atlantic Street
Stamford, CT 06902

14. <u>Severability</u>. If any provision of this Agreement is held unenforceable by any court of competent jurisdiction, all other provisions of this Agreement will remain effective. If any provision of this Agreement is held to be unenforceable only in part or degree, it will remain effective to the extent not held unenforceable.

15. <u>Entire Agreement</u>. This Agreement constitutes the entire agreement of the parties pertaining to the subject matter of this Agreement.[9] It supersedes all prior agreements of the parties, whether oral or written, pertaining to the subject matter of this Agreement.

16. <u>Amendment</u>. This Agreement may not be amended except by an instrument in writing signed on behalf of both parties.

---

[9] Using the word *agreement* three times in a single short sentence is awkward. Using *hereof* to eliminate the third *agreement* would not, however, improve matters.

17. <u>Counterparts</u>. This Agreement may be executed in counterparts, each of which is an original and all of which together constitute one and the same instrument.

The undersigned are executing this Agreement on the date stated in the introductory clause.

SARGASSO HOLDINGS, INC.

By: _____

    Name:

    Title:

_____

NEIL J. PROCTOR

INDEX

About the Author

KENNETH A. ADAMS is a corporate lawyer with the New York law firm Kramer Levin Naftalis & Frankel LLP. Since graduating from the University of Pennsylvania Law School in 1989, Mr. Adams has practiced with major law firms in New York and Geneva, Switzerland. Although a U.S. citizen, until law school he lived in Europe (primarily England) and Africa.